FOURTH EDITION

Psychology A Level Year 1 and AS

THE TEACHER'S COMPANION

Michael Griffin • Rosalind Geillis

Consultant Editor: Cara Flanagan

OXFORD
UNIVERSITY PRESS

OXFORD
UNIVERSITY PRESS

Great Clarendon Street, Oxford, OX2 6DP, United Kingdom

Oxford University Press is a department of the University of Oxford. It furthers the University's objective of excellence in research, scholarship, and education by publishing worldwide. Oxford is a registered trade mark of Oxford University Press in the UK and in certain other countries

British Library Cataloguing in Publication Data
Data available

ISBN 978-0-19-833865-9

10 9 8 7 6 5 4 3 2 1

Paper used in the production of this book is a natural, recyclable product made from wood grown in sustainable forests. The manufacturing process conforms to the environmental regulations of the country of origin.

Printed in Great Britain by Bell and Bain Ltd., Glasgow

Dedications

Michael: Thanks to Rob, the editors, the designers and all at OUP for their support. And thank you to Alana again, who continually loses me to work-related projects!

Rosalind: To Shawn, who continues to support me in everything I do. My friends and family who remind me there is life outside teaching. Finally, my wonderful students old and new.

Acknowledgements
Cover illustrations: Chris Cardwell

Credits
The publishers would like to thank the following for permissions to use copyright material:

Introduction icon (p1 onwards): xpixel/Shutterstock; **p3**: Author image; **p4**: Lukiyanova Natalia / frenta/Shutterstock; **Social Influence icon (p11 onwards)**: Qiun/Shutterstock; **p17**: With thanks to Adrian Frost; **Memory icon (p26 onwards)**: america365/Shutterstock; **Attachment icon (p36 onwards)**: Akinina Olena/Shutterstock; **Psychopathology icon (p49 onwards)**: Palto/Shutterstock; **Approaches in Psychology icon (p60 onwards)**: silvano audisio/Shutterstock; **Biopsychology icon (p69 onwards)**: fabioberti.it/Alamy; p71: (top) Christos Georghiou/Shutterstock; **Research Methods icon (p78 onwards)**: KlektaDarya/Shutterstock; **p101**: niderlander/Shutterstock; **p102**: niderlander/Shutterstock; **p110**: meaculpa_1/Shutterstock; **p113**: (top) © Don Troiani/Corbis; (middle) gielmichal/Shutterstock; (bottom) Stylus photo/Shutterstock; **p131**: vvoe/Shutterstock; **p163**: niderlander/Shutterstock; **p157**: (top) szefei/Shutterstock, (bottom) meunierd/Shutterstock; **p161**: KOUNADEAS IOANNHS/Shutterstock; **p172**: Kristina Stasiuliene/Shutterstock; **p183**: (data) scottlitt/Shutterstock, (feelings) f9photos/Shutterstock, (limitations) Eric Isselee/Shutterstock, (strengths) kungverylucky/Shutterstock, (creativity) 2happy/Shutterstock, (overview) Africa Studio/Shutterstock; **p186**: (top) Lightspring/Shutterstock, (bottom) Nicku/Shutterstock; **p196**: (tl, bl, br) PWT/Shutterstock, (tr) Fuse/Getty Images; **p210–211**: vasabii/Shutterstock; **p219**: (eye) Alexandru Cristian Ciobanu/Shutterstock, (light levels) monbibi/Shutterstock, (sleep/wake) Elena Tkachenko/Shutterstock; **p225**: A1Stock/Shutterstock; **p226**: Christophe BOISSON/Shutterstock; **p239**: cristi180884/Shutterstock; **p241**: (tl) leosapiens/Shutterstock, (tr) Yes Man/Shutterstock, (bl) Stephen Rees/Shutterstock

Although we have made every effort to trace and contact all copyright holders before publication this has not been possible in all cases. If notified, the publisher will rectify any errors or omissions at the earliest opportunity.

Links to third party websites are provided by Oxford in good faith and for information only. Oxford disclaims any responsibility for the materials contained in any third party website referenced in this work.

CONTENTS

Approaching AQA Psychology

Approaching the mark schemes

Assessment objectives (AOs) are set by Ofqual to ensure consistency across different psychology specifications and exam boards. As well as defining the three AOs students are to be tested on, Ofqual also state that at least 10% of the overall qualification will contain mathematical skills equivalent to level 2 (GCSE A*–C) or above and 25–30% of the overall assessment will assess skills, knowledge and understanding in relation to research methods.

When teaching exam technique, a famous quote I (RG) like to share with my students comes from the martial arts actor Bruce Lee, 'Knowing is not enough, we must apply'. If students are unsure what the question is asking them to do then they will not know how to use their knowledge in a way to ensure the question is addressed in their answer. It is helpful to teach students the different AO skills they need to demonstrate and refer to these when introducing activities in lessons, attempting exam questions and giving feedback.

Applying mark schemes – the ladder approach

Choose a level

When marking a student's answer begin at the lowest level (level 1). If the student's answer meets all the criteria for this level then move to the next level.

At this second level (level 2) again consider whether the answer satisfies the criteria stated; if so, the answer climbs to level 3.

When deciding upon a level consider the overall quality of the answer rather than focusing on small areas that may not have been done so well.

Awarding a mark

Once you have identified the appropriate level, take a best-fit approach to identify the mark. For example, in the case of a student whose answer seems to fit into level 3 but has a few elements of level 4, their answer remains at level 3 as they have not satisfied enough of the criteria to move to level 4, but would receive a mark close to the top of the level 3 band.

Using mark schemes with students

Self/peer assessment and teacher feedback

Handouts 1 and **2** can be used for self and peer assessment, as well as teacher feedback by simply colour coding which cells a student's answer has met for the AOs contained in the question. When marking answers, encourage students to annotate AO1, AO2 and AO3 so they are able to break up the various components of the answer before applying the mark scheme. Students will need to be trained in how to apply the mark scheme if self and peer assessment is to be meaningful. A useful activity involves giving students both a high- and a low-scoring answer for the same question. Working in

pairs, students annotate the answer to identify relevant AOs. They then meet with another pair to work as a group of four, comparing their annotations and using the mark scheme (or the appropriate generic mark scheme from **Handouts 1** and **2**) decide on the level, and possibly mark for the two answers. The teacher then shares the actual level and mark with the class explaining what elements of the question lead to the final level and mark. I would recommend buying back a few exam papers each exam series to be used in lessons.

Writing frames

When setting 12-mark (AS route) or 16-mark (A Level route) extended questions, students may benefit from writing frames to direct their attention to the required AOs. Each frame should be specific to the question asked and may include sentence starters to provide a guide as to what needs to be considered. Once students are familiar with these questions, frames can be removed, however those who struggle with literacy may prefer to continue using them.

Approaching schemes of work and revision

The following tips are by no means the definitive answer to planning teaching a course. However, they are pointers I have found useful to bear in mind when I sit down with a blank sheet of paper, textbook, specification and a worried crease across my brow.

When to teach research methods

Research methods is important as a stand-alone topic (Paper 2) but can also be used to create valuable evaluative comments when discussing research from other topics. For example, experiments in memory research and the use of meta-analysis in cross-cultural variations in attachment.

Embedding research methods

Giving a brief introduction to research methods early in the course provides students with a level of understanding that can be applied to other topics. For example, should you choose to study memory near the beginning of the course then teaching the experimental method prior to this topic provides students with an understanding of variables, experimental design and analysis of quantitative data that they can then apply to a range of studies into memory. Students may find it helpful to start the year with a two-week introduction to psychology, where investigations are planned and carried out. This aims to highlight psychology's status as a science and begin to develop their understanding of research methods. See **Handouts 3** and **4** for experimental planning sheets.

Research methods are then further reinforced by making reference to key concepts in research when discussing studies across a number of topics. For example, consideration of ethical issues in social influence research, the use of questionnaires to determine attachment type as a child and their later impact on relationships as an adult.

General notes

Research methods as a stand-alone topic

An alternative pathway would be to teach research methods as a stand-alone topic. Examples of research from other topics on the specification can be used in these lessons to illustrate research methods concepts with the added benefit of revisiting research from other areas of the course.

Having experienced both pathways of delivering research methods I personally prefer delivering this aspect of the course as a stand-alone topic. I found students placed more importance on research methods, and feel the topic was more visible when taught in designated lessons with its own folder, contents page and glossary.

Revision records

With the move to linear examinations, meaning exams at the end of Year 1 for AS-route students and at the end of two years for A Level-route students, creating revision notes across the course is more important than ever. **Handout 5** provides a generic template for a revision record that can be used for both AS and A Level students. These can be completed as homework tasks or time can be given in lessons as a means to check progress. Completion of the record could be set as a paired task with the final record being photocopied so each student received a copy.

The top of the handout requires students to state the topic and also the overall section and paper to help with organisation of revision notes. For example, Topic: the Authoritarian Personality, Section: Social Influence, Paper 1.

Completing the six sentence summary and topic glossary provides an outline of the topic which can be used to address AO1 questions requiring students to state, identify, outline and describe research.

The final four cells encourage students to create PEEL evaluations (AO3). Aim for two strengths and two limitations as exam questions may ask students to describe two limitations for example.

Although the record covers AO1 and AO3 skills the record can be a useful tool for tackling AO2 application questions nearer the exam period. The record can also be used in revision sessions with students giving them to a peer who then asks questions to test their retention of knowledge.

Toolkit of activities and ideas

The most useful thing I (MG) ever did as a teacher (well, as a PGCE student) was to compile a compendium of starters, plenaries, and main lesson activities as I used them, or as I heard ideas from other teachers. Some of you may even have the booklet I produced, *The Psychology Teachers' Toolkit*, which is available on the resource sharing website www.resourcd.co.uk. Now, whenever I am struggling to think of an idea to teach a new topic, I only have to delve into the toolkit for inspiration. On reflection, some of the ideas in there are a little silly and I never use them. However, there are many that I still use and some new ones that I have added in. Here are some of the activities I find most useful:

Starters and plenaries

Question Raffle – At the start or end of the lesson, ask each student to write a question related to the topic and/or lesson objectives on a piece of paper. Fold up the questions, place them in a hat and ask the students to pick out a question and answer it in front of the class.

Blankety Blank – Ever asked students to read part of a sheet or textbook and been frustrated by how little they have taken in? Try setting a time limit and warning them that they will be tested on that information shortly afterwards. Lift quotes from the text they have read and blank out keywords/variables etc. to see if they can remember what those keywords were. This activity works even better if you can create a PowerPoint which mirrors the old game show!

Psychology Jackanory – To start off a lesson, why not consider reading your students a children's story relevant to your lesson? For example, *The Emperors New Clothes* is useful for thinking about majority and minority influence. Last year, I even had one group sitting on the floor with cushions to recreate their primary school circle time – they loved it!

Odd One Out – Display four pictures, keywords or concepts on a PowerPoint or whiteboard and ask students to select which one they think is the odd one out and justify why. You can either deliberately manipulate the odd one out to test knowledge, or purposefully not include an obvious odd one out so that students can make their own links/comparisons between different things.

Quick Sentence – Very easy. Ask a student for a number between say, 20 and 40. Whatever number they select, the students must summarise the lesson in exactly that number of words. Another idea that makes your workload easier.

Jerry Springer – Explain that at the end of his shows, Jerry Springer always does a summing up. It usually starts with the phrase "So… what have we learnt here today? We have learnt that…" Ask the students to complete their Jerry Springer summing up of the lesson. You can then ask some students to read theirs out. Again, for those of the 'gimmick' persuasion, consider buying a humorous Jerry Springer style wig for this moment!

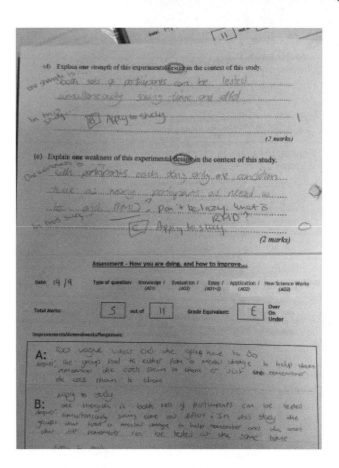

"I have learnt that…" – You and your students may be familiar with the game "My Granny went to the shops and she bought…" This plenary is a variation of that game. Students must write down one thing they have learnt that lesson. Then, the teacher selects one person who must say "I have learnt that…" (then whatever they have written down). Then the teacher should select a second student who must state what they learnt, but also what the first person learnt. And so on… This promotes active listening in students, and if my experience is anything to go by, it can require some practice!

Pictionary – Give students a key word, theory or psychologist, and ask them to attempt to draw this in a visual form that other class members would be able to guess. This could be setup as a whole class activity, or a small group competition.

Mixed Bag – On an A4 sheet of paper write a series of plenary statements such as: "What information is important to remember from this lesson?", "What are the three key words relevant to this lesson?", "How could I have improved my work?", "How could I use the knowledge/skills from this lesson in my other subjects?", "How can I relate what we have learnt in this lesson to my own life?", and "How valuable has my contribution to this lesson been and why?" Cut these questions out and ask students to pick one at random at the end of the lesson. They could then feed back their answers to the rest of the class.

Post-it® Continuum – This is particularly useful for evaluation lessons. Display a continuum on the whiteboard, e.g. low ecological validity to high ecological validity. Give each student a Post-it® note and ask them to place it on the continuum along with a justification of why they have placed it there. You could even introduce a two-dimensional continuum if you are feeling particularly daring!

Making connections – Display lots of key terms/concepts/studies on the board. Ask the students to make three or four pairs and explain their connections. This makes a good starter to a lesson.

Assessment for learning

A B C marking – The current Ofsted framework (as of 2014, I know that it changes every couple of weeks!) talks about marking which engages students in dialogue. I've seen different schools and teachers approach this in different ways. The method I prefer is very simple and genuinely has the potential to move students on in their learning. In the body of the student's answer/essay, ask three questions which you think will help them to move on in their learning and to progress their understanding. Label these questions 'A', 'B' and 'C' and the students can then use **Handout 6** as a template for their responses. With my classes, all assessed work follows this format and their work is then stored in a separate assessment folder. Examples of questions can be seen in **Handout 6**.

Bingo – Students can place the AOs on a bingo grid so they can visualise what information was missing from their own answer. "Examples of questions can be seen in the work below."

Outline Bowlby's monotropic theory of attachment (6 marks).

Showed an understanding of the evolutionary basis of attachment.	Gave examples of social releasers and explained their function.	Explained the concept of a critical period (3–6 months).
Defined the term Monotropy.	Explained the concept of an internal working model and its importance in social relationships.	Showed an understanding of the continuity hypothesis.
Highlighted the difference between primary and secondary attachments.	Made a distinction between the formation of attachment and the consequences of attachment formation.	Mark awarded _____

Students read each cell of the bingo grid and tick comments that refer to aspects they have included in their answer. Alternatively students can colour code each cell of the bingo grid (green – I explained this clearly, yellow – I implied this or my comments were muddled, red – I did not mention this in my answer). Students then re-write any ambiguous areas and add missed information to form a complete answer.

Match me up quickly – Taking inspiration from the 'fastest finger first' game in Who Wants to be a Millionaire, display four key terms/concepts and label them A, B, C and D. Then display the definitions and label them 1, 2, 3 and 4. As soon as the definitions are displayed, the students use their mini-whiteboards to match them up as quickly as possible and hold up their mini-whiteboards when they have finished. This is a good little game at the end of the lesson if you have a series of four/five rounds.

Did you…? – This activity can be used in a number of ways to encourage students to reflect on what needs to be included in a successful answer and can be adapted to suit any AO question as well as those that combine two or more skills. The checklist can be used to cover exam technique (using key terms correctly, including the correct AOs in an answer, writing in PEEL paragraphs) or can relate to actual knowledge and understanding needed to answer the question.

For example,

Outline and evaluate research into the effects of leading questions on the accuracy of eyewitness testimony (8 marks).

Did you…	Muddled/ flawed	Basic	Reasonable	Effective
Did you select relevant research?				
Did you outline procedures accurately?				
Did you state findings accurately?				
Did you use PEEL to structure evaluations?				
Did you….				

The class could work together to create the *Did you?* table before sitting the assessment or could use a table the teacher has produced to engage in self or peer assessment before submitting their answer to be marked.

Essay Oscars – On completing an assessment, provide students with a list of Oscar nominations from which they are to choose one or two they feel their answer could be awarded. This should be done before seeing teacher feedback. For example:

- Concise yet detailed writing style
- Consistent use of evaluation signposts
- PEEL used to structure evaluative comments
- Direct links made to question
- Common words spelt correctly
- Accurate use of specialist terminology.

Once students have identified their particular strengths they are to predict one or two areas they need to improve; seeing other students' answers may help them do this. Only when this has been done, are students then given the teacher feedback and mark. This could be on a sticker that can be stuck at the end of the assessment.

This activity helps students reflect on what they have written rather than rushing straight to the mark they were awarded as well as encouraging student ownership of assessment for learning. A variation of this could be to withhold the mark until improvements have been acted on, then students can be provided with their original mark and their post-improvement mark enabling them to visualise how they have improved.

Making use of students work – Giving students an overview of how the class as a whole is working can be a useful tool when giving feedback and encouraging students to identify their own areas to improve:

1. Share aspects of the assessment that were done well by the majority of the class.
2. Highlight one or two common errors that were seen in the majority of students' answers.
3. Work through these errors by assigning students to groups with a lead learner (a student who did not make that error and asking them to share their assessment) or as a whole class by annotating a model answer or setting a 'fill in the blanks' task to form a model answer.
4. Students then revisit their assessment to reflect on what they did well (step 1) and re-write areas they need to improve (steps 2–3).

Keeping a record – Either at the front of their folder or in a section containing previous assessments, students should keep a record of their assessment marks and targets to improve, along with any improved marks for re-written assessments. This record should be referred to before sitting each assessment to provide a reminder of previous targets to ensure the same mistakes are not being made and focusing students on the areas they need to address when preparing for the up-coming assessment. These records are a valuable source of information for parents' evening and when writing reports.

Objective Venn diagrams – Identify three objectives for the lesson or class task. Display a Venn diagram to the class similar to the one shown here, making sure each objective is clearly displayed. Give each student a Post-it® and tell them to write their name on it and place it on the Venn diagram to show which objectives they feel they have achieved. You could also ask students to give a justification of their choice.

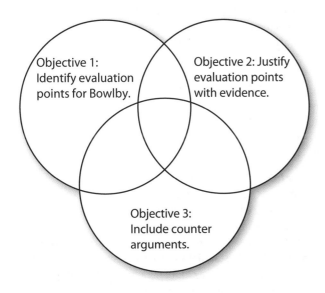

Objective 1: Identify evaluation points for Bowlby.

Objective 2: Justify evaluation points with evidence.

Objective 3: Include counter arguments.

This assessment method encourages students to reflect on their own learning and quickly demonstrates where the class is as a whole. If the majority of students do not meet one objective it may indicate that area needs to be addressed in a different manner. Differentiation could also be addressed with all students aiming to achieve the first objective while more able students are challenged to meet more than one objective.

Peer assessment grid – **Handout 7** can be used to help students assess each other's evaluations, exam answers and essays. Try to anonymize the activity by asking students to write a number between 1 and 999 on their work before giving it in. Give out one piece of work to each student marker with one copy of the peer assessment grid. The student marker should then complete the first box by identifying four key terms that the 'candidate' has used and one key term that they could have used. Then, they pass the work and the peer assessment grid to the person on their left. The second marker then completes the second box, by writing down a good sentence from the work and explaining why it was a good sentence. Then pass to the left... and so on. By the end of the activity the peer assessment grid should be completed and handed back to the original 'candidate' by calling out the numbers on each piece of work. Each 'candidate' will get feedback from four student markers and will have reviewed four different pieces of work themselves. The feedback may vary in quality, but the activity of reviewing four different pieces of work should produce plenty of learning gains. Most importantly, the peer assessment was qualitative rather than quantitative; which I think is much more productive than the usual 'look at the mark scheme and give your mate a score' type of peer assessment.

Collaborative learning

Group work can be incredibly productive, but it is also a perilous activity! The danger is this: diligent students in the group do most of the work, the drama students do most of the feeding back to class, and all of the other students are anonymous in the middle!

The trick to making sure group work is successful is to ensure the tasks you devise are based on the following principles:

- students are dependent on each other in order to successfully complete the task
- students are individually accountable for the work they have done
- students participate equally.

With these aims in mind, here are some simple ideas for structuring your group work:

Random numbers – When setting a discussion question, ask the students to number themselves in their groups. Then make it clear that when you ask the group to feed back their answer, you will randomly choose a number and that person will have to feed back. This ensures that all group members are involved in the discussion and need to pay close attention to what is being said. In addition, it ensures that more gifted students will need to 'teach' their higher-order arguments to the weaker students, so that they are able to feed back that idea.

Group statements – Set your students a discussion question. Individually, students should write their response to that question and elaborate their answers as fully as possible. Following this, students should share their statements with members of their group. Finally, the group should write a group statement which reflects the opinions, arguments and ideas of the group as a whole. This prevents the strongest and most confident students from taking over the activity and writing the statement without input from weaker/less confident students.

Snowballing – Ask students individually to write down 3 ideas in response to a question. For example, 'list 3 evaluation points for Asch's study'. This works better if you give them a short time limit, say 2 minutes. After those 2 minutes are up, tell students to share their ideas with the person on their left and write down any new ideas they hadn't thought of – give them another 2 minutes to do this. Then repeat the process with students who sit across from them. Hopefully, by the end of the activity they should have picked up different ideas from the students around them, and shared their own ideas.

Student dimension line – Display some sort of continuum on your PowerPoint or whiteboard. For example, 'Zimbardo's Prison Experiment was ethical' – strongly agree to strongly disagree. Ask your students to stand along that line to indicate their opinion on this matter. As the teacher, you can now use this line to structure group work. For example, you could 'fold' the line so that the person who most 'strongly agrees' ends up facing the person who most 'strongly disagrees'. Students can then discuss their ideas with the students opposite them (e.g. think, pair, share – see below). Alternatively, you could use a 'systematic sample(!)': go along the line giving students numbers and then asking them to sit in groups, ensuring that your groups are mixed by having people who 'strongly agree', 'agree', 'disagree' and 'strongly disagree' with the original statement. This idea works particularly well when the original question you set is something like: 'To what extent do you understand ethical issues?' Constructing a dimension line like this also means you can sort your students into differentiated, or mixed-ability groups.

Think, pair, share – I am sure many people have heard of this technique already; it is perhaps the most well-known collaborative learning structure. Set your students some kind of discussion question and give them a few moments of thinking time to individually gather their thoughts. Then students should share their ideas with the person next to them. In the feedback phase of this activity, ask students to feedback their partner's ideas as opposed to their own. This encourages active listening and clear communication.

Top 3 starter/plenary – Display around ten key terms/concepts on the board. Ask the students to select the three terms/concepts they would be most confident explaining to the rest of the class. Then, ask students to compare their list with that of the person sitting next to them. The students must explain one term/concept on their list which isn't on their partner's lists and vice versa. Crucially, in the whole-class feedback, the students must explain the new term they have learnt, rather than the term they taught to their partner.

Developing students' skills

For both the AS and A Level routes, skills are split into three AOs. AO1: demonstrating knowledge and understanding, AO2: applying knowledge and understanding, AO3: analysis, interpretation and evaluation. Here are just a few ideas for each AO that can be used to deliver a number of topics from the course.

Activities by skill – AO1 (Demonstrating knowledge and understanding)

Basic to detailed – Often students are not aware that their outlines of theories/studies lack detail. Equally, when our assessment feedback suggests 'needs more detail', the students often do not have a tangible idea of what this might entail. It is only when you talk to the students that this becomes apparent. A very simple activity to help the students understand what is meant by 'detail' is to give them 'basic' outlines for them to improve/annotate. For example, leave out percentages, key terms, definitions… be a bit vague about the procedure etc. After you have taught that study/theory in more detail, set the students the task of improving the 'basic' outline to an 'effective' outline. This should help them to see and understand what is meant by 'detail' and remind them of the type of information they should try and include in future answers. There are a couple of examples of this activity in this book that you can use and copy (see **Handouts 8** and **9**).

Distilling – Ask students to call out key words associated with a certain topic. These words are recorded on the board for all the class to see. Students could be asked to do this from memory as a revision activity or following reading of a passage to identify key features of the information read. As a class the words on the board are then grouped in level of importance: which words should a basic outline include, which additional words would form a reasonable outline and finally, for an effective outline what words would also be needed. Students are then challenged to write an outline using as many of the words as possible. Once completed, students could peer assess colour coding the words included (basic, reasonable and effective) and check the accuracy of the outline produced.

True or false – Students are given a list of statements to determine whether they are true or false. Using their own knowledge or with help from a textbook, students add additional comments to any correct statements and amend any statements which are false. This is a useful way to dispel common misunderstandings as well as encourage students to read a passage in a way more meaningful than simply highlighting sentence after sentence.

Activities by skill – AO2 (Applying knowledge and understanding)

Two-sentence technique – Application questions in research methods often follow the same pattern. They look something like this:

*Outline **one strength** and **one limitation** of this research design in the context of this study (2 + 2 marks).*

There might be some variation in the wording and marks available, but this is a fairly repetitive question. However, 'research design' (underlined) could be replaced by 'correlation', 'sampling technique', 'measure of central tendency' etc. In these types of questions, students are required to show their *knowledge* and their ability to *apply* their knowledge to the situation. So, I (MG) encourage my students to use a two-sentence technique.

Sentence one (show your knowledge): *One limitation of the independent groups research design is that group differences may occur.*

Sentence two (apply to the context): *In this context, the group of participants using the mind map technique may have had better memories than the participants using the repetition technique. This biases the results.*

At the start of the psychology course, I actually insist that students also write in two different colours to drive the message home. This technique can be used across the course, not just in research methods. For example, in the approaches topic, students write a knowledge sentence on one of the approaches and then apply that knowledge to the context given. They can keep doing that until they feel they have answered the question. An example is given on **Handout 8**.

Taking the role of... – Students are assigned the role of a professional working in a field related to the topic being studied, e.g. occupational psychologist, therapist, editor of a psychological journal, and are set a challenge relating to their job role which involves them drawing out key information from a text. If working in groups, the challenge set can be split into clear objectives (relating to higher-order thinking levels) and each group member assigned one to action. Alternatively, a more-able group could be asked to identify their own objectives from the overall aim set by the teacher or even have to work out what the actual problem is that needs to be addressed, and develop their own aims and objectives.

Bridging the gap – Students are provided with two pieces of information and are asked to bridge the gap between the two texts. For example, a passage relating to the experience of depression, such as an extract from the autobiography *Prozac Nation* by Elizabeth Wurtzel (1994) is shown at the top of a piece of paper. At the bottom of the paper is an extract from a textbook outlining the cognitive explanation of depression. Clues could be added along the bridge to scaffold thinking.

Scaffolded application – This activity relies on specimen and past exam papers or the creation of your own scenarios. Provide students with an exam question that requires application of knowledge. Students first highlight the key piece of information contained in the question stem and record this in the stem column of **Handout 9**. In the second column they identify a relevant concept. The final column provides space for the student to apply the concept to the stem (application). You can use **Handout 8** 'AO2 Application of knowledge – an example' to show students how to use this technique.

Activities by skill – AO3 (Analysis, interpretation and evaluation)

Primark and Savile Row – This analogy can be used to explain the importance of creating evaluations that relate specifically to the research being discussed. Basic evaluations are like Primark jumpers: cheap and cheerful, they fit anyone but are pretty disposable. Basic evaluations are those that can be applied to a number of different theories or studies with little direct fit. Comments such as 'this study lacks population validity' would be considered basic. Savile Row suits are expensive and tailored to the individual: they simply wouldn't look right on another individual. Effective evaluations are those which relate explicitly to the research under discussion as they are based on key features of the research and so do not fit anywhere else. When students have written their evaluations ask them to check whether they are Primark (basic) or Savile Row (effective).

Body building – This activity encourages students to add weight to the basic evaluative comment to create an effective evaluative paragraph. Provide students with a range of one sentence evaluations that could apply to a specific research theory or study. Working in small groups, students are asked to develop the muscle behind this evaluative point by adding specific details that link the point to the actual research being discussed. For example, 'Point: The Working Memory model is useful as it has had many real world applications'. Students can build up this evaluation by considering how the model has been used in dyslexia research.

Evaluation Ladders – Hands up who has read and been upset by this comment on their students' essays: 'The ecological validity of the study is low because it is not like real life'?! Aaaaggghhh! Of course, our job as teachers is to help students to elaborate their evaluative comments; something they seem to find really hard, but undoubtedly has a significant impact on their grades if they can develop the skill. Having read the above statement in an Asch essay for the thirtieth time, I decided to try and devise a memorable teaching technique to help students with this skill. And so, the 'elaboration ladders' were born (see **Handout 10**). The central idea behind the elaboration ladders is that students start with an introductory evaluation comment at the bottom of the ladder and then gradually elaborate this comment further and further until they reach the smiley face at the top!

The box on the right-hand side is designed to prompt students into thinking of ways they could elaborate their evaluations, for example, 'have I got evidence?'. To give you an example of how this might work, consider Ainsworth's Strange Situation paradigm:

1. Students could start off by making a generic statement such as: *'It could be argued that Ainsworth's studies lacked ecological validity.'*

2. Students would then need to consider how they could elaborate this. Using the prompts on the right they may decide to include evidence: *'Indeed, Lamb et al. (1995) feels that the Strange Situation is highly artificial (novel and stressful) and therefore might make children more clingy and less likely to look secure.'*

3. Again, students should consider the prompts on the right such as 'Why does this matter?' For example: 'This is a problem because it means that the results of the study may not be generalisable outside of the Strange Situation and that Ainsworth's results may have underestimated the amount of secure attachments.'

4. Once again, students should consider how they might elaborate this response. This time, it could come in the form of a counter argument: *'On the other hand, it may be relatively common that infants would face novel and stressful situations and Ainsworth's study is able to take that into account. In addition, Ainsworth designed the study deliberately to be artificial and create anxiety in order to judge whether the infants would be able to use their attachment figures as a secure base.'*

By going through this process, the hope is that the student is able to discuss their evaluation and its implications in more depth. This visual technique, used in conjunction with the prompts on the right-hand side of the ladders, seems to have been very successful in developing elaboration skills in the students at our school.

Burger evaluation skills – This technique can be used with your students to develop their ability to evaluate theories with studies. I often find that students struggle with the structure of using research evidence to evaluate a theory. What students forget to do is illustrate that they understand how and why the evidence undermines or supports a theory. Instead, they simply describe a relevant study and expect the reader to draw their own conclusions! The burger technique asks students to 'sandwich' their study descriptions with evaluative commentary (AO2). You will see from **Handout 11** that students are first encouraged to outline whether the evidence 'supports' or 'undermines' the theory at the top of the burger. Then, in the middle of the burger they outline that evidence, ensuring that they only outline the relevant information of that study, and not every detail. Lastly, and most importantly, at the bottom of the burger they must explain how that study undermines or supports the theory. Usually, this should involve explaining whether or not the data supports what the theory would have predicted and why. Blank burger templates are given on **Handout 12** where students can attempt the technique.

ICT tips and tricks

Here are just a few ideas you could use to 'jazz up' your lessons!

Rolling shows – These can be created using PowerPoint and essentially consist of a slideshow of images. They are very useful to use when students are coming into lessons. When played with relevant music they create a good atmosphere and let students know that from the moment they walk into your classroom, they are in a learning environment.

Find a series of images related to the content of the lesson. Insert an image onto each slide of your PowerPoint. You could also insert questions for the students to read. When you have finished inserting your images/text, select the <Transitions> or <Animations> tab on the top menu bar. Here you can select which transition you would like to be used to change from one slide to another – I find that 'fade' looks the most professional. Untick the option <On mouse click> and instead select the tick box <Automatically after> and then set the transition to every 5 seconds (or so). Make sure you click the <Apply to all> option beneath this. Lastly, select the <Slide Show> tab from the top menu bar, and then <Set up slide show> from the menu. Clicking the tick box for <Loop continuously until 'ESC'> will ensure that your slideshow will cycle through the images until you want it to stop.

Randomiser – This is another technique that can be used with PowerPoint and enables you to select students randomly, for example to answer a question, or to sort them into groups. Enter your students' names into PowerPoint, with one name on each slide. When you have finished this, follow the procedure outlined above for 'Rolling Shows' exactly, except this time, set the transition between slides to be every 0 seconds – this is important to make the process random as you will see later. To stop the slideshow on one of the names simply press 'S' on your keyboard, this will stop the slideshow. To select another name, simply press 'S' again to start the slideshow.

Although I (MG) have suggested doing this with names, it can also be used to 'randomise' questions, key terms, and even essay titles.

Bluetooth mouse – This idea requires a little investment but is extremely effective if you do not have an interactive whiteboard. Consider purchasing a Bluetooth mouse (search on Amazon, you can get them for around £10 at time of writing). It is essentially a wireless mouse but the signal is much more powerful. This means they can be used at the back of the classroom by your students! You can set up matching games etc. in Publisher, Word, or other software – and your students can play them from their seats! I like to call it the 'Lazy man's interactive whiteboard'. If your laptop or computer is slightly older, you may also need to purchase a 'Bluetooth dongle', perhaps ask your IT technicians about these.

Saving YouTube videos – Is YouTube blocked at your school? Want to download a YouTube video and save to your laptop for future use? There are several websites that will help you to do this; all you have to do is copy and paste the address of the video into the relevant website and the rest is done for you! At the time of writing, these websites were working and available:

keepvid.com/

www.clipconverter.cc/

en.savefrom.net/

Windows Movie Maker – This is a free programme which is installed on most Windows machines (unless the over zealous IT technicians at your school have removed it!). It is an extremely easy programme to use and allows you to edit videos and insert text on top. This is useful to edit videos you have downloaded (e.g. using the websites above) or videos you have recorded on a digital camera (e.g. a re-enacted student version of Milgram!). There are plenty of tutorials for using this programme on the internet; simply search for 'Windows Movie Maker tutorial' on the internet. Alternatively, I wrote a beginners guide for a staff INSET last year which can be found at www.oxfordschoolblogs.co.uk/psychcompanion/blog/

MonkeyJam – This free software is also relatively easy to use and allows students to make animations, with either drawings, themselves, or plasticine. The process takes a while but is ideal for extended projects or after-school clubs. Searching for monkeyjam in Google should be enough to find this software. Again, there are many tutorials available on the internet. A video camera or good webcam are required.

Making cartoons – There are some fantastic websites that allow students to make professional-looking cartoons with images they want to use. For example, they could recreate a discussion between Milgram and his critics by finding images of the relevant psychologists. Here are some easy-to-use websites you might consider: www.toondoo.com and www.stripcreator.com

Great websites

Here are a list of fantastic psychology-related websites on the internet, invaluable to any teacher! I am sure there are more out there waiting to be found, but these are the ones I have come across:

- www.psychlotron.org.uk *A site packed full of ready-to-use worksheets, information sheets, video clips and interactive whiteboard files. Brilliantly organised and updated every week. A fantastic site!*
- www.resourcd.com *This is a teacher sharing site that contains worksheets, PowerPoints, past-exam papers, video clips, ideas, a forum... everything a psychology teacher would ever need!*

- www.holah.co.uk *Although this site is primarily for teachers of the OCR spec, there is invaluable information on this site relevant to AQA content.*
- www.coolpsychologystuff.co.uk *A great site which specialises in psychology-related products for teachers and students. Includes equipment, gifts, DVDs and posters.*
- www.uniview.co.uk *A similar site to that above with products available for your classroom.*
- www.allpsych.com *A collection of links to further sites, organised by topic.*
- www.theatp.org *A great website and association for psychology teachers. They also run a CPD conference each summer which is cheap and well attended.*
- www.teachpsych.org *Lots of resources and ideas for teaching on this website. It is designed for teachers following the American 'APA' qualification but there are still useful ideas that can be gained from this website.*

Blog sites and twitter accounts

The following sites contain thousands of articles related to AQA topics. They are extremely useful for using as extension tasks. Many of the sites allow you to subscribe to their RSS feeds. This means you do not have to search each of the sites every week or so to find related articles; the articles come to you!

Most of these blogs also have twitter accounts you can 'retweet' to your class if your school allows subject twitter accounts. Alternatively, advertise the twitter accounts to your students and try to convince them to give them a 'follow'!

- www.psychblog.co.uk
- www.alevelpsychology.co.uk
- www.bps-research-digest.blogspot.com
- www.oxfordschoolblogs.co.uk/psychcompanion/blog/
- www.mindhacks.com
- www.spring.org.uk
- www.thepsychfiles.com
- www.thesituationist.wordpress.com
- www.in-mind.org
- www.psychcentral.com
- www.whatispsychology.biz
- www.badpsychologyblog.org

Introduction to Lesson notes

Your lesson notes section

This section has been written with some specific objectives in mind:

1. To provide teachers with plenty of ideas for teaching the AS/Year 1 AQA psychology specification.

2. To provide teachers of psychology with a 'toolkit' that helps to alleviate workload, specifically in the planning and creation of resources.

3. To assist teachers in identifying opportunities for differentiation in their psychology lessons and catering for different 'learning styles'.

Plenty of ideas

Within this section we hope you will find plenty of ideas which you might consider using when delivering the AS/Year 1 AQA psychology specification.

We have tried to structure this section in a way that mirrors the AQA course so that you can easily identify how the ideas and resources fit in with your delivery of the specification. As a result, those of you who have purchased *The Complete Companion* will find that our structure is borrowed from the chapter breakdown used in the Student Book.

The lesson notes include ideas for starters, plenaries, main activities and study replications. We have decided not to include detailed lesson plans as there is rarely a one-size-fits-all approach to teaching; it is often more effective for teachers to adapt ideas to suit their own teaching techniques.

Creation of resources

For many of the ideas and activities included in this section, there are accompanying photocopiable handouts which can be used in lessons.

We hope that these handouts will ease some of your workload and bring you closer to that elusive work–life balance!

These handouts can be found on pages 91 to 224. They are numbered so that you can find them easily.

Differentiation

Undoubtedly one of the most challenging responsibilities for a teacher is planning opportunities for differentiation in lessons. In our own experience of the classroom, we have taught students predicted A grades alongside other students who are predicted U grades (yes I know, hard to believe isn't it?!).

Much of the time we are differentiating without even thinking about it. However, if you are anything like us, you may start to panic when asked to identify 'strategies for differentiation' on lesson plans! To a certain extent, the skill is in identifying what we are already doing, as opposed to reinventing the wheel.

Consequently, we have tried to identify how the lesson ideas in this section may provide opportunities to stretch the gifted and talented, while supporting the weaker students so that you can highlight these on your lesson plans and schemes of work.

Your AS and A Level classes will probably have a wide range of abilities and if you are teaching in a sixth form or college with a comprehensive intake, you could have a class with target grades ranging from E through to A. As such, differentiation is a vital component of lessons if we wish all our students to progress.

The lesson notes included show how to adapt activities or offer social support to help students of different abilities access the lesson based on the principles listed below:

- **P**athways – students of different abilities may benefit from being set different tasks based on their current level of skill or understanding.

- **H**igher order – some activities can be adapted or added to, to encourage higher-order thinking such as evaluating, synthesising or creating as mentioned in Bloom's Taxonomy.

- **S**caffolding – scaffolding provides some students with the support needed to access the same activity as others in the class. This may mean providing a list of key words to assist reading of a passage or a writing frame when answering 12- or 16-mark questions.

- **G**rouping – depending on the activity set, students may benefit from working in mixed-ability groups, where more-able students can take on the role of lead learners with the responsibility of directing the group and checking understanding. This in turn helps consolidation of their own knowledge. For other activities, grouping by ability may be more suitable with different groups being set different activities.

- **T**argeted intervention – at some points you may wish to work closely with a certain student or small group of students. This could be to support less-able students or challenge the most able to think beyond the obvious. This is challenging when teaching large classes but can be done if the class is provided with tasks that encourage independent learning and the group develops a culture of collaboration, rather than relying on their teacher to provide all the answers.

TOPIC: Types of conformity and explanations of conformity

Conformity in an elevator

NO HANDOUT

P **H** S **G** T

> The nature of this activity lends itself to higher-order thinking, particularly analysis and application. Using collaborative learning structures (see page 5) can also ensure that your higher-ability students are stretched and that your lower-ability students are supported.

I have always started the Social influence topic in the same way and I (MG) find it is an interesting starting point.

Type in to Google (other search engines are available…etc.) or YouTube, 'conformity in an elevator'. You are likely to come across some excellent candid-camera style pranks where confederates of the film crew stand the 'wrong' way in an elevator (i.e. with their back to the elevator door); this confuses the unwitting stars of the show who invariably conform and slowly turn their backs on the elevator door. At the time of writing, there are two great clips at https://www.youtube.com/watch?v=BgRoiTWkBHU and https://www.youtube.com/watch?v=nPobACr9oL4

Apart from some general introductions, this is pretty much the first thing I show my students in this topic. I ask them a very simple question: 'Why do those people conform?'. You can use the **'random numbers'** or **'group statements'**

techniques to facilitate the discussion (see pages 5 and 6). This is a good starter activity to help students start to consider the different types of conformity and the explanations that underlie them. Students might suggest reasons like 'not wanting to look different' and 'thinking that something might be going on'. You can use these suggestions as stems to introduce concepts such as public and private conformity, compliance and internalisation, and informational and normative social influence.

If you prefer, you could teach these concepts first and ask the students to identify which type of conformity they have witnessed. Ultimately, I think that this is debatable and there is no clear answer, which is why it is such a good clip to start the topic.

As an aside, if you are wondering how this might demonstrate informational social influence, I think I may have a personal anecdote that might help. Having moved to London a few years ago, I braved the

tube to meet a friend at Covent Garden. Anyone who knows that underground station will be familiar with the fact that you have to exit the station via one of the three lifts. So, at the front of the queue, I entered the lift and turned round to face the lift door. As I turned around, and all the commuters piled in, they were in fact facing me. I quickly realised that they had clearly been in this lift before and that we were going to be exiting the lift via a different door. Obviously, I turned around. A classic case of informational social influence and conforming to people who clearly know more than you.

TOPIC: Types of conformity and explanations of conformity

Conformity quotes rolling show

NO HANDOUT

P H S G T

> This activity is not differentiated.

'Rolling shows' are essentially slideshows of images that automatically change after a set period of time – 5 seconds for example. Details on how to setup Rolling Shows using PowerPoint are outlined on page 8.

These slideshows make an excellent start to the lesson. I usually have one running

with some appropriate music before the students arrive, so that from the moment they turn up, the topic and tone of the lesson are clear.

You could fill multiple slides on your PowerPoint show with quotes about conformity. There are some excellent thought-provoking conformity quotes

at http://www.quotegarden.com. Follow the link to 'conformity'.

You could also include some images that illustrate conformity in action: people queueing, students with their shirts untucked etc.

TOPIC: Types of conformity and explanations of conformity

Beans in a jar – conformity demonstration

NO HANDOUT

P **H** S **G** T

> Again, this activity is more of a demonstration than an activity so there is not too much scope for differentiation. However, you could use collaborative learning structures (see page 5) to consider higher-order questions.

Conformity is a great topic to teach, my favourite in fact, and generally the students are enthusiastic about it too.

As we know, the key to generating intrigue and interest around a topic is through well-designed 'starter' activities.

There are several ways you could introduce conformity and social influence, and we've included a fair few in this section. 'Beans in a jar' is just another way to do it.

Beans in a jar

Jenness (1932) conducted an experiment using beans in a jar to demonstrate the power of conformity.

To replicate this activity, fill a jar with beans (or smarties, pasta shells etc). Ask your students to estimate how many beans are in the jar.

In order to determine whether their behaviour is influenced by others, you need to ask the students to write their answers on pieces of paper where previous students have recorded theirs (I told my students I had already asked my tutor group to do it that morning, though of course, I had made up their estimates for the purposes of this demonstration).

Some of the pieces of paper should contain high estimates (group 1), others should have lower estimates (group 2).

Participants in each condition should differ in terms of their mean estimates, as a consequence of conforming to the estimates they see.

This activity and demonstration should help you to introduce the concepts of internalisation, informational social influence and ambiguous scenarios.

You could also use it as an opportunity to ask students research methods questions. For example, what is the independent variable, dependent variable, research design etc.

References

Jenness, A. (1932). The role of discussion in changing opinion regarding the matter of fact. *Journal of Abnormal and Social Psychology, 27,* 279–96.

TOPIC: Types of conformity and explanations of conformity

Which type of conformity?

P · **H** · **S** · G · **T**

A version of **Handout 13** appeared in the previous edition of the *Teacher's Companion* but it has been carefully updated to reflect the new specification content and the demands of application questions.

It is important that we constantly help students to practise applying their knowledge to unseen examples as this is a skill they will be tested on in their exams.

Handout 13 briefly describes a series of conformity examples. Ask your students to identify the types of conformity shown and the motivation that is most likely to underlie that conformity. For example, although an example of conformity might clearly be a case of compliance, is it more likely to be motivated by fear of rejection by the group or by the pursuit of approval?

Although the examples have been written with a specific type of conformity in mind, in the past, students have often been able to articulate alternative interpretations; if these interpretations are fully justified and logical, I think the students should be praised for their original thinking!

Ideally, this should be an independent activity that helps students consolidate their understanding of the types of conformity and helps them practise their application skills – a higher-order skill.

It could be used as scaffolding for weaker students before they attempt application questions because it will help them to structure their answers.

When the students have completed the sheet, make sure that you feed back from students in a targeted way. For example, ask your higher-ability students to explain which types of conformity they have chosen for the research studies at the bottom. Ask your lower-ability students to explain the more obvious examples at the top of the handout.

TOPIC: Types of conformity and explanations of conformity

Conformity table mats

P · **H** · **S** · G · T

This activity can either be used as a starter or consolidation activity.

If you have a lovely technician in your department, ask them to laminate enough copies of **Handout 14** for the class. Then, they should cut out the statements on **Handout 15** and place them into envelopes; there should be enough envelope 'sets' for each member of the class.

In essence, this is a very simple matching exercise. As a more difficult topic starter exercise, ask students to place the 'compliance' statement on the left normative social influence side next to the 'type of conformity' subtitle and the 'internalisation' statement on the right informational social influence side next to the 'types of conformity' subtitle. The students then have to sort all of the other statements into their correct places. This may be difficult because you haven't taught the content, but it is by no means impossible. Students just have to think through what is meant by compliance and internalisation and make educated guesses as to what leads to those types of conformity. In the process, they will gain a better idea of the two explanations of conformity.

Alternatively, you could use these table mats as a simple progress check tool at the end of the topic and as a consolidation activity.

You could use this activity to provide structure and scaffolding for an 'Explanations of conformity' essay.

If this activity is used as a topic starter activity, before you have actually taught the content, students will need to use higher-order thinking skills.

Laminating the table mats and statement sets will save you cutting out the statements again the following year.

TOPIC: Types of conformity and explanations of conformity

Stickman theories

I've used this activity quite often with my students. They tend to remember theories better as a result, as they have to understand the theories in order to illustrate them. Obviously, you need to judge whether this activity is suitable and appropriate for your students. I find it useful with weaker students, but I'm not convinced it has much value with higher-ability students.

Display one of the two explanations of why people conform on your whiteboard (e.g. normative social influence). It is best to break this down for students with simple bullet points so students are not overwhelmed with complex language (see below).

Then give them an allotted amount of time, say 7 minutes, to illustrate how those explanations work in a visual way. Tell students to use simple stick people.

I usually add the rule that they must include the words that I display on the board in bold. They should not use any other words in order to explain their drawings, that is unless they are contained within thought or speech bubbles.

This ensures students do not simply copy out the explanations on the board and then add 'token' images to appease you!

After they have completed the first explanation of why people conform (e.g. informational social influence), give them another amount of allotted time to complete the second.

Suggested bullet-point forms of the explanations to display on the whiteboard are given below:

Normative social influence

- As people we have a **need to be accepted** by others and to **avoid rejection**.
- To gain acceptance from others and make a favourable impression on them we are inclined to **conform**.
- This results in **compliance**, because we might change our behaviour or articulate views **publicly** in order to be accepted or liked, but **privately** we do not.
- It is most likely to happen when we believe we are **under surveillance** by the group.

Informational social influence

- We also have a basic need to **evaluate our ideas and attitudes** in order to check they are accurate or correct.

NO HANDOUT

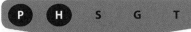

This could be an activity that is set specifically for weaker students who struggle to handle complex language. The activity forces them to think about what the explanations mean and how this applies to real-life situations. In that respect, you could also argue that it requires them to use higher-order thinking skills. Meanwhile, your higher-ability students could be asked to complete a different, more appropriate, activity.

- Therefore, in **ambiguous situations**, where the right course of action or opinion is not clear, we might change (conform) our behaviour or views in line with others.
- This results in **internalisation**, because there is a change in both our **public** *and* **private** attitudes and behaviours.

It is more likely to occur when we believe others to be **experts**.

TOPIC: Variables affecting conformity

Replicating Asch's research

Asch's (1956) study is a fun experiment to replicate with your class. In the previous edition, we included six pages on stimulus lines cards in order to help you repeat the experiment. In hindsight, in the age of PowerPoints and the internet, this was probably a waste of handout space. You could easily make the stimulus and comparison lines on your PowerPoints, or if your skills are not that advanced, I am happy to make these available on our blog.

There are perhaps three ways in which this study could be replicated with your class:

1. If you have a situation where one student is absent, brief the rest of the class on Asch's experiment and enlist them as confederates. In the next lesson when the absent student returns, run the experiment by showing the stimulus lines and comparison line. On 12 out of 18

trials everyone should give the wrong answer. Interview the 'absent' student(s) about what he/she felt and debrief.

2. Prepare a note which 'needs' to be sent to a staff member on the other side of the school. Ask one student to deliver this note. In the time that the student is gone, explain the study to the rest of the class and enlist them as confederates. Make sure the staff member knows the purpose of the student's visit and note, otherwise their confusion may give the game away. (I like to write an awful joke and then ask for the student to deliver the 'very important' message to my lucky colleague.)

3. Prepare instructions for each member of the class detailing their role in the experiment. Every member of the class should receive 'confederate' instructions apart from one, who

NO HANDOUT

P   H   S   G   T

As this is a replication of an experiment, the activity is not differentiated.

However, you could ask different levels of questions about the replication to students of different ability. You could explore the ethics, the type of conformity, the underlying motivation etc.

receives the 'participant' instructions. In this case, it would be important to emphasise to students the importance of not sharing what is written with the people around them, and to not show reactions (e.g. giggling!), which would give away their role as confederates.

This activity should help to embed the procedures of the study and also give some insight into both why people conform and associated ethical issues.

TOPIC: Variables affecting conformity

Asch numbers quiz

HANDOUT 16

P H S G T

Students always remember Asch's research, but that can lead to complacency in their detail. If students are asked to outline this research, it is important that it is full of detail in order to gain the highest marks.

If students are asked to outline Asch in an examination question, it is likely they will be able to achieve basic marks without too much thought. **Handout 16** is designed to take them into the higher mark bands. By focusing their attention on the numbers, students will hopefully be more likely to include these details in their answers, which will undoubtedly help them to pick up more marks.

In addition, I often find that students inaccurately report one particular finding in Asch's original research: "In

Asch's study, 33% of the participants conformed". Of course, this is in fact wrong. Instead, it should read: "In Asch's study, participants conformed, on average, on 33% of the critical trials". This is a crucial difference. The numbers quiz is designed to help them see that, by asking them to calculate the total number of critical trials and then asking them the percentage of those trials where the participants conformed.

You could bring in a competitive edge by giving the answers to the students and asking them to calculate how far out they were on each answer... the student with the lowest score wins.

For reference, the answers are as follows: 123, 3, 5, 18, 12, 1476 (123 X 12), 33%, 25%, 75%, 1%, 5.5%, 9%.

You could vary this activity in a few ways. Firstly, for less-able students, you could allow them to match the numbers at the bottom of **Handout 16** to the correct answers.

For middle-ability students, you could ask them to cover the numbers at the bottom of the worksheet to test their memory of the details.

For more-able students, you could ask them to cover the questions, and to state what the numbers at the bottom of the worksheet refer to (in the style of 'if these are the answers, what are the questions?').

TOPIC: Variables affecting conformity

Asch evaluation ladders

HANDOUTS 17 and 18

P **H** **S** G T

The idea behind, and the technique for, using elaboration ladders is outlined on page 7. In my experience, using the concept of 'ladders' has been one of the most successful visual 'gimmicks' in helping my students to understand the concept of evaluating in depth. A different version of this activity was included in the previous edition, it has been updated here to reflect the evaluative points included in the new *Complete Companion* (page 21).

'Ladders' (see pages 7 and 8) are basically a way to encourage students to write about their evaluative points in more depth and to avoid basic and superficial comments such as "Asch's research cannot be generalised to today because of McCarthyism which made people more likely to conform." Remember that the mark schemes (see **Handout 1**) require students to be good at both description (AO1) and evaluation (AO3), and therefore, students will score lower in the essay mark bands if their evaluation skills are not up to scratch. Our aim here is to try and get students to hit the dizzy heights of levels 3 and 4.

Students start with an introductory evaluation comment at the bottom of the ladder and then gradually elaborate this comment further and further until they reach the top! The box on the right-hand side of the handout is designed to prompt students into thinking of ways they could elaborate their evaluations (see page 21 for examples).

Asch (1956) is a good study to use this technique with because, although the evaluations are relatively simple, students rarely elaborate them effectively.

Handouts 17 and **18** provide the framework and some starting points. **Handout 18** is aimed at brighter students who should be encouraged to think for themselves, whereas **Handout 17** is designed to give weaker students more support. As such, you can provide different pathways to students of different ability. However, if you are teaching the Social influence topic as the first topic of the course, it is likely that students will need lots of support

Evaluating research in depth is undoubtedly a higher-order thinking skill that will stretch and challenge all learners. The 'ladder' handouts provide students with a scaffolded worksheet to help them increase the depth of their evaluative points. **Handout 18** provides much more scaffolding than **Handout 17** and therefore you can offer students different pathways according to their ability.

completing 'ladders'. The more 'ladders' they complete the more independent your students will start to become.

References

Asch (1956) Studies of independence and conformity: I. A minority of one against a unanimous majority. *Psychological Monographs: General and Applied, 70(9)*, 1–70.

TOPIC: Conformity to social roles

How would you behave if...?

Conformity to social roles is actually quite an abstract idea so it makes sense to start with an activity that helps to give students a more tangible feel for what it means.

A simple way to do this might be to ask the students to imagine how their behaviour might change if they were in a different scenario. For example, how might your behaviour be different if:

- you are a police officer on the 'beat'?
- you are a football fan at a match against your rivals?
- you are a teacher in front of a class?
- you are a university student in a university bar?
- you are a parent at a parents' evening?
- you are a politician in the House of Commons?
- you are an inmate in a prison?
- you are a Year 7 student in a maths class?
- you are a Year 10 student in a maths class?

I would ask students to just bullet point two to three adjectives that would describe their behaviour or attitude in these scenarios. At the end of this, you can ask the students to share their ideas and it is likely that there will be similarity in their answers. Where does this similarity come from?

Following this, you could move the discussion on slightly. For example, how might your behaviour change if:

- you are a police officer at home with your family?
- you are a teacher at the weekend seeing your friends at a pub?
- you are an inmate who is released from prison seeing your mother for the first time as a free individual?
- you are a university student at a job interview?

These examples may help your students to consider how the behaviour of people changes depending on the situations and role they are playing, despite the

NO HANDOUT

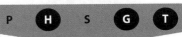

This activity is fairly loose in its structure. Hopefully, the nature of the discussion will lead to higher-order thinking because students will examine the nature of social roles, conformity and behaviour. To make the activity more structured and differentiated, there is a good opportunity to use **collaborative learning structures** for parts of the discussion (see page 5). Alternatively, highly-skilled questioning could be targeted at appropriate students according to their ability.

fact they are the same people. Why does our behaviour change in this way?

A good way to end this discussion might be to ask students to summarise the discussion in 24 words (a random number, just to help students identify to main point of the discussion).

TOPIC: Conformity to social roles

Flipped learning: The Stanford Prison Experiment

We all know that students like to watch videos. Mainly, I might uncharitably suggest, because it means they can relax and not do any writing. Well, not in my classroom!

I have a very simple rule for my lesson planning and that rule states that if a video is over ten minutes long, there must be a worksheet that goes with it.

However, a really interesting new concept that has been gathering pace is that of 'flipped learning'. A really useful summary is here: http://www.edudemic.com/guides/flipped-classrooms-guide/ Essentially, the idea is that the lecture (or in this case, watching a video) occurs outside the classroom, the lesson in the classroom is used to explore the themes and ideas.

I would advocate using this idea to explore the Stanford Prison Experiment (SPE). Documentaries about this experiment (and the BBC replication

years later) are often available to buy on the internet (albeit they are quite expensive), search for the 'Quiet Rage: Stanford Prison Experiment' DVD which features interviews and commentary from Zimbardo himself. Alternatively, give students a list of YouTube videos to watch for homework. Above all, 'flipped learning' saves lesson time which is extremely useful for such a content-heavy course.

During the homework and 'flipped learning', students should write comments on what they see which they can discuss in the next lesson. To give this homework some structure, provide the students with themes they should comment on. For example:

- behaviour which showed the prisoners had conformed to their social roles
- behaviour which showed the prison guards had conformed to their social roles

NO HANDOUT

Structure can be provided in this activity by giving themes/categories that students must comment on when watching the clips of The Stanford Prison Experiment.

During class feedback and discussion, higher-order questioning should be targeted at more-able students. In contrast, retention and comprehension questions can be targeted at lower-ability students.

- evidence that shows the participants were initially 'normal' people, without a history of rebellion or aggression
- aspects of the study that might be judged as ethical
- ways to defend the ethics of the SPE
- evaluation of the research method used.

TOPIC: Conformity to social roles

Dimension line. Conformity to social roles?

The activity on **Handout 19** is designed to help students evaluate the conclusions of the Stanford Prison Experiment (SPE). One interpretation of the study is that the 'normal' participants conformed to their social roles of prisoner or guard and this is what resulted in their rebellious and aggressive behaviour. However, it is possible to challenge the validity of these claims and provide alternative explanations.

On **Handout 19**, each box presents evidence for or against the idea that the SPE shows the participants conforming to social roles. The students should decide which boxes provide evidence for and which boxes provide evidence against.

Having done that, the students should then decide the *strength* of that evidence. They can represent their decisions visually by writing the evidence letter on the dimension line. For example, if they think that evidence A strongly supports the 'conformity to social roles' argument, they can write 'evidence A' on the left hand side on the arrow. They should also write a brief justification for their decision.

As a teacher, you could decide to make more of this activity by asking the students to draw the dimension line on A3 paper so that the students have more room to articulate their decisions. They could also cut out the boxes and stick them on the dimension line.

Once the students have completed this for all of the evidence boxes, they can use the visual representation of the strength of evidence to help them write a short conclusion. On the weight

of evidence, does the SPE illustrate the power of conformity to social roles?

Support for less-able students

The interpretation of this evidence is not easy. For less-able students, you could provide a 'cheat sheet' that helps prompt their responses and decisions. For example:

Evidence A: If the participants know they are not being watched, can their behaviour be due to demand characteristics? If not, what else can explain their behaviour?

Evidence B: Did the prisoners automatically become aggressive and rebellious in this study? What would we expect if the participants had automatically conformed to their social roles? Does this suggest conformity to social roles is always automatic? What might make conformity to social roles more likely?

Evidence C: The behaviour of the soldiers in Iraq was very similar to those in the SPE. Why do you think the soldiers and guards behave in similar ways? Does this real-life example support the conclusions of the SPE? Do the results generalise outside of the SPE? What type of validity is high if results do generalise outside of the study?

Evidence D: If these participants were judged as 'normal' before the study, why did their behaviour change? Why do all the psychological tests before study strengthen the argument that conformity had occurred?

Evidence E: Which side could this evidence be used for? It might be worth combining this evidence with evidence D.

> This activity requires higher-order skills; it involves both evaluation and analysis of evidence.
>
> The activity can be completed 'as is' by more-able students, but you may wish to provide the 'cheat sheet' support for less-able students. The 'cheat sheet' support guidance is included below in the lesson notes.

Evidence F: If these students, who did not take part in the study, were able to guess the aim of the study, why might that make us concerned about the original study? How is this related to the concept of validity – the aim to measure what you intend to measure?

Evidence G: What are investigator effects? Why might they be relevant in this case? How are they related to the concept of validity – the aim to measure what you intend to measure?

It might be useful to photocopy these prompts for your students.

References

Banuazizi, A. and Movahedi, S. (1975) Interpersonal dynamics in a simulated prison: A methodological analysis. American Psychologist, 30, 152–60.

Haslam, S.A. and Reicher, S.D. (2012) Contesting the 'nature' of conformity: What Milgram and Zimbardo's studies really show. PLoS Biology, 10(11).

TOPIC: Situational variables affecting obedience

Demonstrating obedience

As the teacher, ask the class to do something, e.g. "Can everyone please stand behind their chairs. Place your right hand on your right hip. Now place your left hand in the air, and then slant/bend your body to the left (I'm a little teapot!)."

This excellent idea was submitted by Sara Berman in an old incarnation (the specification before the last one!) of *The Teacher's Companion*:

'Ask the class to do strange things, e.g. get them to sit in a row according to birthdays; lots of chat relaxes them. Then ask them all to stand behind their chairs, on their desks, with some A4 paper, tear it carefully into strips, drop every fourth strip on the floor, all those with birthdays between March and June get down and pick up paper, etc. Nothing dangerous or embarrassing but keep going until someone asks 'Why?'

It's extremely interesting to see how far they will obey totally absurd requests.

You can then discuss why they obey. What was it about the situation, my role, their role, the socialisation process of school behaviour?

This can also lead to discussion of Orne's research on demand characteristics.

Orne (1962) observed that people behave in quite unusual ways if they think they are taking part in a psychology experiment. For example, in one experiment he asked participants to add up columns of numbers on a sheet of paper and then tear the paper up and repeat this again. If people believed this was part of a psychology experiment some were willing to continue the task for over six hours! This led Orne to develop the idea of *demand characteristics*.

People taking part in an experiment want to please an investigator and want their performance to be helpful. A demand characteristic acts as a confounding variable.

NO HANDOUT

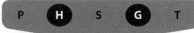

P **H** S **G** T

A discussion about the nature of obedience can provide good opportunities to ask higher-order questions. For example: Why do humans obey so easily? Could there be an evolutionary component to obedience behaviour? Predict variables which are likely to increase/decrease obedience etc. Ensure that your more-able students are challenged with questions which stretch their thinking.

References

Orne, M.T. (1962). On the social psychology of the psychological experiment: With particular reference to demand characteristics and their implications. *American Psychologist, 17*, 776–83.

TOPIC: Situational variables affecting obedience

Teaching with cartoons

What follows is an exceptionally good idea that was included by Adrian Frost in the previous incarnation (the specification before last!) of *The Teacher's Companion*. So good it seemed a shame to not include again! Although, I would argue that this type of activity should mainly be used with less-able students who find the details of studies difficult to memorise. More-able students should be using more time to refine their evaluative skills and applying their knowledge:

I (AF) do make quite a lot of use of visual learning, mainly because I like doodling on the board.

Some kind of visual approach is useful for the social influence section of the specification because it helps students to keep track of what's going on in the studies.

Research like that of Asch, Crutchfield or Moscovici can get very confusing for students over time, as they try to keep track of the varying stimulus material, majorities, minorities, confederates, dissenters and experimenters. I always find it best to draw the varying conditions on the board, even if I only use stick men. Little speech bubbles can be added and I do genuinely find that it helps the students remember the material.

If you're not big on drawing, get the students to do it for you. Some students

just like to draw, and can be relied upon to produce excellent visual aids and revision material. A surprising amount of material can be crammed into one image (see the Milgram example below).

Some students really like this approach, others groan.

Ask students to produce cartoons

Get a big compilation book of cartoons. Books of newspaper cartoons like 'Peanuts' or 'Calvin and Hobbes' work best, as they contain hundreds of images of the same people, drawn at about the same size, wearing the same clothes in each frame. Photocopy lots of different figures and then cut out and stick them onto a sheet of A3 paper. This is time consuming but you only have to do it once.

Photocopy this A3 'resource sheet' and distribute to students. Ask them to cut out figures and stick on paper, and then they have to add speech bubbles of their own. This works well with two characters where they have to debate a particular issue, with each figure holding a viewpoint and the argument alternating between the two viewpoints, so that you end up with something like 'Calvin and Hobbes debate the ethics of Milgram's research', with one character presenting the criticisms and the other presenting

NO HANDOUT

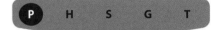

P H S G T

This type of activity is mainly aimed at less-able students.

counterpoints. This really helps the students to produce balanced argument, discussion and debate, rather than rote learn AO2 points.

One you've got the sheets, you only have to rustle up scissors and glue anytime you want to use the exercise. (In my experience, groups like the exercise so long as they are only ever asked to do it once or twice. The results look great if photocopied onto coloured card and it is guaranteed that other staff will ask to photocopy your mastersheet.)

TOPIC: Situational variables affecting obedience

The David Bailey school of teaching

The previous activity is fairly time-consuming and is only really focused on knowledge retention; therefore, it is aimed only at the less-able students.

However, all students struggle to remember the vast array of studies they are required to have knowledge of on the AQA course.

A fun, simple and quick way to help the students remember the studies is to have a visual reference point in your classroom. When teaching a new study, consider using a few of your students to perform a very quick 'freeze-frame' representation of the study. Take a digital photograph of all of these and make a classroom display.

NO HANDOUT

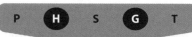

This activity is not differentiated.

For Milgram, all you need is three chairs, a few electrical wires from your Science department, a lab coat, a card with some word pairs, and a make-shift wall. Try and squeeze in as many memorable details as you can!

TOPIC: Situational variables affecting obedience

Milgram's obedience barometer

In Milgram's (1963) original study of obedience, he found that 65% of participants continued to shock the learners up to 450 volts. This was the maximum voltage and far beyond what was marked 'Danger: Severe shock'.

Milgram (1974) then carried out a series of variations of the obedience experiment in order to identify some of the influencing factors. It is clear that in the new specification, there will be more emphasis on the variations of Milgram's original research.

Some of those variations are described at the bottom of **Handout 20**, and the suggested activity is that students place these variations onto the 'obedience barometer' to indicate the obedience level they think was found. They should also justify their estimations.

Answers

Touch-proximity: 30% of participants continued to 450 volts

Different location: 48%

Experimenter-absent: 22%

Teacher's discretion: 2.5%

Two peers rebel: 10%

Proximity: 40%

HANDOUT 20

This activity requires the higher-order thinking skill of prediction. You could also use **collaborative learning structures** (see page 5) to ensure more-able students are stretched and less-able students are supported.

References

Milgram, S. (1963). Behavioural study of obedience. *Journal of Abnormal and Social Psychology, 67*, 371–8.

Milgram, S. (1974). *Obedience to authority: An experimental view*. New York: Harper and Row.

TOPIC: Situational variables affecting obedience

Discussing Milgram's internal validity

I always find that students are able to gain a greater understanding of internal and external validity when teaching Milgram's study.

I've used versions of **Handout 20** and **Handout 21** for several years now and found them to be something of a game changer with several students. **Handout 20** is designed to help students evaluate Milgram's research and truly engage with what is meant by internal validity. The students can then move onto **Handout 21** and start to understand the difference between internal validity and external validity.

The instructions for **Handout 21** are fairly self-explanatory, but as the teacher, your job is to make sure the students are moving beyond generic statements such as 'this affects the internal validity'. Ask the following questions:

• Why does it affect the internal validity?

• What is internal validity?

• What did Milgram intend to measure (prompts are at the top of the handout)?

• If the study was affected by demand characteristics, did he measure what he intended to measure?

Ideally, with your guidance, students will be able to write something more along these lines: "If the participants did not really believe they were causing harm to the learner, this questions the internal validity of Milgram's study. Milgram intended to measure whether people would obey an authority figure, even if it resulted in harm, but if the participants did not think they were actually harming the learner, then he did not measure exactly what he intended."

References

Orne, M.T. and Holland, C.C. (1968). On the ecological validity of laboratory deceptions. *International Journal of Psychiatry, 6(4)*, 282–93.

HANDOUT 21

Scaffolding is provided in **Handout 21** to help students structure their evaluative points and increase the depth of their comments.

This is a difficult activity and the teacher should provide more personalised one-to-one support for less-able students as they complete the activity.

Perry, G. (2012). Behind the Shock Machine: The untold story of the notorious Milgram psychology experiments. Brunswick, Vic: Scribe Publications.

TOPIC: Situational variables affecting obedience

Discussing Milgram's external validity

Before attempting **Handout 22** with your students, I would urge you to complete **Handout 21** first and read the relevant lesson notes.

Handout 22 is designed to follow **Handout 21** and to help students' understanding of the difference between internal and external validity.

As the teacher, your job this time is to make sure the students are moving beyond generic statements such as 'this affects the external validity because the results cannot be generalised'. Ask the following questions:

- Why does it affect the external validity?
- What is external validity?
- What is different about Milgram's situation compared to the Holocaust?

(e.g. in Milgram's study, the participants were led to believe the shocks would have no long-term damage; in contrast, the perpetrators of the Holocaust invariably knew what the consequences of their actions would be.)

- Why then, does this mean the results and conclusions cannot be generalised to the Holocaust? What else might we need to explain the events of the Holocaust? (Mandel believes variables such as racism and discrimination are required, not the 'obedience alibi'.)

References

Mandel, D.R. (1998). The obedience alibi: Milgram's account of the Holocaust reconsidered. *Analyse and Kritik: Zeitschrift für Sozialwissenschaften, 20,* 74–94.

Blass, T. (1999). The Milgram paradigm after 35 years: Some things we now know about obedience to authority. *Journal of Applied Social Psychology, 29,* 955–78

P **H** **S** G **T**

Scaffolding is provided in **Handout 22** to help students structure their evaluative points and increase the depth of their comments.

This is a difficult activity and the teacher should provide more personalised one-to-one support for less-able students as they complete the activity.

TOPIC: Explanations of obedience

The case of Sandor Képíríó

The case of Sandor Képíríó is briefly outlined on **Handout 23**. If you are able to gain access to the documentary that interviews Képíríó, it is well worth a watch. At the time of writing, it could be found here: https://www.youtube.com/watch?v=vCJpd6_RGfU There are also plenty of websites and news outlets that describe his case. Again, this may be a good opportunity to try 'flipped learning' (see page 15).

In many ways the interview with Képíríó and the defence he put forward in his trial perfectly reflect the legitimate authority explanation of obedience.

When discussing this with your students and supporting their explanations (see bottom of **Handout 23**). you may wish to draw out the following themes:

Agentic state: Képíríó feels that he was 'just following orders' and therefore the actions were not his own.

Responsibility: Képíríó claims that he demanded written confirmation from whoever gave the orders to state that they accepted responsibility for the consequences (although there is no evidence that the written confirmation was ever provided).

Legitimate authority: Képíríó's orders came from his superiors and the Nazi officers who were occupying the country at that time.

Institutional structure: Képíríó's job and role existed within a clearly defined institutional structure with explicit chains of command.

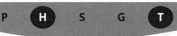

P **H** S G **T**

This activity requires higher-order application skills which will stretch and challenge the students. To support your less-able students, you may wish to provide them with targeted one-to-one support to structure their answers and provide prompts.

Self-image: When faced with the consequences of his actions (e.g. photos from the raid and subsequent massacre), Képíríó feels sorry for what happens but feels relatively guilt-free because he does not feel responsible. This helps to maintain a positive self-image.

TOPIC: A dispositional explanation: The authoritarian personality

Questionnaire 1: The California F-scale (authoritarian personality)

It is nice to have resources that can help students get a feel for what an authoritarian personality is like. In my opinion, one of the best ways to do this is to get the students to take the questionnaire themselves.

The questionnaire on **Handout 24** is adapted from Adorno's (1950) original. Due to the nature of the questions, this activity may cause considerable debate amongst the students. I think it would be important to tell the students that this is a shorter version of the questionnaire which was written a long time ago. I would be wary of students sharing their results in the class or with each other because of the obvious connotations with the authoritarian personality and

the actions of those in the Holocaust. Given today's culture and context, I would very much doubt that the majority of the students would score highly on this test; in addition, I have removed some of the most controversial questions and religious questions which may mean that the student's score are artificially inflated (because they would probably score low in the removed questions).

Bearing all of that in mind, I'll leave it up to you whether you share the general scoring instructions.

Scoring instructions

Add up all of the scores and divide by 16.

HANDOUT 24

| P | H | S | G | T |

This activity is not differentiated.

0–3 in the original scale would have indicated someone with more liberal thinking.

3–4.5 would indicate someone within the normal limits.

4.5–5.5 would indicate someone with more right-wing views.

Any score over 5.5 would indicate someone with an authoritarian personality.

References

Adorno et al. (1950). *The Authoritarian Personality*. New York: Harper and Brothers.

TOPIC: A dispositional explanation: The authoritarian personality

Questionnaire 2: The right-wing authoritarianism (RWA) scale

Robert Altemeyer (1981) refined the concept of authoritarian personality by identifying a cluster of three of the original personality variables that he referred to as 'right-wing authoritarianism' (RWA). According to Altemeyer, high-RWA people possess three important personality characteristics that predispose them to obedience:

- conventionalism: an adherence to conventional normal values
- authoritarian submission: uncritical submission to legitimate authorities
- authoritarian aggression: aggressive feelings toward people who violate these norms.

Handout 25 is an adapted version of Altemeyer's (2006) RWA questionnaire for your students to complete and/or consider.

Once again, if you do ask your students to complete this questionnaire, please read the previous lesson notes for **Handout 24** and consider how to prepare students beforehand; this type of questionnaire can cause difficult scenarios with students.

Scoring instructions

The first two questions should be ignored, Altemeyer calls these 'warm-up questions'.

For questions 6, 9, 11, 12, 13 and 14, the following scoring system applies:

-4	1 point
-3	2 points
-2	3 points
-1	4 points
0	5 points
1	6 points
2	7 points
3	8 points
4	9 points

For the rest of the questions (which are shown with a *), the following scoring system applies:

-4	9 points
-3	8 points
-2	7 points
-1	6 points
0	5 points
1	4 points
2	3 points
3	2 points
4	1 point

HANDOUT 25

| P | H | S | G | T |

This activity is not differentiated.

The lowest possible score is 12 and the highest possible score is 108. Altemeyer suggests that his Canadian college students were scoring around an average of 35 and their parents around 45.

Extra activity

You could ask your students to identify the questions on the scale that measure each of the three personality variables.

References

Altemeyer, R. (1981). *Right-Wing Authoritarianism*. Winnipeg: University of Manitoba Press.

Altemeyer, R. (2006). *The Authoritarians*. Page 10-15. Altemeyer, R (2006). *The Authoritarians*. Page 10-15. http://members.shaw.ca/jeanaltemeyer/drbob/TheAuthoritarians.pdf

TOPIC: A dispositional explanation: The authoritarian personality

Post-it® picture: Situational or dispositional?

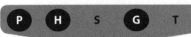

An idea for a plenary when teaching the explanations of obedience is to display powerful images from a historical event, e.g. from the Holocaust or Rwandan Genocide.

Give each student a Post-it® note and ask them to write their views on the following:

- Was this historical event mostly the result of situational or dispositional factors?

Their summary argument should include brief references to psychological explanations, evidence and/or evaluation.

This plenary activity encourages students to summarise the research they have studied in class and formulate their own opinions based on the evidence.

The activity can also help you to create thought-provoking displays for your classroom. Buy a cheap frame to display the Post-it® notes, with the image in the middle.

> This activity requires students to formulate their own views based on the available evidence and is therefore good for stretching the most-able students.
>
> You might consider using **collaborative learning structures** such as **group statements** and **random numbers** (see pages 5 and 6) to help support the less-able students before starting the substantive activity.

TOPIC: A dispositional explanation: The authoritarian personality

Debates

You could actually precede the 'Post-it® picture' activity with a full-blown debate. Although a scary prospect for a classroom teacher, debates do provide students with an opportunity to develop the public speaking and communication skills so vaunted by higher education institutions and employers.

Debates scare me! I once planned a lesson with a 30-minute debate in mind. It lasted about 5 minutes, with a 25-minute black hole in my lesson ensuing!

The mistake I made was not providing sufficient structure and guidance for the students. There are many different ways you could do this: there is no one-size-fits-all approach, since every debate is different in its requirements and characteristics. However, I'll describe some of the ways my colleagues have conducted debates with some success, and hopefully you will be able to adapt some of those ideas. The debate surrounding situational and dispositional explanations of obedience provide us with an excellent opportunity to do this.

Students could be assigned to debate teams, and given a position to defend. For example, 'Some individuals are always more likely to obey authority figures simply because of their personality, even if that obedience results in harming others', and vice versa.

Students should then be given time to prepare for the debate, perfect their arguments and prepare for rebuttals. It is often students' confidence that inhibits their participation in debates, so this period of reflection is quite important.

It might also be useful to formalise the debate by having a specific order to adhere to. For example, the debate should begin with one team presenting their arguments to support their position. The opposing team is then given the opportunity to rebut those arguments. Then, depending on the time available, the original team could answer those criticisms. There may also be opportunity to open the debate to the floor, with the teacher acting as facilitator.

House of Commons

An interesting variation to this would be contextualising the debate within The House of Commons, with one group presenting a bill with some relevance to the ethics debate, and the other team opposing the bill (for example, a bill which seeks to tighten the ethical rules within which psychologists have to operate). Students must also address each other in accordance with the proper parliamentary rule: "My Right Honourable Friend…"!

> This activity requires students to formulate arguments based on the available evidence: a higher-order skill.
>
> As a teacher, you can ensure that the groups are mixed ability and that debate roles are given to appropriate students according to their skills/ability.

Court Cases

'Is Képírió guilty of being personally responsibility for the murder of Jews and Serbs at Novi Sad' (see page 19 and 113).

You could also frame the debate in such a way that students either argue for guilty or not guilty positions.

You really could go to town on this by assigning students different roles according to their skills and confidence.

Possible roles that could be used include a prosecution team, a defence team, expert witnesses (e.g. the defendant, expert psychologists from the dispositional and/or situational perspective, the victims) and a jury. Those with active roles must research their parts before the trial, whereas the jury must write notes during the trial, and then present a reasoned decision afterwards based on the arguments.

TOPIC: Resistance to social influence

Rolling show – resisting obedience

I've outlined the idea of a 'rolling show' a few times already. On page 8 you can find instructions for creating a rolling show and some of the reasons why they are such a great start to the lesson.

Resisting conformity and obedience is a particularly poignant topic for using the rolling show, as there are so many examples from history where resistance from social influence could have prevented terrible events. It will also follow nicely and contrast with the rolling show on conformity (see page 11).

For the rolling show you could use images from the Holocaust, the Rwandan Genocide, Jonestown, Abu Ghraib, the Suffragettes, Rosa Parks, Fathers for Justice, the student loan protests etc.

NO HANDOUT

| P | H | S | **G** | T |

This activity is not differentiated, but if it results in a discussion, the teacher can make sure that questioning of the students' understanding is targeted by ability.

TOPIC: Resistance to social influence

Is it better to be resistant or obedient?

Another way to introduce the topic is by discussing the following question:

Is it better to be resistant or obedient?

Think about using one of the collaborative learning structures outlined on page 5, particularly '**group statements**' or '**random numbers**'.

NO HANDOUT

| P | H | S | **G** | T |

Using collaborative learning structures (see page 5) can also ensure that your higher-ability students are stretched and that your lower-ability students are supported.

TOPIC: Resistance to social influence

Questionnaire 3: Rotter's (1996) locus of control scale

I like this topic, not just because of its links to social influence, but also because it can be a tool to help students become aware of their thought tendencies; you can discuss their attribution style in terms of examination success, friendships, general behaviour etc. In fact, I like to talk about Arsene Wenger in this lesson (apologies to Arsenal fans), who has a tendency to attribute failure to external reasons (e.g. referees, the pitch) and attribute success to internal reasons (e.g. the right tactics, quality of the players). Perhaps I am being unfair. Anyway...

The term **locus of control** (Rotter, 1966) refers to a person's perception of personal control over their own behaviour. It is measured along a dimension of 'high internal' to 'high external'. High internals perceive themselves as having a great deal of control over their behaviour, and are therefore more likely to take personal responsibility for it (e.g. "That happened because I made it happen"). In contrast, high externals perceive their behaviour as being caused more by external forces or luck (e.g. "That happened because I was in the wrong place at the wrong time").

Some of the research in this area has indicated that high internals are less likely to rely on the opinions of others, and better able to resist coercion from others.

Handout 26 provides you with a questionnaire to give to students so that they can work out their own locus of control. This questionnaire is Rotter's I-E scale.

You could also combine this with a survey of some kind on the ability to resist coercion from others in order to undertake a correlational analysis between the two variables.

Scoring instructions

Score internal statements as follows (question numbers 2, 3, 5, 7, 9, 11, 12, 13, 14, 15, 16, 20).

HANDOUT 26

| P | H | S | **G** | T |

Using collaborative learning structures (see page 5) can also ensure that your higher-ability students are stretched and that your lower-ability students are supported.

Give each statement a score between 1 and 6, where the answer 'agree very much' = 1 and 'disagree very much' = 6.

Score external statements as follows (questions numbers 1, 4, 6, 8, 10, 17, 18, 19).

Give each statement a score between 1 and 6, where the answer 'agree very much' = 6 and 'disagree very much' = 1.

Add up total score. Score range from 20 to 120. A low score indicates an internal locus of control.

References

Rotter, J.B. (1966). Generalised expectations for internal versus external control of reinforcement. *Psychological Monographs, 30(1)*, 1–26.

TOPIC: Resistance to social influence

Application skills: The two-sentence technique

If your schemes of work and lesson planning follow the order of the AQA specification, it is likely that Social influence will be one of your first teaching topics. As such, it is an excellent time to develop all of the skills in your students that they will require for the rest of the course.

One of the most difficult for students to master is the skill of application. For the past few years, I have taught students the 'two-sentence technique' (see page 7). This technique is outlined on **Handout 27** and students can read through a worked example which is relevant to the social support topic.

Essentially, the 'two-sentence technique' is a writing structure to help students illustrate both the appropriate selection of material, and then the appropriate application of that knowledge to a new scenario; both required by the AQA mark schemes to secure top level scores.

So, go through **Handout 27** with the students, and then ask them to complete **Handout 28** which requires them to select appropriate knowledge from the resistance to social influence topic (locus of control in particular).

The 'two-sentence technique' is a little rigid in its structure and does not always

HANDOUTS 27 and 28

| P | H | **S** | G | T |

> **Handouts 15** and 16 provide scaffolding to students attempting application questions towards the start of the AS/A Level course.

lend itself easily to some application questions. However, at the start of the course, it is an excellent teaching tool and scaffolded support for the students. As the course progresses, more-able students will learn to use the technique in a more flexible way whilst the technique remains a good crutch for less-able students.

TOPIC: Minority influence

Where would we be without minority influence?

Display a definition of minority influence on your whiteboard:

"A form of social influence where people reject the established norm of the majority of the group members and move to the position of the minority."

Then, using a collaborative learning structure such as **'group statements'**

or **'random numbers'** (see pages 5 and 6), set the following discussion question, asking students to fully elaborate and justify their responses:

'Where would we be without minority influence?'

NO HANDOUT

| P | H | S | **G** | T |

> Using collaborative learning structures (see page 5) can also ensure that your higher-ability students are stretched and that your lower-ability students are supported.

TOPIC: Minority influence

Maximising your 'outline' marks

I have found myself in the last few years writing 'needs more detail' in some of my essay marking feedback. Of course, this is pretty useless feedback for students who genuinely do not understand what is meant by 'detail'. It is much easier to *show* them and *illustrate* to them what is meant by 'detail' and how this translates into examination marking.

It is feasible that within this topic the following question might be asked in an AS examination: *'Outline **and** evaluate one or more research studies into the role of minority influence.'* [12 marks]

Suppose that you have taught your students one key study, Moscovici et al. (1969), and so they need to outline this study in good detail. This activity should help them to know what 'good detail' means. Try using **Handout 29** with your students after you have outlined the study to them in detail.

Handout 29 outlines the Moscovici et al. (1969) study accurately, but with vague

details. The students should add details to the description by using the table at the bottom of the handout.

Suggested additions

1. In particular, the role of consistency in minority influence
2. 4
3. Someone who is unaware of the purpose of the research
4. 2
5. In contrast, the confederates were aware of the purpose of the research and were asked to follow specific instructions by the researchers
6. Of varying shades
7. In two-thirds of the trials
8. In one-third of the trials
9. 8% of the trials
10. 1% of the trials
11. 0.25% of the trials, where there were no confederates present

HANDOUT 29

| P | H | **S** | G | **T** |

> This provides less-able students with a tangible example of what examiners mean by 'detail'. It could be given to less-able students in order to increase their examination skills and to structure their answers.

12. They set different 'threshold' points for what counted as 'green' and 'blue'. Those in the consistent condition judged more of the chips to be green than those in the inconsistent condition
13. Because the effect remained even outside of the influence of the minority being present

References

Moscovici, S., Lage, E. and Naffrenchoux, M. (1969). Influence of a consistent minority on the responses of a majority in a colour perception task. *Sociometry, 32*, 365–80.

TOPIC: Minority influence

Flipped learning: Twelve Angry Men

The concept of flipped learning was outlined earlier in this chapter (see page 15). The 1957 film, 'Twelve Angry Men' provides another opportunity to get your students to consider psychology outside of the classroom.

Minority influence is brilliantly dramatised in the film 'Twelve Angry Men'. You will need to purchase a copy of the DVD. In this film, 12 jurors preside on the case of a young man who is accused of killing his father. In the film, 11 of the jurors initially judge the man to be guilty, only to *all* be persuaded by one man that there is reasonable doubt to acquit the defendant.

Ask your students to watch the film, or a segment of the film, for homework. Ask them to write a 400–500 word report on:

- How Henry Fonda (the main character) was able to influence the majority.
- What successful techniques he used in order to persuade the majority.

The report should recall and draw upon psychological research in order to provide **evidence** for your explanations (e.g. Moscovici). When watching the film, the students should scribble down some notes, quotes and examples from the film to source the report.

They could use the following headings to structure their notes and/or report:

- Consistency
- Flexibility
- Commitment
- Snowball effect
- Conversion.

NO HANDOUT

P (H) (S) G (T)

Structure can be provided in this activity by giving themes/categories that students must comment on when watching the clips of 'Twelve Angry Men'.

During class feedback and discussion, higher-order questioning should be targeted at more-able students. In contrast, retention and comprehension questions can be targeted at lower-ability students.

References

Moscovici, S. and Zavalloni, M. (1969). The group as a polarizer of attitudes. *Journal of Personality and Social Psychology*, 12, 125–35.

TOPIC: Social influence processes in social change

Change the world!

For those of us who have migrated from the old AQA 'A' specification, the 'social change' topic will be familiar…

I have changed the way I teach the social change topic at least five times. Only recently did I settle on using versions of **Handout 30** and **31** in these lessons as a way of helping students grasp the conclusions of Moscovici's (1980) social change research by using their own tangible social change examples. The students do tend to enjoy this activity and have been good at remembering the general principles outlined by Moscovici.

Essentially, the activity asks students to think of one way they would like to change society; this can be in a small way, or more profound way. The students often find this the most difficult part! In the past, my favourite ideas from my students have been:

- making sure people always give up their seat on the tube for older people and pregnant women

- changing society so that 'gay' is no longer seen as a derogatory term.

The students then have to articulate and consider Mosovici's social change principles in the context of their own ideas.

One place where you may need to check the students' understanding is on box two: 'cognitive conflict'. Students see the word 'conflict' and think that it just means the two positions having an argument; help them to understand that this actually means two thoughts (cognitions, beliefs, opinions) that are inconsistent with each other. For example, 'women cannot be trusted to vote in elections' and 'women *can* be trusted to vote in elections'. Once cognitive conflict is created, people have to think more deeply about which cognition is true (which they may not have ever done, had the minority not drawn 'attention' to this cognition in box two).

HANDOUTS 30 and 31

P (H) (S) G T

Handouts 30 and **31** require higher-order application skills and provide scaffolding for students to work through the principles of social change, as described by Moscovici (1980).

Anyway, this activity is good fun and also helps prepare your students to approach modern life in Britain positively. (This sentence may seem random, but actually reflects the new Ofsted guidance for the inspection of Sixth Forms; as a current Head of Sixth Form, it has been on my mind!)

References

Moscovici, S. (1980). Towards a theory of conversion behaviour. In L. Berkowitz (Ed.) *Advances in experimental social psychology*, 13. New York: Academic Press.

TOPIC: End of Social influence topic summary

Confidence ratings

The confidence rating handout could be annotated in a number of different ways. You may wish to set a percentage in each cell (25%, 50%, 75%, 100%) for students to colour code as they revisit each area as part of their revision. An alternative method could be to colour code a cell (red: cannot achieve this, amber: can achieve with some support, white: feel comfortable, green: feel confident).

Again as topics are revisited through revision cells above, the original colour can be highlighted to correspond with current confidence levels.

Additional activities

The checklist could be used to form targeted revision groups and students can sign up to sessions that cover the areas they are least confident in.

Students may wish to reflect on their own progress through the unit as an individual or as part of a peer discussion. Alternatively the checklist could form part of a one-to-one discussion with a student who is of particular concern.

TOPIC: Characteristics of memory: STM and LTM

Super simple summary: Capacity of STM

P   H   **S**   G   **T**

This activity encourages students to consolidate their understanding into a simple revision sheet that can be used closer to examinations. It helps students identify any areas of misunderstanding or missed information.

Ask students to complete a summary for each of the following:

- Digit span technique
- 7+ −2
- Chunking
- Influence of stimuli
- Influence of size of chunks
- Influence of age.

The first three phrases relate to knowledge of short-term memory (STM) capacity and can be used to answer 'outline' and 'describe' questions.

The 'influence of…' phrases relate to research that suggests it is too simple to claim the capacity of STM is 7+/−2 items. For example, research has suggested people had a shorter memory span for larger chunks. Further consideration can be given to the nature of capacity experiments which are often laboratory based using artificial stimuli such as strings of digits. However, such evaluative comments need to directly address the investigation of capacity, not generic memory research.

Students should now use their summaries to help them answer the following questions:

- What is meant by the term 'capacity' in relation to memory? (2 marks)
- How have psychologists investigated the capacity of STM? (4 marks)
- Evaluate research studies into the capacity of STM. (4 marks)

Once completed, the summaries can be used in later lessons as a game of Taboo in which teams are challenged to describe the key term for a team mate to guess. An additional level of challenge can be added by banning certain words in their description such as 'Miller' and 'Magic' for 7+/−2.

More-able students can be challenged to complete each summary without using their revision notes then, using a different coloured ink, add any missed information from their class notes. Less-able students may need to use their class notes to complete each key phrase or cards could be created for each phrase for students to match up. Allowing students time after working alone to share with a peer may help them identify any missing information or inaccuracies.

References

Miller, G.A. (1956). The magic number seven, plus or minus two: Some limits on our capacity for processing information. *Psychological Review, 63,* 81–93.

Simon, H.A. (1974). How big is a chunk? *Science, 183,* 482–8.

TOPIC: Characteristics of memory: STM and LTM

Encoding in STM and LTM

P   **H**   S   **G**   T

Let battle commence

This classroom game can be used for a wider variety of topics. Once you have created a PowerPoint template you can easily change the questions depending on the area of psychology under study to create an active progress check.

The Template – Divide the PowerPoint slide in half vertically using a line or colours and assign a team name to each side (this could be two local football teams, famous actors or even musicians). Using the custom animation function, add a textbox at the top of the slide that drops down 'on click' to reveal a question. This slide can then be copied as many times as needed, changing the question each time.

The groups – Split the class in half, mixed ability works best, and each group nominates a scribe. The scribes wait at their side of the board, pen in hand ready to answer the drop-down question. The first scribe to write down (in legible handwriting!) the correct answer called out from their group wins a point. A new scribe is nominated for each question.

Typical questions:

- What is meant by the term encoding?
- What forms can encoding take?
- Finish the sentence: STM usually encodes…
- How is information usually encoded in LTM?
- Give two semantically similar words
- Give two acoustically similar words
- What type of experiment did Baddeley conduct?
- Who suggests STM can encode visually?

This is a team game so ensure groups are mixed ability. Questions range from simple knowledge recall to higher-order thinking in terms of making links to wider knowledge of research methods.

References

Baddeley, A.D. (1966a). The influence of acoustic and semantic similarity on long-term memory for word sequences. *Quarterly Journal of Experimental Psychology, 18,* 302–9.

Baddeley, A.D. (1966b). Short-term memory for word sequences as a function of acoustic, semantic and formal similarity. *Quarterly Journal of Experimental Psychology, 18,* 362–5.

TOPIC: Characteristics of memory: STM and LTM

The duration of STM

Some questions on **Handout 34** target knowledge and understanding with links to research methods; identifying the IV and DV, use of distraction task and drawing a line graph. Other questions relate to methodological issues which impact on the validity of the research findings.

Students may wish to conduct this investigation themselves using a PowerPoint slide to display a constant syllable such as THX-512 then counting backwards for a set time. Different

intervals between learning and recall could be tested. This would help students' appreciation of research methods in terms of importance of standardisation, threat of extraneous variables etc.

References

Peterson, L.R. and Peterson, M.J. (1959). Short-term retention of individual verbal items. Journal of Experimental Psychology, *58*, 193–8.

HANDOUT 34

Assigning students to mixed-ability groups will support less-able students and help more-able students consolidate their understanding as they take on the role of group leader. The final box (bottom, right-hand corner) may be deemed suitable for students seeking a stretch activity.

TOPIC: Characteristics of memory: STM and LTM

The duration of LTM

Students may wish to highlight each of the exam responses shown on **Handout 35** to illustrate outline comments and evaluative comments before marking and providing improvements.

Candidate A: This candidate has identified some of the findings but failed to include data from free-recall tasks. An attempt is made to evaluate the findings but this is vague and no real point is made. As such, this answer would fall into the level 1 mark band.

Candidate B: This response is an improvement on that of Candidate A in terms of outlining findings as both photo-recognition and free-recall for both 15 and 48 years are noted. However, evaluation is missing from this answer and so it remains at level 1.

Candidate C: Both aspects of the question are addressed well here so it would meet the requirements for level 2. The outline of findings is

accurate and detailed while a clear evaluative comment is made. This could be further improved by mentioning that rehearsal of the yearbook is an extraneous variable that should have been controlled. Another issue may be how popular a person was at school; those who had a wider social network or became involved in more extra-curricular activities may be able to remember more of their classmates than those with a limited circle of friends.

As an introduction to the duration of LTM I (RG) find beginning the lesson with a quiz from the students' childhood really gets them thinking about how powerful their own LTMs are. Each round targets a specific year / age in their life. Topics such as cartoon characters and pop music are often well recalled while news events less so leading to a discussion on why some events and experiences form strong LTMs, while others are barely recalled at all.

HANDOUT 35

Students may benefit from discussing Candidate A, awarding a mark and giving suggested improvements before considering Candidates B and C. As students work through marking and making suggestions as to how to access the level 2 mark band, the teacher is free to work with students who may be struggling to identify outline or evaluation comments, or find it difficult to appreciate the level of detail required. More-able students could be challenged to create a similar activity for the duration of STM and share this with the class.

References

Bahrick, H.P., Bahrick, P.O. and Wittinger, R.P. (1975). Fifty years of memory for names and faces: A cross-sectional approach. *Journal of Experimental Psychology: General*, *104*, 54–75.

TOPIC: The MSM

Describing the MSM

Handout 36 encourages students to use specialist terminology in their description of the multi-store model (MSM) and can be further utilised to highlight structure and processes named in the model, both of which need to be discussed in an accurate outline of the model.

Prior to this activity students may find it useful to draw the model or complete a 'label the diagram' task to familiarise themselves with the terminology.

HANDOUT 36

Less-able students may benefit from being provided with a key word sheet to support them in re-writing each statement using psychological terminology. Other students may wish to use a textbook or class notes to identify terms, while more-able can be challenged to use their memory of the model to complete the task.

TOPIC: The MSM

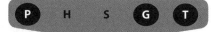

MSM essay practice

Ask your students to highlight AO1 and AO3 comments in the extract. Weaker students often see the word 'limited' and mistake this as an evaluative comment rather than simply an outline of the properties of STM. This extract allows for discussion of the importance of signposting evaluative comments clearly, ('This may be a limitation of the model...') as well as giving an example of an underdeveloped evaluative comment. Students may also wish to consider whether they prefer to write all their AO1 outline comments then their AO2 evaluation, or discuss strengths / limitations as opportunities arise during their outline of the model.

This paragraph models an effective evaluative comment. Students should be reminded that in extended answer questions, consideration needs to be given to outline and evaluating concepts/research. Ask them to highlight PEEL sections in the extract.

This handout can be used to provide students with a scaffold before attempting an exam question such as, 'Outline and evaluate the multi-store model' or 'Discuss the multi-store model of memory'.

Getting students to create their own drawings of the MSM helps consolidate knowledge of the basic structure but students must remember to describe both structure and process: how information moves through the system (such as attention and maintenance rehearsal) and how information is lost from the system (displacement, decay, interference). Students can then use this as a guide to translate visual information to a written description. Revision can take the form of a simple 'fill in the blanks' task using a basic diagram of the three stores.

Less-able students may find it useful to have an explanation of the terms 'linear' and 'unitary' in order to understand what is meant by the statement 'MSM is a linear model comprised of unitary stores'.

Students can be paired to work through both highlighting activities on **Handout 37**. For example, two students of similar ability regarding understanding of essay structure can work through each task at their own pace, discussing their ideas. Students who quickly identify the different elements of the PEEL evaluative paragraph can be challenged to create their own to share with the class or improve the evaluative comment from the first extract.

References

Atkinson, R.C. and Shiffrin, R.M. (1968). Human memory: A proposed system and its control processes. In K.W. Spence and J.T. Spence (Eds). *The Psychology of Learning and Motivation.* Vol 2. London: Academic Press.

Glanzer, M. and Cunitz, A.R. (1966). Two storage mechanisms in Free Recall. *Journal of Verbal Learning and Verbal Behaviour, 5,* 351–60.

TOPIC: The working memory model

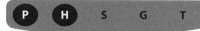

Baddeley et al. (1975a)

In my experience most students quickly become adept at identifying IVs and DVs in research studies but lose valuable marks by not operationalising each variable, so I take any chance available to reinforce this skill. This also applies to writing hypotheses: they understand what a directional (or non-directional) and null hypothesis are stating but fail to clearly state each variable. Allowing class time to work in pairs to identify these then model a 'top marks' answer on the board is a useful activity.

The later questions on **Handout 38** consider the impact of word length effect on previous notions of STM capacity in that it may be better to see capacity in terms of time rather than quantity. In respect of chunking, Baddeley's findings can be related to research into the effect of the size of the chunk on recall (see **Handout 38**).

In addition, ask your students if they can think of any real-life examples of dual tasks? For example: fill in the blanks – 'Without my working memory I would not be able to listen to music while I painted a picture'. Similar sentences could be given to students on paper, or displayed on the board, with space available for them to add two tasks (see underlined phrase in the example above) that use different slave systems.

References

Baddeley, A.D., Thomson, N., and Buchanan, M. (1975a). Word length and the structure of short-term memory. *Journal of Verbal Learning and Verbal Behavior, 14,* 575–89.

More-able students could be assigned the task of running a version of this experiment with the rest of the class acting as participants. This will reinforce the planning of research while the participants will consolidate their understanding of the procedure.

Initial questions relating to research methods provide the opportunity to practise understanding in this area while later questions access higher-order thinking in terms of making links and predictions.

TOPIC: The working memory model

Baddeley et al. (1975b)

Handout 39 aims to break down the study into smaller sections to help students understand the different components of the procedure. As with **Handout 38** (Baddeley 1975a) this study can be used to evaluate the working memory model (WMM) and develop understanding of laboratory investigations.

References

Baddeley, A.D., Grant, S., Wright, E. and Thomson, N. (1975b). Imagery and visual working memory. In P.M.A. Rabbitt and S. Dornic (Eds). *Attention and performance*, Vol V. London: Academic Press.

HANDOUT 39

P **H** S G **T**

Students often find Task 1 in this experiment difficult to understand and it often helps if you carry out these two tasks with the class. Model task 1 using a PowerPoint slide explaining the 'top' and 'bottom' line then ask students to visualise the letter while, on a separate slide, using the animations function to create a moving dot (or use a laser pen in a darkened room).

The making links question at the bottom of the handout targets higher-order thinking as students are required to consider a range of issues relating to validity. Being really strict with students and forcing them to side with one method or the other can generate real discussion or assign a method for a formal debate. Less-able students can vote following the arguments presented.

TOPIC: The working memory model

Key questions

Students who struggle with tackling extended answer questions may find it less daunting if the whole response is broken down into a series of smaller questions. When considering evaluative comments, students should be reminded of the importance of PEEL structure and explicit links to the usefulness of the model.

Questions to support students in writing an outline of the WMM (AO1):

- Does the WMM relate to sensory register, STM, LTM or the whole memory system?
- What is the role of the central executive?
- What are the two components of the phonological loop and what are their responsibilities?
- What sub-systems are involved in the visuo-spatial sketchpad's processing of visual information?
- What is the function of the episodic buffer?

Questions to support students to write an evaluation of the WMM (AO3):

- Why might this model be seen as an improvement on the MSM of memory?
- How can the WMM explain case studies such as KF?

- What support is derived from laboratory experiments using the dual-task technique?
- To what extent does the word-length effect support the concept of a phonological loop?
- What criticisms have been made of the concept of a central executive in working memory?

A scenario for your students to consider is of Katya, a successful business woman who is able to converse in French, English and Spanish. She regularly travels for business and enjoys experiencing new cultures. However, she frequently gets lost when visiting cities despite having detailed directions.

How might Katya's abilities be explained by the WMM? (Application (AO2))

Possible answer: Language ability could be related to the phonological loop in that Katya is able to hear different sounds within languages and can easily associate written words with different sounds. However, her visuo-spatial sketchpad does not seem to be as powerful as she struggles to navigate her surroundings and translate information from a 2D map to her 3D environment.

NO HANDOUT

P **H** S G **T**

Students select which questions they can answer as an individual, with peer support or with targeted help from you, the teacher. These questions can be used to scaffold an extended answer requiring an outline and evaluation of the working memory model. An application activity is included for students who wish to complete an extended answer assessing all three skills:

Discuss the WMM with reference to Katya's talents and abilities.

Students interested in working memory may wish to read around this topic by visiting

http://dyslexiahelp.umich.edu/professionals/dyslexia-school/working-memory which discusses working memory in relation to dyslexia.

References

Baddeley, A.D. and Hitch, G.J. (1974). Working memory. In G.H. Bower (Ed.), *The psychology of learning and motivation, Vol. 8*. London: Academic Press.

TOPIC: The working memory model

Visual representation

As with the MSM, asking students to draw the WMM helps consolidate their understanding and forms a useful revision tool. Students may wish to draw (either by hand or using images from the internet) each component based on their roles, e.g. the central executive as a briefcase (the 'boss'), the phonological loop as headphones and visuo-spatial sketchpad as an artist's easel. You could hold a mini art competition for the most creative (detailed and accurate!) entry.

References

Baddeley, A.D. and Hitch, G.J. (1974) Working memory. In G.H. Bower (Ed.), *The psychology of learning and motivation, Vol. 8*. London: Academic Press.

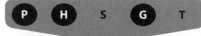
TOPIC: Types of LTM: Episodic, semantic and procedural

Types of LTM

Colour coding the bricks on **Handout 40** provides students with the phrases that might be used when asked to *'explain what is meant by episodic/semantic/procedural memory'*. Once each phrase has been identified, students can be challenged to create these definitions and use the bricks to peer assess another student's attempts. This activity can be used as a progress check during or at the end of a lesson.

The first two questions of 'Deepen your thinking' on the handout assess basic understanding of the similarities or differences between the three types of LTM. The final two questions require students to make links between types of LTM and wider research studies and the MSM. These are more challenging and some students may require targeted support or would benefit from clues. These clues could be provided face down on the table and students encouraged to look at them only after using textbooks and discussion with peers. Clues might include, 'What areas of the brain have brain scans identified when different memories are accessed?' or 'How might brain scans be used to show LTM is not located in one single store?'

HANDOUT 40

'Deepen your thinking' questions are based on Bloom's taxonomy of higher-order thinking. The questions progress in terms of complexity and so can be used as a means to challenge students at different levels of understanding. Students may choose to focus on those they find difficult or questions can be assigned to groups of students based on ability. Each group can then feed back answers to the class.

TOPIC: Types of LTM: Episodic, semantic and procedural

Making links

Using their *Complete Companion* page 44 or class notes, in **Handout 41**, students have to apply their knowledge of research focusing on the physiology of memory to form effective evaluations (following the PEEL paragraph structure). For example,

P - The case of HM suggests a distinction can be made between procedural and declarative memories.

Ev - *HM was able to form some types of LTMs after his surgery but not others. He was able to learn a new skill: mirror drawing. However, he could not remember learning this skill.*

Ex - This showed HM had procedural memory but had no recollection of learning which implies no episodic or semantic LTMs.

In this example a suitable sentence starter for less-able students might be, *'What activities was HM able to perform following his surgery? What was he able to recall?*

Prior to this activity, students may find it helpful to reflect on the different areas of the brain. Draw and label a diagram or take advantage of the various websites or apps showing tours of the brain.

As an introduction to research using patients suffering from brain damage, you can tell students of Claparède (1911), a Swiss psychiatrist who on shaking hands with an amnesiac patient, pricked her hand. The next day, she refused to shake his hand but couldn't remember why she didn't want to greet him. Ask students to detail how this finding could be explained.

HANDOUT 41

Handout 41 may be more suited to more-able students in the form presented here, as the students are required to apply their knowledge of research into the biological basis of memory to form completed evaluative paragraphs. Less-able students may benefit from sentence starters in the evidence box to guide their thinking and may wish to ignore the final link which requires consideration of wider research issues.

References

Claparède, E. (1911). Recognition and 'me-ness'. Trans. D. Rapaport. In D. Rapaport (Ed.) (1951). Organization and Pathology of Thought: Selected Sources. New York: Columbia University Press.

TOPIC: Explanations for forgetting

Proactive and retroactive interference

Using **Handout 42**, students are first required to identify whether the example given relates to PI or RI as a means of checking their understanding of the two concepts. Molly – PI, Ajay – RI, Sam – RI, Dylan – PI.

The second activity introduces a study of RI and provides the opportunity to revise some aspects of research methods (independent measures design, choice of stimulus material in relation to participants being tested). This study showed the effect of RI as the children who learnt both picture lists showed poor recall when asked to recall the images on the first list. This implied the second list had a negative impact on their memory for the first list they had seen. A stretch activity can be added for more-able students in which they are encouraged to consider the abilities of participants based on their age/level of education. Students might suggest using word lists when testing adult participants as their reading ability would be better than that of young children.

In the third activity on the handout, an example of RI is given. Students are required to identify this form of forgetting by making reference to the past learning (French) and the present learning (Spanish). They should then apply relevant research, such as Howe (1995) or the notion that interference only explains some forgetting, i.e. in cases where the two memories are quite similar. If you wished to use this as an assessed piece of work marks could be awarded as follows:

One mark for identifying RI, a further mark for making use of the question

HANDOUT 42

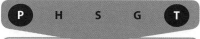

Students can be assigned different tasks from **Handout 42** as each task progresses in levels of challenge. Students can take ownership of their learning by deciding their current level of understanding and selecting tasks that move them beyond this.

stem to explain this conclusion. One mark for brief link to relevant research, a further mark for elaboration on research with explicit link to the question stem.

References

Howe, M.L. (1995). Interference effects in young children's long-term retention. Developmental Psychology, *Vol 31(4)*, Jul 1995, 579–96. doi: 10.1037/0012-1649.31.4.579

TOPIC: Explanations for forgetting

Research into interference

This natural experiment considers the impact of a naturally occurring event (intervening games (IV)) on players' memory (recall of team names (DV)). Revisiting operationalization of variables and hypothesis writing, as well as interpretation of graphs, provides an opportunity for further research methods practice. Being able to identify variables and interpret data from a novel scenario is an important exam skill.

Drawing the study in a simple cartoon strip can create a helpful revision tool. There are a number of free online sites allowing students to create their own strip, one such site being http://bitstrips.com/create/comic/ However, care must be taken to ensure detail is not lost in the translation of text to images. Once the cartoon is completed, a simple peer assessment exercise would be to provide a mark scheme with one point for each of the key features identified, e.g. natural experiment: 1 point, rugby players: 1 point, missed games due to injury/illness: 1 point. The grid on **Handout 43** will provide a summary of the key details and help highlight areas that have been missed.

References

Baddeley, A.D. and Hitch, G.J. (1977). Recency re-examined. In S. Dornic (Ed.)

HANDOUT 43

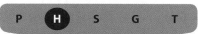

On completion of the task on **Handout 43** students could be challenged to give the strengths and limitations of carrying out forgetting research for real information, rather than artificial tasks such as word lists generated by the researcher. Comments should relate specifically to Baddeley and Hitch's (1977) rugby study to be deemed effective.

Attention and performance. New Jersey: Erlbaum.

TOPIC: Explanations for forgetting: Retrieval failure

Investigating cued recall

Students have the opportunity to carry out a classroom version of Tulving and Pearlstone's (1966) free recall/cued recall. **Handout 44** gives basic instructions but requires students to make some timing decisions for learning and recall phases and provides an opportunity to discuss the importance of standardised instructions and procedure. Knowledge of research design, variables and data analysis can be practised through completion of the investigation. Materials for the procedure can be found on **Handout 45.**

Students could be challenged to design a study to investigate context-dependent memory in which participants learn and recall information in the same or different locations around the school. Their study can be carried out as an extra-curricular activity with students using their findings, combined with previous research, to possibly provide revision advice, e.g. revise in a similar setting to the exam room (quiet, no distractions, use categories to help recall). Students might disagree with this advice and could be challenged to find alternative evidence for creating a different revision environment.

References

Tulving, E. and Pearlstone, Z. (1966). Availability versus accessibility of information in memory for

HANDOUTS 44 and 45

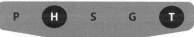

Less-able students may need some support in compiling data and drawing conclusions on **Handout 44** . Other students who are confident mathematicians have the opportunity to take on the role of lead learners working with a small group of their peers. More-able students may wish to consider any confounding variables that may impact on the data gathered.

words. *Journal of Verbal Learning & Verbal Behavior* 5(4), 381–91.

TOPIC: Explanations for forgetting: Retrieval failure

Evaluating research into retrieval failure

HANDOUT 46

P H **S** G **T**

Using their *Complete Companion* page 54, or class notes, students are asked to read each evaluative comment then decide which aspects could be considered the key elements of the evaluation. Following this identification, additional details are added to develop the critique before students formulate their own conclusion. **Handout 46** can be used as a revision tool nearer the exam period but also demonstrates the importance of building up detail within a commentary to produce an effective evaluation that is able to access the higher levels of the mark scheme.

Prior to this activity, students could be placed in groups of four and be assigned one evaluative point each, given time to read the comments and produce a

market stall to share their information with others in the class. How students design their stall is up to them and a variety of presentation methods would add interest to the lesson; for example PowerPoint, mini-lecture, research poster. One student then remains with the stall while the other members of the group visit each of the other stalls (notepad in hand). The visiting students are taught by the stall holder, then return home to teach their stall holder what they have learnt. More-able students are effective stall holders as they clearly explain their information and are keen to question their returning group members to ensure they have a good understanding of the other stalls.

Some students may benefit from having comments prepared for them to match to the relevant evaluative points. From there they are free to consider which comments are key elements and which are additional, leaving them to write their own conclusions. Other students may benefit from targeted support or working in small supportive groups.

TOPIC: Accuracy of eyewitness testimony: Misleading information

Spot the leading question

NO HANDOUT

P H **S** G T

A quick introduction activity to the effect of misleading information is 'Spot the leading question'. This helps students focus on the potential impact of leading questions and can be related to research studies which have tested the effect of misleading information on memory for events, e.g. 'How fast was the car going when it 'smashed' into the other

car?'. Students are given the following information: *You have been asked to question a witness of a crime. It is thought that the crime was committed by a local youth who usually wears red trainers, a blue baseball cap and a distinctive yellow leather jacket. He has the nickname Blogsy.*

This activity is helpful for students who may need support in understanding the concept of misleading information included in questions. Students could be challenged to re-word leading questions into more open ones, e.g. what was the perpetrator wearing?

TOPIC: Accuracy of eyewitness testimony: Misleading information

Loftus and Palmer (1974) – The broken glass study

HANDOUT 47

P H **S** G **T**

Students are required to decode each picture in the cartoon on **Handout 47** and using their *Complete Companion* page 56, or class notes, they should complete the dialogue box below each to explain what part of the procedure or findings the images represent. The aim of this activity is to get students noticing the details of the procedure and to produce a visual revision sheet of the study.

This revision sheet can be used to address questions such as 'Describe **one** study related to the effect of leading questions on eyewitness testimony.' (5 marks)

References
Loftus, E and Palmer, J. (1974). Reconstruction of automobile destruction: An example of the interaction between language and memory. *Journal of Verbal Learning and Verbal Behaviour*, Vol 13 (5), 585–9.

Individual students may benefit from targeted support for this activity or support can be scaffolded by providing students with completed text to cut and stick onto the correct dialogue box on the **Handout 47**. In the conclusion section of the handout less-able students may find a set of questions helps formulate their ideas such as, 'What was the leading question given to participants?', 'How did researchers know this leading question had an effect on memory of the event?', 'Did the misleading information affect all participants?' Student understanding needs to be checked here: the leading question was the seriousness of the incident implied through the question wording, either 'smashed' or 'hit'.

TOPIC: Accuracy of eyewitness testimony: Misleading information

Evaluating research into misleading information

Students match text boxes to create developed evaluations (PEEL) with students. This activity could be carried out in the form of a cut and stick task and less-able students may find it helpful to physically manipulate each box allowing them to check and change their answers a number of times before sticking the correct version in their notes.

The activity encourages students to read for meaning and organise the information presented into a coherent form. The overall aim is to further develop students' understanding of how to create effective evaluations that relate specifically to the concept under discussion.

The structure is based on a commonly used method of teaching paragraphing: the PEEL method. (P) make your **P**oint; (Ev) give the **Ev**idence, state additional evidence or commentary; (Ex) **Ex**plain how the evidence relates to the point, consider associated research; (L) **L**ink back to the question.

The evaluation of research into EWT provides an opportunity to reinforce key concepts in research methods such as the artificial nature of tasks used in laboratory based studies and how much importance participants might place on recall of meaningless film clips compared to actually witnessing an event. Students could be asked to vote on which method they think is more suitable giving detailed explanations for their choice.

References

Braun, K.A., Ellis, R., & Loftus, E.F. (2002). Make my memory: How advertising can change our memories of the past. *Psychology and Marketing, 19,* 1–23.

Foster, R.A., Libkuman, T.M., Schooler, J.W. and Loftus, E.F. (1994). Realism and eyewitness person identification. *Applied Cognitive Psychology, 8,* 107–21.

Lindsay, D.S. (1990). Misleading suggestions can impair eyewitnesses' ability to remember event details. *Journal of Experimental Psychology: Learning, Memory, and Cognition, 16,* 1077–83.

HANDOUT 48

P H S G **T**

Boxes on **Handout 48** could be left blank for students to add in their own comments; for example, showing the point and expansion but challenging students to find a suitable study from their textbook or class notes. Another version would be to show the point and evidence but ask students to create their own expansions. Less-able students may find the matching task more accessible if their attention is drawn to the words used in each text to develop the initial point; for example, the word 'vulnerable' is repeated throughout the evaluation.

Schacter, D.L., Kaszniak, A.W., Kihlstrom, J.F. and Valdiserri, M. (1991). The relation between source memory and aging. *Psychology and Aging, 6(4),* 559–68.

Yuille, J.C. and Cutshall, J.L. (1986). A case study of eyewitness testimony of a crime. *Journal of Applied Psychology, 71,* 291–301.

TOPIC: Accuracy of eyewitness testimony: Anxiety

The effect of anxiety on the accuracy of EWT

Handout 49 asks students to apply their knowledge of research into the effect of anxiety on EWT to a novel situation. Emphasis should be placed on applying research to the crime described to allow students the opportunity to practice their AO2 application skills. For example, Loftus et al. (1987) found eye movements of witnesses showed tracking of the weapon rather than of the person's face. The petrol station staff may have followed the movement of the gun and so paid little attention to the masks or other features. The scar on the left wrist may have been noticed as the gunman may have been holding the gun in this hand. However, research by Christianson and Hubinette (1993) suggests the staff may have accurate recall of events, especially staff who were behind the counter and so were directly threatened by the robbers.

A simple true or false game could be created to test students' recall of the key features of studies into anxiety. Awarding points adds an element of competition especially if there is some kind of small prize to be won. Questions should be created by the students and could include, *'In which country did Christianson and Hubinette conduct their research?'*, *'How many bank robbery witnesses were interviewed?'* This activity highlights the importance of giving accurate and detailed outlines of research procedures and findings.

References

Christianson, S.-Å. and Hubinette, B. (1993). Hands up! A study of witnesses' emotional reactions and memories associated with bank robberies. *Applied Cognitive Psychology, 7,* 365–79.

Deffenbacher, K.A., Bornstein, B.H., Penrod, S.D. and McGorty, E.K. (2004). A meta-analytic review of the effects of high stress on eyewitness memory. *Law and Human Behavior, 28,* 687–706.

Loftus, E.F., Loftus, G.R. and Messo, J. (1987). Some facts about 'weapon focus'. *Law and Human Behaviour, 11,* 55–62.

HANDOUT 49

P H **S** G T

Students may benefit from a hint sheet to help them focus on the key aspects of the scenario that could be related to research into anxiety. For example, one member of staff mentions focusing mainly on where the gun was pointing which can be related to Johnson and Scott's (1976) bloody knife/greasy pen study. More-able students could consider not only the Yerkes-Dodson effect as an explanation of why recall might improve or decline but also the difference between research using artificial-type materials (such as films) and research using real-life crimes.

TOPIC: Improving the accuracy of eyewitness testimony

The cognitive interview

Matching the component to an example of how it might be introduced in an interview, then exploring the reasons behind using that technique creates a detailed outline of the cognitive interview.

You can ask students to create their own mnemonic to aid their recall of the four components of the cognitive interview. For example:

Mostly (Mental reinstatement of original context)

Rabbits (Report everything)
Chew (Change the perspective)

Carrots (Change the order).

As mentioned previously if students can create a visual image of their mnemonic and include a brief sentence for each component they have created a useful revision tool for their exam.

References

Anderson, R.C. and Pichert, J.W. (1978). Recall of previously unrecallable information following a shift in perspective. *Journal of Verbal Learning and Verbal Behavior, 17,* 1–12.

HANDOUT 50

P **H** S G T

Once they have completed the match-up task on **Handout 50** students can be challenged to complete the sentence, *'One goal of the cognitive interview is to overcome pre-existing schemas because…'.* Students should explain why pre-existing schemas can hinder accurate EWT and how the changing the order of components and the perspective can reduce the impact of these schemas.

TOPIC: Improving the accuracy of eyewitness testimony

Evaluating the effectiveness of the cognitive interview

This activity could be carried out in the form of a cut and stick task and less-able students may find it helpful to physically manipulate each box allowing them to check and change their answers a number of times before sticking the correct version in their notes. Once completed, students can use the three aspects of evaluation shown at the top of **Handout 51** to create a final link comment (PEEL).

The handout encourages students to read for meaning and organise the information presented into a coherent form. The overall aim is to further develop students' understanding of how to create effective evaluations that relate specifically to the concept under discussion.

The structure is based on a commonly used method of teaching paragraphing: the PEEL method. (P) make your **Point**; (Ev) give the **Ev**idence, expand through supporting evidence or commentary; (Ex) **Ex**plain how the evidence relates to the point, consider associated research; (L) **L**ink back to the question.

The evidence relating to the point and explanation concerning Stern & Memon's (2006) study is less clear than other PEEL groupings (as Brazil is not mentioned in the evidence section).

P: Research into the effectiveness of the cognitive interview (CI) technique has been useful in improving the interview techniques in Brazil, where police traditionally use interrogation, torture and ill treatment. **Ev:** Stein & Memon showed university cleaning staff a video of an abduction. Compared to standard police interviews the CI showed an increased amount of correct recall. For example, detailed descriptions of the man holding the gun were obtained from the witnesses. **Ex:** These findings suggest the CI technique could be used to develop a new approach in interviewing witnesses in Brazil. Hopefully, this will lead to a reduction in the amount of miscarriages of justice.

Stretch activity: **L:** This research demonstrates a useful aspect of the CI: its use in real-life situations to improve the quality of witness statements.

Students should be able to work out the Stern & Memon connections by a process of elimination as the other PEEL groups have clear clues in the wording. However, textbooks (page 60 in the *Complete Companion*) could be made available for students to check their groupings.

Students could then create a final evaluation by providing a 'point' such as, *'The Cognitive Interview may be*

HANDOUT 51

P H S G **T**

Less-able students may benefit from first working as a group to identify which boxes are 'points' which could be classed as 'evidence' and which are 'expansion' boxes. Drawing students' attention to how we are able to work out each box based on language such as, *'These findings suggest…'* will model how to introduce and structure evaluative ideas as well as support development of a wider vocabulary for extended writing.

particularly useful when interviewing older adults who have witnessed a crime'. Using the *Complete Companion,* page 60, class notes or their own internet research they should identify evidence, then expand upon this with either further supporting research, contradictory research or commentary on the usefulness of the evidence presented.

References

Kebbell, M.R. and Wagstaff, G.F. (1996). Enhancing the practicality of the cognitive interview in forensic situations. Psychology [on-line serial], 7(6), Available FTP: Hostname: Princeton.edu Directory: pub/harnard/Psychology/1996.

Stein, L. and Memon, A. (2006). Testing the efficacy of the Cognitive Interview in a developing country. *Applied Cognitive Psychology, 20,* 597–605.

TOPIC: End of Memory topic summary

Confidence ratings

P   H   S   **G**   **T**

The confidence rating **Handouts 52 and 53** could be annotated in a number of different ways. You may wish to set a percentage in each cell (25%, 50%, 75%, 100%) for students to colour code as they revisit each area as part of their revision. An alternative method could be to colour code a cell (red: cannot achieve this; amber: can achieve with some support; white: feel comfortable; green: feel confident). Again as topics are revisited through revision cells above, the original colour can be highlighted to correspond with current confidence levels.

The checklists could be used to form targeted revision groups and students could sign up to sessions that cover the areas they are least confident in.

Students may wish to reflect on their own progress through the unit as an individual or as part of a peer discussion. Alternatively the checklist could form part of a one-to-one discussion with a student who is of particular concern.

TOPIC: Caregiver – infant interaction

Caregiver – infant interaction crossword

A crossword may seem a little too juvenile for A Level students but, as an activity, it certainly has its merits (and in my (MG) experience, there is no such thing as *too* juvenile for A Level students!). This activity can be used to force students to engage with textbook material in more depth and to read for meaning; the clues on this crossword are designed to encourage this. The crossword would work well with page 70 of the *Complete Companion*.

The answers are as follows:

Across

1. interactionalsynchrony
2. imitated
3. innate

Down

1. reciprocity
2. attachment
3. infancy
4. nonverbal
5. behaviouralcategories

References

Meltzoff, A.N. and Moore, M.K. (1977). Imitation of facial and manual gestures by human neonates. *Science, 198,* 75–8.

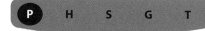

HANDOUT 54

P H S G T

It is likely that some students will finish earlier than others. This is because some will be able to work out the answers more easily and may read more quickly than others. As such, you may wish to have an extension activity up your sleeve. You could ask students to add two to three questions/answers to the crossword using the text provided.

TOPIC: Caregiver – infant interaction

Plenary questions

'Plenary Questions' is a very simple and effective idea. It is a good way to end the lesson and ascertain the main themes, concepts and key words that the students have picked up on during the lessons. Essentially, the activity simply involves cutting up the plenary questions and asking the students to select one from the hat. You can then have a feedback session with the students. Alternatively, if you have lots of time left, the students could answer as many questions as they can on the handout.

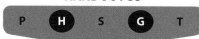

HANDOUT 55

P H S G T

You could pair the students so that there is a high-ability student and a low-ability student. The job of the high-ability student is to select the question and teach the answer to the low-ability student; in the whole-class feedback session, it is the low-ability student that must answer. Several of the questions do entail higher-order thinking (e.g. synoptic links) and therefore your higher-ability students are also being stretched.

TOPIC: The development of attachment

Which stage of attachment?

'Just because you've taught it, doesn't mean they've learnt it.' I'm not sure where I heard that phrase, but I've tried never to forget it when teaching A Level psychology. The mistake we can sometimes make is to go over content in the textbook or information on a PowerPoint and then expect the students to simply know and retain it. Ultimately, we need to find ways to help the students consolidate that knowledge. Simple activities, such as the one on **Handout 56** help students to do that. The activity is self-explanatory, but the 10 minutes it will take students to complete is certainly worth the teaching time.

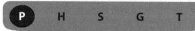

HANDOUT 56

P H S G T

For lower-ability students, it might be best to give them the titles of the stages before they begin in order to help them sort the statements, i.e. Stage 1: Indiscriminate attachments, Stage 2: The beginnings of attachment, Stage 3: Discriminate attachment, and Stage 4: Multiple attachments.

TOPIC: The development of attachment

Maximising your 'outline' marks

I have found myself in the last few years writing 'needs more detail' in some of my essay marking feedback. Of course, this is pretty useless feedback for students who genuinely do not understand what is meant by 'detail'. It is much easier to *show* them and *illustrate* to them what is meant by 'detail' and how this translates into examination marking.

Although this handout might suggest that detail just always means 'more', it is important to note that sometimes 'detail' may mean adding key words into their writing. Conversely, this may mean that they actually write less (because using that word is more detailed than an everyday explanation). It might be worth discussing this with the students afterwards.

It is feasible that within this topic the following question might be asked in an AS examination: 'Outline the stages

of attachment identified by Schaffer.' (6 marks)

Try using **Handout 57** with your students after you have outlined the stages to them in detail.

The handout outlines the stages accurately, but with some vague detail in places. The students should add details to the description by using the table at the bottom of the handout.

Suggested additions:

1. Indiscriminate attachments
2. Whether they are animate or inanimate
3. Responding to the action of the caregiver with a similar action
4. The caregiver and infant start to mirror each other's facial and body movements

5. The beginnings of attachment
6. Fear or unease in the presence of people they do not recognise
7. Discriminate attachment
8. Called separation anxiety
9. The person they are most comforted by
10. The quality of the relationship was more important (e.g. quickly responding to 'signals')
11. Multiple attachments
12. These are called secondary attachments.

TOPIC: The development of attachment

The role of the father: True or False?

Handouts 58 and **59** provide another activity designed to encourage students to read textbook content carefully and a way to ensure that students are more likely to retain and understand that knowledge.

Various statements are included on the handouts and mirror the content from pages 72 and 73 in the *Complete Companion*. Students need to decide whether they think that statement is

true or false. If the statement is true, they should develop that point with more detail. If the statement is false, the students should correct the statement.

Answers

1. False, 2. False, 3. True, 4. True, 5. False, 6. True, 7. False, 8. True, 9. True

---

TOPIC: Animal studies of attachment

Brief summaries

This is a fantastic idea stolen (with permission!) from Jo Gotts at www.resourcd.com).

Essentially the activity involves students summarising information and as such, choosing the most important to retain in the synopsis. The information they need to summarise is on page 74 of the *Complete Companion*. Each 'brief' will be a summary of an evaluation point on either Lorenz's or Harlow's animal research. Alternatively, the students could research the studies on the internet and aim to understand how each of the key terms is relevant. One rule that should be maintained is that the students write full sentences. The idea here is that students have to read an evaluation, process it, understand it and then write it back down in summarised form; this stops

students simply copying text into their notes without actually thinking about what they are writing or understanding it.

Handout 60 therefore provides the visual prop of four briefs in which to write 'brief summaries' of evaluations of animal studies on attachment.

Beneath each 'brief' are some key words/studies which students should aim to include in their summary. You could change/adapt this sheet to suit your needs.

References

Guiton, P. (1966). Early experience and sexual object choice in the brown leghorn. *Animal* Behaviour, *14*, 534–8

Harlow, H.F. (1959). Love in infant monkeys. *Scientific American, 20(6),* 676–84.

Lorenz, K.Z. (1935). Der kumpan in der umwelt des vogels. *Journal of Ornithology, 83,* 137–213. Published in English (1937) The companion in the bird's world. *Auk, 54,* 245–73.

TOPIC: Learning theory of attachment

What's missing?

An effective lesson activity, in my experience, is to give students a series of key terms (e.g. from a theory) and ask them to create a concept map which links those concepts together; I feel this helps them to understand the 'bigger picture' of a theory and understand it in more depth.

A quicker, but similar activity, is useful in helping students to process psychological ideas; this activity, on **Handout 61**, displays the concept map, but asks students to identify the concepts/key terms that are missing. This is a sort of 'reverse links' activity. It may seem like a glorified 'fill in the blanks' exercise, but I would argue it is slightly more effective and helps students to see the connected nature of some psychological explanations.

This activity would work particularly well with the description of the operant conditioning explanation of attachment on page 76 of the *Complete Companion*.

Depending on the version of operant conditioning you use, different key words may be suitable. But for guidance, the following may be the type of terms that students should enter into the concept map:

• Drive

• Pleasure

HANDOUT 61

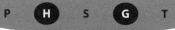

Less-able students could be provided with the words which need to be added to the boxes, although this may make the activity too simple. But the completed **Handout 61** might also be very useful and provide scaffolding for extended writing.

• Rewarding
• Primary reinforcer
• Secondary reinforcer
• Attachment.

TOPIC: Bowlby's theory of attachment

Baby face!

To introduce Bowlby's idea that attachment is innate and adaptive, show students images of young mammals and ask them if they notice similarities.

This is related to the *baby face hypothesis* and the idea that young mammals have the same distinctive features (big eyes, large forehead, squashed up nose).

You can find some excellent images for this at weheartit.com/from/www. thingsthatmakeyougoaahh.com

Your students will almost certainly 'aaawww' at the sight of these cute images. Drawing on this, ask them why these characteristics in young mammals might have evolved. You could also use a collaborative learning structure (see page 5) in which to do this.

Bowlby suggested that these features acted as 'triggers' for parenting behaviour, which is necessary for a young animal's survival. They elicit our desire to look after and care for babies.

NO HANDOUT

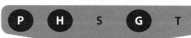

The use of collaborative learning structures (see page 5) could be used here. There is potential with this activity to ask higher-order questions where the more-able students can support the less-able ones; for example, Why would these characteristics have evolved? Predict what might happen if an infant mammal did NOT have these characteristics, etc.

TOPIC: Bowlby's theory of attachment

Connect 5

Bowlby's theory of attachment contains many different elements, principles and terms which students have to be aware of.

However, even if they understand and are aware of all these different elements, they can often still lack an overall understanding of the theory as a whole and how it fits together.

Handout 62 is an activity which aims to encourage students to link different elements of the theory together.

In the grey shaded areas, students should articulate their understanding of the principles i.e. social releasers, adaptive/innate, critical period, sensitivity/reciprocity/interactional synchrony, and monotropy. They could do this using their textbooks (in the *Complete Companion* the relevant pages are 78 and 79).

In between the grey shaded areas, students should try and explain how the elements of the theory link together. For example, social releasers are adaptive because they elicit parenting behaviour which helps them to survive; they are innate because they enhance survival and so the trait is naturally selected.

If you and your students are feeling especially creative, you could even run this activity with different coloured strips of paper in order to make a Bowlby-themed paper chain!

The end result is hopefully that students have a more holistic understanding of Bowlby's theory, and they are encouraged to use higher-order thinking skills.

HANDOUT 62

The instruction to define key terms is a lower-order thinking skill which requires knowledge and understanding.

The instruction to 'link' elements of the theory together constitutes a higher-order thinking skill which some of the students may find more difficult.

As such, you could group students in mixed-ability pairs and give the students different roles to complete the activity, i.e. less-able students complete the definitions, more-able students complete the links. Crucially however, in the whole-class feedback session, reverse the roles so that you ask less-able students about the links and more-able students about the definitions. This will ensure that all students are accountable for all aspects of the work and the students work collaboratively to understand all aspects.

TOPIC: Bowlby's theory of attachment

Burgers

The 'burger' evaluation technique specifically aims to help students to use studies when evaluating theories/explanations; an area where many students appear to lack confidence.

The principles of this technique are outlined earlier on page 8.

Handout 63 provides students with instructions on how to use this technique in order to evaluate Bowlby's theory of attachment.

Deconstruct this technique with your students, and then ask them to evaluate the learning theory explanation of attachment using Sroufe et al. (2005), Rutter et al. (2010), Belsky and Rovine (1984) and the Czech twins.

References

Belsky, J. and Rovine, M. (1987). Temperament and attachment security in the Strange Situation: A rapprochment. *Child Development, 58,* 787–95.

Rutter, M. and Sonuga-Barke, E.J. (2010). Conclusions: Overview of findings from the era study, inferences, and research implications. *Monographs of the Society for Research in Child Development, 75(1),* 212–29.

Sroufe, L.A., Egeland, B., Carlson, E. and Collins, W.A. (2005). *The development of the person: The Minnesota study of risk and adaptation from birth to adulthood.* New York: Guilford.

HANDOUT 63

P H S G T

Handout 63 provides scaffolding for students' paragraphs which should support all students, particularly the less able. If students are finding this too hard, you could also instruct them on the general area of Bowlby's theory that each study supports or undermines, e.g. 'Use Sroufe et al. (2005) to support the internal working model and continuity hypothesis.'

You can also make it an expectation that more-able students should attempt to provide extra commentary and/or counter arguments at the bottom of their 'burgers'.

TOPIC: Ainsworth's Strange Situation: Types of attachment

Role playing Ainsworth

I have to confess that the idea of using role play fills me with absolute horror! Ros and I used to work at a performing arts school (actually, Ros still does) where the students take their drama very seriously. Combine that with the fact that I am extremely uncomfortable with performance myself, and you'll understand why role play does not find its way into my lesson plans!

However, I am well aware that role play can be an excellent tool for helping students remember and understand psychological studies. I would just caution that I don't think long periods of lesson time should be given over to role play because the learning gains are relatively low. BUT, as a fun homework task (i.e. the preparation/rehearsal for the role play is done outside of lesson time), I can certainly see the benefit. So, for those of you who are confident and willing, Ainsworth's Strange Situation does seem to lend itself particularly well to this kind of activity.

In Ainsworth's original research, observers recorded infant behaviour under five categories:

1. proximity and contact-seeking behaviours
2. contact-maintaining behaviours
3. proximity and interaction-avoiding behaviours
4. contact and interaction-avoiding behaviours
5. search behaviours.

Every 15 seconds, the observers made a note of which of the above behaviours were being displayed, also scoring the behaviour for intensity on a scale of 1 to 7.

To role play with students, ask for three groups of volunteers. In each group there should be a caregiver, stranger and infant. In Group 1 the infant should act as securely attached. In Group 2 the infant should act insecure-avoidant, and in Group 3 insecure-resistant.

Using information from their textbooks, each group should act out the episodes

NO HANDOUT

 P H S G **T**

I'm not sure it is possible to differentiate this activity. However, you may decide that it is only an activity that your less-able students complete if they struggle to retain information and understand the procedures of studies.

of the Strange Situation. This provides the rest of the class (those who do not act as stranger, caregiver, or infant) with the opportunity to practise making observations (and find out just how hard this is). Observers should record behaviours over the 8 episodes of the Strange Situation (it might be prudent for them to design a grid on which to do this).

Afterwards class members can compare their results using descriptive statistics (e.g. measures of central tendency, graphs etc.) and consider their conclusions (which infant was which attachment type).

TOPIC: Ainsworth's Strange Situation: Types of attachment

Insecure attachments – spot the difference

Students, understandably, can get confused between the two major insecure attachments types: avoidant and resistant.

Using **Handout 64**, students could complete a 'spot the difference' exercise to help them remember and understand the differences between the two attachment types.

Students should construct simple drawings that illustrate the differences in the willingness to explore, stranger anxiety, separation anxiety, and reunion behaviour of infants who have insecure-avoidant and insecure-resistant attachment types.

These drawings can be really simple. I often tell my students to use little stickmen style infants and caregivers, and to use thought and speech bubbles to present their understanding, especially if they are not confident in their artistic expression!

HANDOUT 64

Like the last activity, you may find that this one is less necessary and/ or suitable with more-able students who have a clear understanding of the attachment types. Instead, it should be an activity given to those students you have identified as confused.

The handout can then be used to structure a student's answer to the following exam question:

'Outline **two** differences in behaviour that might be expected from infants with insecure-avoidant and insecure-resistant attachment types.' (4 marks)

TOPIC: Ainsworth's Strange Situation: Types of attachment

Attachment table mats

This activity can either be used as a starter or consolidation activity. If you are using this as a starter activity, then you must give some general input on the nature of each attachment type, i.e. secure = strong, can use caregiver as a secure base; insecure-resistant = inconsistent, infant is unsure; insecure-avoidant = child is indifferent towards the caregiver.

You need to laminate enough copies of **Handout 65** for the class. Then, cut out the statements on **Handout 66** and place them into envelopes; there should be enough envelope 'sets' for each member of the class.

In essence, this is a very simple matching exercise. The students have to sort all of the statements into their correct places. This may be difficult because you haven't taught the content, but it is by no means impossible; essentially the students are having to hypothesize the behavioural reactions of infants with each attachment types by making educated guesses. In the process, they should gain a better idea of the attachment types and you will have the opportunity to challenge misconceptions.

Alternatively, you could use these table mats as a simple progress check

HANDOUTS 65 and 66

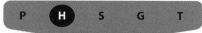

If this activity is used as a topic starter activity, before you have actually taught the content, then students will need to use higher-order thinking skills (see lesson notes).

tool at the end of the topic and as a consolidation activity.

Laminating the table mats and statement sets will save you cutting out the statements again the following year.

TOPIC: Ainsworth's Strange Situation: Types of attachment

What happened next?

You can play a simple plenary game to assess your students' knowledge of the Strange Situation and the characteristics of the attachment types.

To do this, simply present the students with the follow events, and ask them 'What happens next?':

1. The mother of a securely attached child leaves the room.

2. The mother of a child with an insecure-avoidant attachment type leaves the room.

3. The mother of a child with an insecure-resistant attachment type re-enters the room.

4. The mother of a securely attached child attempts to soothe their distressed child.

5. A stranger attempts to comfort a distressed child with an insecure-avoidant attachment type.

Showdown

To make this game a little more competitive, consider putting your students into small teams and playing 'showdown'.

Present event 1 to the students and ask them to consider 'What happens next?' Each team member must *individually* write down their answer. When the teacher gives the signal, all team members reveal their answers at the same time. If all the answers in the team are correct and match each other, that team gets 5 points.

And so on, until all events have been presented.

NO HANDOUT

This activity is mostly designed as a progress check, and therefore opportunities for differentiation are slim and not necessarily appropriate. However, in the feedback, you could target the questioning towards appropriate students depending on the difficulty.

TOPIC: Cultural variations in attachment

Where in the world is that? Individualism vs Collectivism

Now you can test the geographical skills of your A Level students! Collectively, as a class, they might be able to help each other out!

The Van Ijzendoorn and Kroonenberg (1988) research includes data from many different countries and from both individualist and collectivist cultures. Students need to have a basic understanding of these concepts before they engage with the conclusions of the research.

Individualism vs Collectivism

My recommendation is that you first briefly outline what is meant by individualist and collectivist cultures. I would display the following definitions on the board:

- *Individualist: A culture which values personal interest and independence.*
- *Collectivist: A culture which values group needs and consensus.*

Then, give students a series of statements to sort into the two cultures:

- Emphasis on loyalty, dependence on each other and cooperation (C)
- Large families often live together (extended families) and pool their financial resources (C)

- Ties between individuals are loose (I)
- Society is organised into cohesive groups (C)
- People are expected to be responsible for their own well-being and to look after themselves (I)
- From birth, individuals will belong to strong communities (C)
- Emphasis in society is on personal achievement (I)
- Emphasis in society is on working together to achieve common goals (C)
- Families may be important but relationships are less dependent e.g. children move out of the home when they can afford to (I)
- Emphasis in society is on competition (I).

Once students have done this, they are much more likely to have a basic understanding of the differences in the types of cultures and start to think about how they might affect child-rearing values.

West vs East

The next thing your students need to understand is the pattern and spread of individualist and collectivist cultures across the world.

The statement sorting aspect of this activity is best done as a whole-class question and answer session. Therefore, ensure that you ask students questions of appropriate difficulty.

A good way to do this is to display a map of the world on the board and ask students to identify where each of the countries in Van Ijzendoorn and Kroonenberg's (1988) study are on it. When the students have done this, you can mark which of those countries are individualist (e.g. West Germany, Great Britain, Netherlands, USA, Sweden) and which are collectivist (e.g. Japan and China). Ask the students if they notice a pattern. You may need to add more countries to the map if they are struggling. What you want them to spot is that that individualist countries are more likely to be in the West and collectivist countries are more likely to be found in the East.

References

Van Ijzendoorn, M.H., and Kroonenberg, P.M. (1988). Cross-cultural patterns of attachment: A meta-analysis of the Strange Situation. *Child Development, 59,* 147–56.

TOPIC: Cultural variations in attachment

Cultural variations in attachment

Surprisingly perhaps, I think this has to be one of the most difficult topics to teach in the developmental psychology section of the specification. The students that I have taught always seem to find it very difficult to remove themselves from the area they live in order to understand cultural variations in child-rearing values and how they influence attachment types. But having a full and deep understanding of these concepts is crucial for being able to explain, analyse and evaluate research into cultural variations in attachment.

Ask your students to read **Handout 67**. This sheet outlines the child-rearing values of two different cultures: Japan and Germany. Of course, these values are somewhat simplistic and not generalisable to the whole of those cultures, but are useful for the purpose of this activity. You could perhaps discuss how these values are different to what we are familiar with in the UK.

Next, get your students to attempt the worksheet on **Handout 15**. Using the information they have read, students are asked to make predictions about how infants from each culture would behave if placed in the Strange Situation, and the percentages of attachment types that would be found.

The students should also justify their predictions with reference to the information outlined in **Handout 67**. By asking the students to do this, the aim is that they will be able to understand the link between cultural variations in child-rearing values, and the behaviour of infants from different cultures in the Strange Situation.

Following this activity, students will hopefully be in a position to study Van Ijzendoorn & Kroonenberg's (1988) research, and be able to explain some of the results. They can also compare their predictions from the worksheet with the findings of their meta-analysis.

For this activity, you could group students in mixed-ability pairs and give the students different roles to complete the activity. For example, more-able students should complete the Japan box and very clearly explain their answers to the less-able students. Following this, the less-able students should complete the Germany box with the support of the more-able students.

References

Van Ijzendoorn, M.H., and Kroonenberg, P.M. (1988). Cross-cultural patterns of attachment: A meta-analysis of the Strange Situation. *Child Development, 59,* 147–56.

TOPIC: Cultural variations in attachment

World Restaurant Cup!

One of the most compelling evaluations of studies like Van Ijzendoorn and Kroonenberg (1988) is that the use of the Strange Situation is not a valid way of measuring cultural variations in attachment: it is culturally biased. The Strange Situation was created in the USA and reflects the norms and values of American culture, but assumes behaviour has the same meaning in all cultures.

In Japan for example, infants are rarely separated from their mothers. As a result, elements of the Strange Situation pose more of a threat to these infants than infants in the USA. This means infants from Japan are more likely to be classed as insecurely attached and a negative judgement made on Japanese mothers. As such, the Strange Situation could be said to be ethnocentrically biased.

However, this is a very difficult evaluation to teach to AS students, particularly the weaker ones.

World Restaurant Cup

While tearing my hair out trying to help my students understand this evaluation, I had the idea of relating these concepts to something they know and are enthusiastic about: eating and food!

Present your students with the idea that a 'World Restaurant Cup' competition has been launched by the USA and that the following criteria for judging the restaurants have also been announced:

1. Speed/quality of service (20 points)
2. Cost of food (15 points)
3. Quality of food (10 points)
4. Choice/variety of food (5 points).

Students should then be given information which details cultural values regarding food and restaurants in France, USA, and China. For example:

France: *Restaurant food is taken very seriously in France and they really value the quality of food. In addition, they tend to believe that visiting a restaurant should be an all-round social experience; and not just to simply 'eat food.' As a result, people are far more likely to want to wait longer for their food so that they can enjoy their conversations and be safe in the knowledge that the chefs are taking good care, time and preparation over their food.*

United States: *Just like the British, Americans also have a tendency to like a bargain; so the price of food is important. In addition, Americans tend to lead very busy lives and so the speed of service is often vital. People in restaurants are very quick to complain if the food is taking too long to appear.*

China: *Sharing the meal in China is very important and individual meals/portions are a rarity. This reflects Chinese culture as a whole which is collectivist and values the idea that everything is equal and shared.*

NO HANDOUT

P **H** S G **T**

This is a difficult thinking activity that will stretch the most able. The less able will need your targeted support during the activity and will need tangible examples of why the criteria used to judge the competition may not be fair to all cultures.

The custom in many Chinese restaurants is to call for service when it is required, as opposed to waiting for somebody to serve you. This can lead to confusion when Western people travel to China because they can end up waiting and become frustrated that no one is serving them!

Students should then use this information to evaluate the fairness (validity) of the criteria for judging restaurants in France, USA, and China, as well as drawing overall conclusions at the end.

I found that when using the activity, students had a far better understanding when we related their evaluations to the use of the Strange Situation to measure attachments across cultures. The following activity '**World Attachment Competition**' is designed to naturally follow on from this activity.

References

Van Ijzendoorn, M.H., and Kroonenberg, P.M. (1988). Cross-cultural patterns of attachment: A meta-analysis of the Strange Situation. *Child Development, 59,* 147–56.

TOPIC: Cultural variations in attachment

World Attachment Competition!

This activity is a continuation from the previous '**World Restaurant Cup**' task. Students will find it much easier to complete if they attempted and understood the previous task.

In essence this task is the same but with a slight difference. This time the students are asked to consider the validity of the Strange Situation criteria as a measure of attachments across cultures.

Explain to the students that a 'World Attachment Cup' has been launched by the USA. Thousands of attachments between mothers and infants have been assessed across the world to determine which country has the most 'secure' attachments. The competition organisers have said that the attachments will be assessed using Ainsworth's Strange Situation technique, and the criteria for judging each type of attachment will be the same as Ainsworth's criteria for judging a secure attachment.

However, some countries have already expressed their concern about the ethnocentric bias in the competitions' judging criteria... Why?

Using **Handout 15** again, ideally, the students will conclude something similar to the evaluation of Van Ijzendoorn and Kroonenberg (1998) outlined on the previous page.

"One of the most compelling evaluations of studies such as Van Ijzendoorn and Kroonenberg (1988) is that the use of the Strange Situation is not a valid way of measuring cultural variations in attachment: it is culturally biased."

NO HANDOUT

P **H** S G **T**

Like the previous activity, this is a difficult thinking activity that will stretch the most able. The less able will need your targeted support during the activity and will need tangible examples of why the criteria used to judge the competition may not be fair to all cultures.

References

Van Ijzendoorn, M.H., and Kroonenberg, P.M. (1988). Cross-cultural patterns of attachment: A meta-analysis of the Strange Situation. *Child Development, 59,* 147–56.

TOPIC: Bowlby's theory of maternal deprivation

Snowballing: Reasons for separation

Disruption of attachment refers to a situation where the attachment between an infant and their primary attachment figure has been damaged or lost; this can lead to maternal deprivation and Bowlby believed it would have severe consequences for the child.

This disruption is invariably caused by a physical separation from the caregiver that results in a loss of emotional care.

However, there can be many causes of this physical separation, which students should be aware of.

Use the collaborative learning structure '**snowballing**' (see page 6) with your students to brainstorm the possible, different causes of physical separation between infant and caregiver.

Some of the reasons students could suggest are: day care, hospitalisation, death, divorce, mental illness, school, holiday etc.

> The use of a collaborative learning structure (see page 5) has the potential to ensure less-able students are supported and more-able students can support them.

TOPIC: Bowlby's theory of maternal deprivation

Developing your maternal deprivation evaluations

You may meet similar activities throughout this *Teacher's Companion*. When teaching psychology, I am always trying to think of as many different ways to illustrate to students the need to develop and elaborate their basic evaluation points.

The activity on **Handout 69** is one of those activities; it is very simple, but shows the students how to use the simple PEE structure for evaluations. In completing the activity, they are also considering the evaluations of Bowlby's maternal deprivation research.

Answers:

1. One strength of Bowlby's ideas is that they had real-world applications. In the past, children were separated from their parents when they spent time in hospital. Visiting was discouraged or even forbidden. Bowlby's research led to social change in the way that children were cared for in hospital.

2. Rutter (1981) argued that Bowlby's view of deprivation was too simplistic. This is because the term does not take into account whether the child's attachment bond had formed but been broken, or in fact had never

formed in the first place. He argued that if the latter, the *lack* of emotional bond would have more serious consequences. As such, he used the term 'privation' to refer to the failure to form attachment and 'deprivation' to refer to when one had formed but been lost.

3. A further evaluation relates to the fact that there are individual differences in the reaction to separation. This is supported by Barrett (1997) who reviewed various studies on separation and found that securely attached children sometimes cope reasonably well, whereas insecurely attached children become especially distressed. This suggests that the effects of maternal deprivation are not experienced in the same way and do not affect children in a uniform way.

4. Research studies do tend to support the idea that maternal deprivation can have long-term effects. Bifulco et al. (1992) studied women who had experienced separation from their mothers at an early age because of maternal death or temporary separation of more than a year. Bifulco et al. found that about 25% of the women later experienced

> This activity provides students with a demonstration of the PEE and may therefore provide scaffolding for students' future attempts at evaluation.

depression or anxiety, compared to 15% in a control group. The effects were much greater when the separation occurred before the child was 6. This supports the idea that maternal deprivation leads to a vulnerability in terms of negative outcomes later in life. It also supports Bowlby's notion of a critical period.

References

Bifulco, A., Harris, T., and Brown, G.W. (1992). Mourning or inadequate care? Re-examining the relationship of maternal loss in childhood with adult depression and anxiety. *Developmental and Psychopathology, 4,* 433–49.

Barrett, H. (1997). How young children cope with separation: Toward a new conceptualisation. *British Journal of Medical Psychology, 70,* 339–58.

Rutter, M. (1981) *Maternal Deprivation Reassessed (2nd edn).* Harmondsworth, Middlesex: Penguin

TOPIC: Romanian orphan studies

Rolling show – Romanian orphanages

Rolling shows are essentially slideshows of images that automatically change after a set period of time; 5 seconds for example. Details on how to setup Rolling Shows using PowerPoint are outlined on page 8.

These slideshows make an excellent start to the lesson. I usually have one running with some appropriate music before the students arrive, so that from the moment they turn up, the topic and tone of the lesson are clear.

The effects of institutionalisation is a pertinent topic to try this technique with as there are some very moving images available on the internet illustrating the conditions of Romanian orphanages in the 1980s–90s. Simply using a search engine will provide you with many possible images to use.

For those unsure of the history, Romania's orphan problem began under the Communist rule of Nicolae Ceauşescu who banned abortion and denied access to contraception at a time of severe food and energy shortages. Many Romanians abandoned their newborn children, leaving thousands to suffer at under-funded, state-run orphanages.

NO HANDOUT

P	H	S	G	T

This activity is not really a task that the students complete, but after the rolling show you could ask students a series of questions about what they have seen.

These questions could range from knowledge retention (e.g. name one thing you remember seeing) to predicting (e.g. what do you think the behaviour of those children is like now that they are adults?). As the teacher, you can ensure that you target the questions appropriately, taking into account the student's ability.

TOPIC: Romanian orphan studies

Post-it® picture

An idea for a plenary when teaching the effects of institutional care is to display an image of a child living in one of Romania's under-funded, state-run institutions (see last activity). For example, try here: http://answer-question.org/tanya/romanian-orphanages/.

Give each student a Post-it® note and ask them to write the following information on it:

- Explain one way in which this child's situation might affect him or her later in life.
- Justify this with evidence.
- Extension: give a counter argument or determining factor.

This plenary activity encourages students to summarise the research they have studied in class. This particular task works best after teaching Rutter and Sonuga-Barke's (2010) longitudinal study of Romanian orphans, but might be equally adaptable to other studies of institutionalisation, e.g. Hodges and Tizard (1989). Several studies are mentioned on the 'Romanian orphan studies' spread of the *Complete Companion* (pages 86 and 87).

When I've taught this topic in the past, I bought a large and cheap frame to display the Post-it® notes, putting the image in the middle. That frame is now up in my room and provides quite a thought-provoking display for other students to read.

References

Hodges, J. and Tizard, B. (1989). Social and family relationships of ex-institutional adolescents. *Journal of Child Psychology and Psychiatry, 30,* 77–97.

NO HANDOUT

P	H	S	G	T

This activity involves application skills and so all students will be stretched.

For less-able students you could provide a writing frame e.g. One way he/she may be affected is... This is supported by...

More-able students should be given the expectation to try and include a counter argument, based on their knowledge of the research and evaluation of the methodology.

Rutter, M. and Sonuga-Barke, E.J. (2010). Conclusions: overview of findings from the era study, inferences, and research implications. *Monographs of the Society for Research in Child Development, 75(1),* 212–29.

TOPIC: Romanian orphan studies

Flipped learning: Documentaries on Romanian orphanages

We all know that students like to watch videos. Mainly, I might uncharitably suggest, because it means they can relax and not do any writing. Well, not in my classroom!

I have a very simple rule for my lesson planning and that rule states that if a video is over ten minutes long, there must be a worksheet that goes with it.

However, a really interesting new concept that has been gathering pace is that of 'flipped learning'. A really useful summary is here: http://www.edudemic.com/guides/flipped-classrooms-guide/. Essentially, the idea is that the lecture (or in this case, watching a video) occurs outside the classroom. The lesson in the classroom is used to explore the themes and ideas.

Type 'Romanian orphanages' into YouTube and you will be spoilt for choice on videos you can ask your students to watch in their own time which you can then discuss in class. To give this homework some structure, provide the students with themes they should comment on. Although these themes will depend on the documentary you choose for them to watch, the following questions should feature:

- What are the conditions like?
- Comment on the children's physical care.
- Comment on the children's emotional care.
- What are the consequences of this care likely to be for emotional and social development?

Structure can be provided in this activity by giving themes/categories that students must comment on when watching the clips of the documentary or documentary clips.

During class feedback and discussion, higher-order questioning should be targeted at more-able students. In contrast, retention and comprehension questions can be targeted at lower-ability students.

- Do you think it is possible for the children to recover from these circumstances?
- What do you think would make that recovery more likely?

TOPIC: Influence of early attachment on child and adult relationships

Flipped learning: Good Will Hunting

Good Will Hunting, in my opinion (MG), is a superb film which explores a condition known as reactive attachment disorder. Will Hunting is a seemingly confident and brash janitor with a serious anger problem. He is also a genius. His potential is identified by a university professor who takes Will under his wing but insists that he goes to therapy. It is during therapy that Will's background as an orphan is explored. Meanwhile, Will engages in a romantic relationship with a girl but pushes her away when she gets too close to him emotionally.

The film suggests that Will's behaviour is the result of a defence mechanism: the need to push people away before they get too close to him and let him down. The links to Bowlby's theory and developmental attachment are very clear. It is best that you watch this

film yourself and then think about the questions you will set students to answer as their 'flipped learning' homework (see previous activity), but I would suggest some or more of the following:

- What is significant about Will's childhood background?
- According to Bowlby, what might this mean for Will's development? Think about the roles of maternal deprivation, his internal working model, the continuity hypothesis etc.
- On the park bench, what point is Will's therapist (played by Robin Williams) trying to make about Will's experiences?
- Why is Will so scared of going to California with his girlfriend? Think beyond Will's own explanation of this. Why is he pushing her away?

Structure can be provided in this activity by giving themes/categories that students must comment on when watching the clips of the movie.

During class feedback and discussion, higher-order questioning should be targeted at more-able students. In contrast, retention and comprehension questions can be targeted at lower-ability students.

- Why doesn't Will trust anyone according to his therapist?
- What is a defence mechanism and why is it relevant to this film?
- What is Will diagnosed with? What does it mean?

TOPIC: Influence of early attachment on child and adult relationships

HANDOUT 70

Psychology storytime: Internal working model

Why not transport your students back to primary school circle time, turn the lights out, and read them a story…

Something strange but endearing happens to students when they enter the Sixth Form; they seem to regress to an earlier stage of development! For example, sixth form students at the schools I have worked at (female and male) will badger, cheat, and sell their souls for the chance of being rewarded with one of our department's custom-made psychology stickers! So much so that this year we now award psychology t-shirts to those students who achieve a collection of 10 stickers in a year! Now, try this technique with year 10 and 11, and you may get an altogether different reaction…!

On **Handout 70** is a story you can read out, or ask your students to read. It is a silly story but may help students start to think about the concepts of the internal working model.

Set some time in the future, the story describes a girl who receives an 'Edward Bear' for her birthday. This is a futuristic toy (hopefully your students will have the necessary imagination) which is essentially created by the child and behaves just like a 'living being'. However, the girl does not like what she has created…

'Disappointed with the fruit of her labour, Katie stuffed Edward into a dark cupboard, leaving him to contemplate his bleak future.'

Stop the story at this point and ask your students to consider the following question (your students will need to stretch their imagination somewhat!):

1. The bear's first experience of the world is being rejected by its creator and stuffed in a dark cupboard. Based on this first experience, what do you think the bear thinks about himself?

The nature of the questions that go with this activity lend themselves to higher-order thinking skills. As such, it is also a good opportunity to use collaborative learning structures (see page 5) which is a useful way to ensure all your student ability groups are catered for.

2. What do you think the bear thinks about other 'living beings'?

3. Based on your answers, how do you think the bear will behave in the future? Think about its social and emotional development.

Then finish reading the story. Ask your students why they think you read them the story, and what relevance it might have to attachment and developmental psychology. You could then introduce the concepts of the internal working model, and the continuity hypothesis.

TOPIC: Influence of early attachment on child and adult relationships

HANDOUT 71

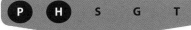

Love quiz

Hazan & Shaver's (1987) study can be said to have provided evidence in support of Bowlby's internal working model and continuity hypothesis.

Bowlby's theory of attachment suggests that the infant's relationships with his or her caregiver forms the basis of the child's internal working model of relationships. This will affect the child's expectations about what relationships (including romantic ones) will be like. Therefore, we would expect a link between early attachments, attitudes about romantic relationships and actual romantic relationships. This is called the *continuity hypothesis*.

Hazen and Shaver's study

Hazan and Shaver (1987) tested Bowlby's hypothesis with their 'love quiz'. The quiz, which contained nearly 100 questions, was published in the *Rocky Mountain News*. They received 620 replies to their questionnaire and drew the following conclusions:

Securely attached adults:

- had certain beliefs about relationships (love is enduring)
- reported certain experiences in relationships (e.g. mutual trust)
- were less likely to have been divorced.

Insecurely attached adults:

- felt true love was rare, and fell in and out of love easily

- found relationships less easy
- were more likely to be divorced.

Analysis of the data revealed that infant attachment style predicted attitudes towards love (internal working model) and experience of love (continuity hypothesis).

In the short version of the quiz on **Handout 71** the questions make assessments as follows:

- Q 1, 2 and 3 assess attachment history.
- Q 4, 5, and 6 assess adult attachment type.
- Q 7, 8 and 9 assess mental models of relationships

Ethics briefing

This study involves questions that may be related to sensitive information about an individual's early-life experiences, which may suggest problematic adult relationships. When replicating this study, always seek informed consent beforehand, where possible, and offer a thorough debriefing, including the right to withhold individual data.

It should also be emphasised that the suggested correlation between early experience and later relationships is not 100%; there are many individuals who overcome early unfavourable circumstances. In addition this correlation is not proven.

The activity mainly involves students simply answering the questions on the 'quiz'. However, as an extension task you could ask your more-able students to also jot down evaluations of the research method, for example, social desirability, demand characteristics, retrospective evidence etc. Often the more-able students read through and answer the questions more quickly so they are likely to have a few minutes in order to complete the extension task.

A further point to make is that the original survey involved nearly 100 questions, whereas this shorter version involves just nine. Therefore, the validity of this exercise will be low, so little can be read into the results.

That said, it is a useful exercise to undertake to understand how Hazan and Shaver collected the evidence which is often used to support Bowlby's hypothesis.

To work out scores use the table below.

References

Hazan, C., and Shaver, P.R. (1987). Romantic love conceptualised as an attachment process. *Journal of Personality and Social Psychology, 52,* 511–24.

Question	a	b	c
Part C			
1	secure	insecure avoidant	insecure resistant
2	secure	insecure resistant	insecure avoidant
3	insecure resistant	secure	insecure avoidant
Score for part A (the dominant category chosen (secure, insecure-avoidant or insecure-resistant) =			
Part B			
4	insecure resistant	insecure avoidant	secure
5	secure	insecure resistant	insecure avoidant
6	insecure avoidant	secure	insecure resistant
Score for part B (the dominant category chosen (secure, insecure-avoidant or insecure-resistant) =			
Part A			
7	insecure avoidant	insecure resistant	secure
8	insecure avoidant	secure	insecure resistant
9	insecure resistant	secure	insecure avoidant
Score for part C (the dominant category chosen (secure, insecure-avoidant or insecure-resistant) =			

	Secure adults	Resistant (anxious) adults	Avoidant adults
Different love experiences	Releationships are positive	Preoccupied by love	Fearful of closeness
Adult's views of relationships	Trust others and believe in enduring love	Fall in love easily but have trouble finding *true* love	Love is not durable nor necessary for happiness
Memories of the mother-child relationship	Positive image of mother as dependable and caring	Conflicting memories of mother being positive *and* rejecting	Remember mothers as cold and rejecting

TOPIC: Influence of early attachment on child and adult relationships

What's going on?

Combining students' learning of developmental psychology and their understanding of research methods is crucial; it is only by identifying and exploring these links that students gain a deeper understanding of psychology and its flaws.

The activity on **Handout 72** is designed to help students with this. In particular, it is designed to help students practise their interpretation of graphical information and to explore the limitations of correlational research.

HANDOUT 72

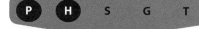

There are a series of extension questions that you could display on the board for more-able students to complete:

- What are the co-variables in this study?

- Is r = +.52 large enough for us to conclude that the results are significant?

- Why is correlational research useful in the context of this study (think ethics, think practicalities)?

- What is the potential problem with quantifying infant and adult attachment scores?

TOPIC: End of Attachment topic summary

Confidence ratings

The confidence rating handout could be annotated in a number of different ways. You may wish to set a percentage in each cell (25%, 50%, 75%, 100%) for students to colour code as they revisit each area as part of their revision. An alternative method could be to colour code a cell (red: cannot achieve this; amber: can achieve with some support; white: feel comfortable; green: feel confident).

Again as topics are revisited through revision, cells can be highlighted to correspond with current confidence levels.

Additional activities

The checklist could be used to form targeted revision groups and allow students to sign up to sessions that cover the areas they are least confident in.

HANDOUTS 73 and 74

P H S **G** **T**

Students may wish to reflect on their own progress through the unit as an individual or as part of a peer discussion. Alternatively the checklist could form part of a one-to-one discussion with a student who is of particular concern.

TOPIC: Definitions of abnormality

An introduction to statistical infrequency

As an introduction to the concept of statistical infrequency a quick class poll could be taken for a range of common phobias.

Draw the following table on the board:

Phobic item	No fear	Mild fear	Moderate fear	Strong fear	Intense fear

NO HANDOUT

P **H** S G **T**

Following the class poll (see below) discussion questions can be targeted at different students in the class. Alternatively, questions could be assigned to pairs or groups of students who are then asked to feed back their ideas to the class.

Students can identify a range of common phobias to be added to the table such as heights, spiders and the dark. Taking a white board marker students come to the board and tick their level of fear for each item.

This activity offers a range of discussion points:

- What are the limitations of using fixed choice answers to assess level of fear?
- How might social desirability influence responses be given in this activity?
- Are there any ethical issues with such an activity?
- At what rating do we consider a person to be phobic?

- Why are phobias seen as undesirable behaviours?
- How might evolutionary psychologists explain some of the phobias identified?

In my (RG) experience this activity is well received by the class and students enjoy the opportunity to share their phobias. Links can often be made to personal experience (in which case behavioural explanations and social learning theory can be discussed) but some phobias seem to develop without a fearful event triggering the response (leading to consideration of biological preparedness).

TOPIC: Definitions of abnormality

Statistical infrequency

Students are required to apply their understanding of statistical infrequency to the scenario given. This activity provides the opportunity to practise writing responses that make explicit links to the question stem (AO2 skill). For example, *'Both Frank and Ralph's responses would be considered abnormal as they are statistically infrequent, meaning that the level of fear they feel towards spiders does not fall within the normal distribution of fear ratings for the population sampled. Frank has a much higher fear than most respondents and so might possibly be considered as having a phobia, which would be seen as an undesirable behaviour. Ralph has a much lower fear rating than most people and so might also been seen as abnormal. However, Ralph might argue his behaviour*

is desirable as it allows him to keep spiders as pets, a hobby he enjoys.'

You can pose further questions to the class regarding the scenario included in **Handout 75**.

- Researchers contacted Frank for a follow-up interview based on his questionnaire responses. In this interview Frank revealed he is so afraid of spiders that he will not enter a room without switching a light on first in case a spider is present, has to check around his room and under his bed before he sleeps at night, and will not carry out any gardening work in case spiders are present. How might we apply the definition 'failure to function adequately' to Frank's behaviour?

HANDOUT 75

P **H** S G T

Following the multiple-choice questions in this activity, students have the opportunity to challenge themselves with the extension questions shown in each arrow box.

The final two questions require students to apply their understanding of statistical infrequency and one of the issues this definition faces: that of deciding the cut-off point in determining abnormality.

If this research were to be carried out in countries where poisonous spiders are a threat to humans, such as Australia, would we need to alter how we viewed level of fear?

An introduction to deviation from social norms

At the start of the lesson students are exposed to a range of cultural experiences (some suggestions are given below) and asked if they would join in (showing an image relating to each example adds to the effect). This activity reinforces the social norms we are used to but can also be used to highlight cultural relativism.

Would you eat a Century egg?

A delicacy in Chinese cuisine a duck, quail or chicken's egg is buried for several months until the yolk has turned a dark, soft green and the white has become a dark brown jelly. The egg smells similar to ammonia and is eaten with rice or as a side dish.

Would you wear a series of neck rings?

The Kayan people live on the mountain border between Burma and Thailand. From the age of five women wear a brass coil that increases in size as they age. Over the years this coil presses on the clavicle resulting in the appearance of a long neck, a sign held in great esteem by the tribe.

Would you fear the evil eye?

Bedouin tribes of the Middle East spend a lot of time and energy in counteracting the effects of the evil eye. The evil eye is seen as a dangerous force which explains much misfortune experienced in the harsh desert conditions.

NO HANDOUT

| P | H | S | **G** | T |

Following the class activity students can work in smaller, mixed-ability groups to identify social norms in their own culture, and the wider UK. Students can be given discussion questions to deepen their thinking once a list of norms has been identified (see lesson notes).

Discussion questions

- How do we learn these social norms?
- How have these norms changed over time?
- Why might norms change for different ages?
- Why might norms change for different genders?
- How do we feel when we observe people breaking these norms?

Deviation from Social Norms

Handout 76 follows Bloom's taxonomy in terms of level of thinking required to complete each task. Students decide which level of thinking they should start at.

Application task

Aisha might not have been considered deviating from social norms if her behaviour was less extreme. Lots of people hold superstitions regarding lucky items. However, her reliance on her teddy has become all-consuming and she now feels her success is solely due to the presence of the teddy. Taking the teddy everywhere, especially as an adult, would be seen as unusual as the majority of people would not do this.

Analysing task

This real-life example illustrates that social norms change over time and so the definition might become outdated. Links can also be made here to who decides what is and what is not acceptable behaviour? In terms of the law, those who hold the most power in the country have the opportunity to influence social norms based on their own opinion as to what is normal and abnormal.

Evaluating task

Encourages students to create effective evaluations rather than simply listing ideas. Quality over quantity.

Creating task

The continuum is based on public figures (celebrities) who hold personal interest for many students so should motivate them to attempt this final activity. When considering each figure students should take into account the context of their behaviour, e.g. elaborate costumes as part of a stage show would not be seen as deviation from norms due to the context in which the behaviour occurs. Furthermore, some behaviour might seem abnormal to us but in the social groupings of the famous might seem more commonplace for example, extreme plastic surgery.

References

Szasz, T.S. (1974). Ideology and insanity. Harmondsworth, Middlesex: Penguin.

HANDOUT 76

| **P** | **H** | S | G | T |

Students first review all tasks before making a decision as to which level they need to begin working at. For example, a more-able student does not need to begin at the 'knowledge level' if they are already able to give examples of social norms.

Independent learning is encouraged at the top of **Handout 76** with suggestions as to where information can be found rather than relying on teacher input.

TOPIC: Definitions of abnormality

An introduction to Failure to function adequately

Think – pair – share

Think: Students are asked to work alone to develop a definition for the term 'Failure to function adequately'. Hints may help here such as, *'think about what someone with mental ill health might find difficult'*. Students may find it easier to focus on a specific mental illness such as depression, OCD or a phobia to allow them to give concrete examples of activities a sufferer may find challenging to perform.

Pair: Students join with a friend (or you can assign them into pairs) to formulate a definition that incorporates both their ideas.

Share: Pairs then form groups of four, to identify common themes and discuss new ideas to either add to a final group definition or remove from the definition following group discussions.

Share the group definitions with the class and vote for the best definition.

The group could then compare their definition to that of Rosenhan and Seligman (1989) who suggested the following characteristics that define failure to function adequately: Suffering, Maladaptiveness (danger to self), Vividness & unconventionality (stands out), Unpredictably & loss of control,

NO HANDOUT

| P | H | S | **G** | T |

Pairing a less-able student with a more-able student may be a supportive relationship. The less-able student will be exposed to more developed ideas while the more-able student, through explaining their thinking, has the opportunity to consolidate their understanding.

Irrationality/incomprehensibility, Causes observer discomfort and Violates moral/ social standards.

References

Rosenhan, D.L. and Seligman, M.E.P. (1989). *Abnormal Psychology. Second edition.* New York: W.W. Norton

---

TOPIC: Definitions of abnormality

Failure to function adequately

This activity requires noticing skills and the ability to make links between comments. In order to access the level 4 mark band in the AS route, students need to produce commentary that is *'effective'*; the A Level route states *'thorough and effective'*. Simply listing evaluative points will exclude answers from the higher mark bands as will generic comments. I (RG) have found students need time to develop this skill and benefit from repeated modelling and opportunities to practise writing AO3 comments. As such, I would suggest

introducing this exam skill early and revisiting it repeatedly throughout the course.

This activity can be completed through colour coding boxes to group them together or carried out as a cut and stick activity. While cut and stick does take longer, less-able students might benefit from having the opportunity to manipulate the boxes and make repeated adjustments to arrive at their final decision. These can then be stuck into notes in the form of completed PEEL paragraphs.

HANDOUT 77

| P | H | S | G | **T** |

This independent activity enables you to work with students who find it difficult to make the connections between comments that can be used to build developed evaluations. Students might find using a textbook helpful to support them in this match-up activity. For students struggling with the course, supporting them to create reasonable evaluations (matching the first three columns only) may be more suitable.

TOPIC: Definitions of abnormality

Deviation from ideal mental health

Handout 78 includes a number of tasks to develop students' understanding of this definition of abnormality. The first task requires students to compare a previously learnt definition to the current definition being taught. This reinforces prior learning and highlights important features of Ideal mental health. The second activity supports students in outlining the six categories identified

by Jahoda (1958). The final activity gives students the opportunity to practise AO2 application skills by noticing aspects of Jahoda's definition in the case study.

Once the activity is completed, students can complete the exemplar exam question: *'Briefly outline the deviation from ideal mental health as a definition of abnormality.'* (4 marks)

HANDOUT 78

| P | **H** | S | G | T |

A stretch question is included for students who wish to make links between Deviation from ideal mental health and Failure to function adequately. While Failure to function adequately differs in its focus (presence of maladaptive behaviours versus presence of adaptive behaviours), links can be made. For example, the absence of ideal mental health means Chris is no longer functioning in his professional and personal life.

References

Jahoda, M. (1958). *Current concepts of positive mental health.* New York: Basic Books.

Level	Marks	Description
2	3–4 marks	Outline is clear and accurate. Main features of definition are included.
1	1–2 marks	Outline is clear but incomplete or partially accurate.
	0 marks	No relevant content/ another definition of abnormality outlined.

TOPIC: Definitions of abnormality

Act like an examiner

On **Handout 79, Candidate A** could not be considered as providing a strong answer to the practice exam question. The student initially identifies one limitation but does not develop the concept much beyond the suggestion that the six criteria Jahoda identifies are unrealistic. Their questions hint at suitable developments but are not elaborated upon and so do not receive credit. The second comment does not receive credit as this is a strength of the model not a limitation (comments here are also brief). One mark is awarded out of four.

Candidate B performs much better. The use of paragraphing and sentence wording makes it easy for the examiner to identify two separate limitations. Both are structured using PEEL structure which has led to developed evaluations earning four out of four marks.

The question and mark scheme on **Handout 79** can be used as a class assessment for other definitions of abnormality.

HANDOUT 79

P H **S** G **T**

A set of assessment questions can be provided for students who struggle to apply the mark scheme:

1. Are two separate limitations easily identified in the answer?
2. How did the candidate introduce each limitation (point)?
3. Was there a development of the limitation initially identified (evidence)?
4. Did the candidate include an example to develop the limitation they identified (expansion)?

TOPIC: Definitions of abnormality

Cultural relativism

Fill in the blanks answers

Statistical infrequency: rare – common – hearing voices – God

Failure to function: adequate – diagnosis – lower classes – non-white

Social norms: culture – white – middle class – panic attacks

Ideal mental health: Jahoda – incidence – individualist – collectivist.

As an extension activity, you could challenge students who are interested in this particular area to research examples of culture-bound syndromes and consider recent revisions to DSM (DSM-5). Simply typing 'culture bound syndromes' into an internet search engine produces a wide range of articles. Students should be reminded to consider the expertise and intentions of the authors of such sites.

HANDOUT 80

P H **S** G T

Less-able students might benefit from terms being linked to the relevant circle as this will then help them to decide the order in which each word should be used.

You can challenge the more-able students by removing the key terms and asking them to fill in the blanks themselves. The most-able students could be given empty boxes with no words or passage, leaving them to create their own summaries.

TOPIC: Mental disorders

Characteristics of mental disorders

Students first select three colours; one for each characteristic. Working as group, students decide how to complete the task. This could mean assigning one example to each student who then teaches the others, or they all work systematically through each example as a collaborative exercise. This activity encourages noticing skills in students: an important skill for application (AO2) questions. Discussion questions following completion of this activity might include:

1. Which characteristics do you feel are most challenging for the patient?

2. Which characteristics are most noticeable to others?

3. How would you define the terms 'emotional', 'behavioural' and 'cognitive' characteristics?

Students may find completing a revision table a useful activity at this point which can then be revisited nearer exam time.

HANDOUT 81

P H S G T

This is a great revision opportunity for students who are able to quickly identify the emotional, behavioural and cognitive characteristics of each disorder. By applying different definitions of abnormality to each example, students are consolidating their understanding of the characteristics of each disorder as well as the criteria proposed by each definition. For example, the OCD patient's rituals (behavioural characteristic) have the potential to make her unable to work (failure to function).

Characteristics	Phobias	Depression	OCD
Emotional			
Behavioural			
Cognitive			

TOPIC: The behavioural approach to explaining phobias

The behavioural approach: the two step model

Handout 82 predominately relates to Mowrer's (1947) two-step model as an explanation of the development and maintenance of phobias. The tasks provide an opportunity for students to practice their AO2 application skills as they are required to use concepts from the behavioural approach to explain Ali's phobia.

Completion of this activity may help students structure their answer to the following practice exam question. Using the Ali scenario on **Handout 82**, students attempt the question, *'Suggest how the behavioural approach might be used to explain Ali's phobia of dogs. (4 marks)'.*

Students can then self- or peer-assess the answer using the mark scheme shown below.

Level	Marks	Descriptor
2	3–4 marks	AO1 - Knowledge of the behavioural approach is clear and mostly accurate. The answer is generally coherent with effective use of terminology related to the behaviourist approach. AO2 - The material is used appropriately to explain Ali's phobia of dogs. For example, candidates may refer to the two-step model as an explanation of the acquisition and maintenance of the phobia.
1	1–2 marks	AO1 - Knowledge of the behavioural approach can be seen in the answer although comments may not always be explicitly linked to how phobias are acquired. The answer lacks details and may be partially inaccurate. Use of specialist terminology is absent or inappropriate. AO2 - References to Ali's fear of dogs might not always be effective.
	0 marks	No relevant content.

HANDOUT 82

P H S G **T**

Less-able students may find it difficult to identify the different components of the classical conditioned response in Ali's case (UCS, UCR etc). Modelling this process in a visual form for Watson and Rayner's (1920) Little Albert might help students *(see Complete Companion, p104).*

References

Mowrer, O.H. (1947). *On the dual nature of learning: a re-interpretation of 'conditioning' and 'problem-solving'.* Harvard Educational Review, *17*, 102–48.

Watson, J.B. & Reyner, R. (1920). Conditioned emotional reactions. *Journal of Experimental Psychology, 3*, 1–14.

TOPIC: The behavioural approach to explaining phobias

Extended answer analysis

Handout 83 builds upon the previous activity in requiring students to write their own explanation of the behavioural approach to phobias, making reference to Ali's phobia **(Handout 82)**. Students should then identify the key components of a successful evaluation (tasks 1 to 6) to model exam technique. Marks have not been assigned to this activity to make it applicable to both AS (12 marks) and A Level routes (16 marks).

References

Di Nardo, P.A., Guzy, L.T. & Bak, R.M. (1988). Anxiety response patterns and etiological factors in dog-fearful and non-fearful subjects. *Behaviour Research and Therapy, 26(3)*, 245–51.

Öst, L.G. (1987). Age of onset in different phobias. *Journal of Abnormal Psychology, 96*, 223–9.

Seligman, M.E.P. (1970). On the generality of the laws of learning. *Psychological Review, 77*, 406–18.

Sue, D., Sue, D. & Sue, S. (1994). *Understanding Abnormal Behaviour (4th edn)* Boston: Houghton Mifflin.

HANDOUT 83

P **H** S **G** T

Group your students into mixed-ability pairs as this will support less-able students. The pair may decide to tackle separate tasks then share their findings with each other. The less-able students can circle key terms and underline references to Ali , while identifying PEEL sections in each paragraph could be the responsibility of more-able students. A suitable stretch task could be to challenge students to create an alternative evaluation paragraph focused on the statement, 'the two-step process ignores cognitive factors'.

TOPIC: The behavioural approach to treating phobias

Create your own desensitisation hierarchy

Set your students the task of creating a poster explaining the behavioural approach to treating phobias. Working in pairs, ask them to create a desensitisation hierarchy for a specific phobia; either of their own choosing or one assigned to them. As well as the hierarchy they devised, their poster is also expected to include key aspects of Systematic desensitisation: progressive muscle relaxation, classical conditioning, reciprocal inhibition, relaxation techniques, visualising a peaceful scene and counterconditioning.

References

Wolpe, J. (1958). *Psychotherapy by Reciprocal Inhibition*. Stanford, CA: Stanford University Press.

NO HANDOUT

P **H** **S** G T

Some students might benefit from a checklist to ensure key components of Systematic desensitisation are included in their poster.

If any of your students wish to carry out their own research, they might find the following website interesting:

http://www.psychotherapy. net/video/wolpe-systematic- desensitization-video

Here they will be able to watch a short video of Joseph Wolpe (1958) explaining how he developed the treatment.

TOPIC: The behavioural approach to treating phobias

Cut it down and build it up

Students use their understanding of different behavioural treatments to create outline of varying degrees of detail. This activity supports students' understanding of the difference between detailed and basic outlines in terms of the level of information included, provides a useful revision tool and provides the opportunity to develop précis skills.

Cut it down (flooding): A detailed outline of flooding is given which students gradually reduce down to key terms that should appear in any outline of the technique.

Build it up (systematic desensitisation): Key terms pertaining to Systematic desensitisation are shown. From this vocabulary students build up the level of detail with each progressive step; moving to a simple sentence such as, *'Using relaxation, patients gradually move through a hierarchy of feared scenes',* then adding detail to create a basic and finally an effective evaluation.

As an extra activity, your students could create a Venn diagram to compare the similarities and differences between the two treatments. For example, both use relaxation and aim to associate this state with the feared object. However, while Systematic desensitisation is gradual, flooding begins at a point of intense fear.

HANDOUT 84

P H **S** G T

Less-able students might find sentence starters helpful as a guide to create more detailed outlines. For example:

- Counterconditioning forms the basis of the therapy because…
- Reciprocal inhibition refers to…
- One relaxation technique taught to patients is…
- The therapy proceeds through gradual steps…

TOPIC: The behavioural approach to treating phobias

Behavioural treatments: evaluation graph

Students need to recreate the graph shown below on a piece of A3 paper.

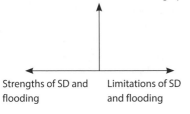

Students cut out each text box on **Handout 85** and decide where to place each comment on the evaluation graph. The stronger the evaluation the further from the centre line the textbox needs to be placed.

Once complete, you could challenge your students to create their own PEEL evaluations using the information contained in the evaluation graph.

References

Choy, Y., Fyer, A.J., and Lipsitz, J.D. (2007). Treatment of specific phobia in adults. *Clinical Psychological Review*, *27*, 266–86.

Comer, R.J. (2002). *Fundamentals of Abnormal Psychology* (3rd Edn.) New York: Worth.

Craske, M.G., Kircanski, K., Zelikowsky, M., Mystkowski, J., Chowdhury, N. and Baker, A. (2008). Optimizing inhibitory learning during exposure therapy. *Behavioural Research and Therapy*, *46*, 5–27.

Freud, S. (1909). Analysis of phobia in a five-year-old boy. In J. Strachey (ed. and trans.). *The Complete Psychological Works: The Standard Eedition* (vol. 10). New York: Norton, 1976.

Klein, D.F., Zitrin, C.M., Woerner, M.G. and Ross, D.C. (1983). Treatment of phobias: II. Behavior therapy and supportive psychotherapy: Are there any specific ingredients? *Archives of General Psychiatry*, *40*, 139–45.

McGrath, T., Tsui, E., Humphries, S. and Yule, W. (1990). Successful treatments of a noise phobia in a nine-year-old girl with systematic desensitisation in vivo. *Educational Psychology*, *10*, 79–83.

Őhman, A., Eriksson, A. and Olofsson, C. (1975). One-trial learning and superior resistance to extinction of autonomic responses conditioned to potentially phobic stimuli. *Journal of Comparative and Physiological Psychology*, *88*, 619–27.

Working in groups is helpful for this activity as students can discuss their ideas as to the strength of the evaluative comment. For example, Freud's case of Little Hans might only be considered an effective limitation if you accept Freud's wider theoretical stance. However, care should be taken when considering findings from a single case study.

Students might find it beneficial to annotate each textbox once stuck down, in order to record the ideas discussed.

TOPIC: The cognitive approach to explaining depression

The cognitive approach: the ABC model

The questions shown below, whether used to check of level of detail when making notes or as a test of knowledge retention, can be marked using the following mark scheme (however, it should be noted this mark scheme is not representative of exam board schemes – see sample and past papers for suitable questions and mark schemes if your wish to conduct a formal exam assessment). I would advise regularly checking past papers and examiner's reports to identify any subtle changes with each examination.

1. **Outline Ellis' ABC model (4 marks)**
   Two marks for naming and explaining A(Activating event), B(belief), C(Consequence).
   Two subsequent marks for examples illustrating each component A,B,C.

2. **Ellis proposed the key to mental disorders, such as depression lay in irrational beliefs. The source of these irrational beliefs lies in mustabatory thinking. What is meant by the term mustabatory thinking? Give examples in your answer. (4 marks)**
   One mark for explaining that this involves thinking certain ideas or assumptions must be true in order for the person to be happy.
   One mark for each of the three most important irrational beliefs Ellis identified (three marks in total).

3. **Explain why mustabatory thinking increases the likelihood of depression. (2 marks)**
   One mark for stating that the person who holds the irrational belief risks becoming depressed when the 'must' is not fulfilled. Often musts reflect very unrealistic standards so disappointment is likely.
   One mark for giving an example, e.g. depressed due to irrational belief regarding failure: *'I must always do well so failing the test means I am stupid').*

Stretch question: Predict how cognitive psychologists might attempt to treat depression.

An additional activity could be a Post-it® assessment. Before students hand their answers in to be marked, give them the opportunity to comment on each other's work. Students rotate around the room

You could set these questions as a research activity with students using class notes and/or textbooks to answer the questions, or use them as an assessment activity to check retention of information.

A stretch question is included which requires students to consider how the ABC model might influence treatment of depression, e.g. identify the mustabatory thinking, help the patient see this thinking is unhelpful and try to remove this thinking style, replacing it with more adaptive cognitions.

looking at other students' work. They use one colour Post-it® note to record any strengths of the student's work, using a different coloured note to record one way they think the work could be improved. These are stuck onto the work. Once you have marked it, these coloured notes, if accurate, can form the basis of feedback and targets to improve.

References

Ellis, A. (1962). *Reason and emotion in psychotherapy*. New York: Lyle Stuart.

TOPIC: The cognitive approach to explaining depression

The cognitive approach: Beck's negative triad

Ask your students to read the *Complete Companion* p108 closely. Using **Handout 86**, they should then identify the true and false statements. Encourage your students to then expand upon these statements.

1. FALSE: explanation focused specifically on depression.

2. TRUE: depressed patients also lack any perceived control over events in the world.

3. TRUE: could give an example, e.g. schema for restaurant means we know how to act when visiting a new establishment for dinner.

4. FALSE: developed during childhood due to variety of factors, including parental/peer rejection, criticism by teachers.

5. TRUE: example of expecting to fail (schema) and exam (event) could be given.

6. FALSE: leads to 'cognitive' biases in thinking.

7. FALSE: there are three key elements.

References

Beck, A. T. (1976). *Cognitive therapy and emotional disorders*. New York: International Universities Press.

HANDOUT 86

| P | H | S | **G** | T |

Working in groups enables students to check their answers and collaborate to identify relevant details from the text that can be used to expand upon the statements.

Students can be challenged to consider the similarities between Beck's explanation of depression and Ellis' ABC model. For example, both see irrational thinking as a source of the disorder and the presence of an activating event.

TOPIC: The cognitive approach to explaining depression

Get creative - Beck's negative triad

In preparation for linear exams students benefit from making revision tools throughout the year that can be revisited during the course and used intensively in the run up to exams. Designing a visual representation of Beck's negative triad, either hand-drawn or using images from the internet provides students with a revision poster that can be displayed at home.

References

Beck, A. T. (1976). *Cognitive therapy and emotional disorders*. New York: International Universities Press.

NO HANDOUT

| **P** | H | S | G | T |

The *Complete Companion* (p108) illustrates the key elements of the triad using the example of thoughts relating to appearance. You can challenge your students to think of an alternative example to build their triad around, for example, *I am a failure* (self), *I am going to fail my exams as I cannot achieve anything* (world), *I am never going to amount to anything and will remain uneducated and unemployed* (future).

TOPIC: The cognitive approach to explaining depression

Evaluating the cognitive approach

Handout 13 requires students to create developed evaluations that show consideration of two sides of an argument (*Complete Companion*, p109).

The first set of bubbles focuses on the argument surrounding irrational thinking as a cause of depression or merely another symptom of the disorder.

The second set of bubbles relates to the approach's focus on mental state when situational factors might have real implications for the patient.

Students should be encouraged to record ideas in their own words rather than simply copy from the Student Book.

In addition, prior to this activity you could give your students statements to consider and feed back to the class:

• Do irrational thoughts cause depression or does depression cause irrational thoughts?

• Could depression run in families? If so, why?

• Who does the cognitive approach blame for the depression experienced?

• What do you think causes depression?

Students' ideas lay the foundation for the reading they need to engage in to complete the evaluation task in **Handout 13**.

References

Alloy, L.B and Abrahmson, L.Y. (1979). Judgement of contingency in depressed and non-depressed students: Sadder but wiser? *Journal of Experimental Psychology, 108*, 441–85.

HANDOUT 87

| P | **H** | S | G | T |

The thought bubbles direct more-able students to other commentary than can be applied to the central argument. The first set of speech bubbles regarding irrational thinking as a cause can be developed by considering that in some cases depressed people actual have more realistic outlooks (Alloy & Abrahmson 1970). The second set of speech bubbles consider the role of situational factors which can be developed in terms of other contributing factors such as genetic influences.

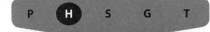

TOPIC: The cognitive approach to treating depression

Treating depression with CBT

HANDOUT 88

P **H** S G T

Students are required to apply their knowledge of CBT to the case of Greta (AO2 application skill). Make sure that as they outline the components of CBT (specifically REBT, homework, behaviour activation and unconditional positive regard) their comments relate explicitly to Greta's case. For example, Greta's previous relationship was abusive and so it is important her psychologist shows unconditional positive regard to convince her of her worth as a human being.

In addition, you could challenge students to summarise CBT for a range of different people, e.g. a Year 7 student, an adult who is about to attend their first CBT session, a biologist who argues depression is a result of genetic vulnerability. Students should consider what language they would use when talking to each person and which aspects of the treatment they would emphasise.

Once the task is completed, more-able students can be provided with reading related to the strengths and limitations of CBT as a treatment for depression. Using this information, students should predict any potential issues that may prevent Greta from achieving a successful outcome.

References

Ellis, A. (1962). *Reason and emotion in psychotherapy*. New York: Lyle Stuart.

TOPIC: The cognitive approach to treating depression

Peer assessment

HANDOUT 89

P H **S** G T

This activity has two stages:

First, ask your students to write their evaluation of CBT on a piece of lined paper.

Secondly, students should use **Handout 89** to structure their peer assessment of another's work. Ask them to select two of their peer's paragraphs to assess but if you wish them to consider the whole evaluation (time permitting) simply photocopy **Handout 89** back-to-back to provide feedback for four paragraphs.

This activity reinforces the use of PEEL as a means to creating developed evaluative comments and reflects

the wording used in the exam mark schemes. Specific marks have not been shown allowing the activity to be used for AS or A Level route teaching.

Alternatively this form could be used to enable less-able students to work with those more able, completing the forms together in preparation for an extended writing assessment. This acts as a writing frame for students who struggle with structuring their written work. This handout can be modified to allow it to be used with other topics in the specification.

Less-able students might find sentence starters helpful when writing their evaluative paragraphs, possibly presented in a PEEL writing frame to help structure their evaluations. For example,

Point	CBT might be less suitable for people who hold irrational beliefs that are rigid and resistant to change.
Evidence	
Expansion	
Link	

TOPIC: The biological approach to explaining OCD

Triplets

HANDOUT 90

P H S G **T**

The words shown at the start of **Handout 90** all relate to genetic explanations for OCD (part of the biological approach). For each set, students choose three words that link together. The lines to the right of the set give students the opportunity to explain the connection between the words.

In addition, ask students to suggest what key terms would form a general introduction to genetic explanations for OCD and create a fourth triplet, e.g. inherit, concordance, genes.

You can set this activity as an individual challenge with students using their class notes or textbook (*Complete Companion*, p112) to build their triplets. This means you can sit with students who may struggle with the biology of mental disorders and support them in making links.

TOPIC: The biological approach to explaining OCD

Team teaching

Once assigned a topic (either abnormal levels of neurotransmitters or abnormal brain circuits) students use their textbook (*Complete Companion*, p112) to make their own notes, recording them on **Handout 91**. They should create a simple outline of the topic in 50 words (helping them to consolidate their understanding), then record research relevant to the topic along with key terms specific to the explanation of abnormality they are researching. The textboxes entitled 'interesting points' and 'links to other areas' encourage students to consider wider issues connected to their given topic.

It is important students record information using note form and in their own words to ensure they have a secure understanding of the explanation rather than copying text with little awareness of what they are reading.

Once research time is completed (this will depend on your class needs and SOW timetable), students need to decide on a format to supplement their teaching; for example, a poster, PowerPoint, A5 flash cards, diagram. Once teaching tools are created, the groups split to form pairs (one student from each original group) who then teach each other their information.

To test how effectively each pair taught each other a mini quiz could be given for each pair to complete without the use of their information sheet or teaching tools. The pair who scores the highest in both sections is the winner.

HANDOUT 91

P H S **G** T

I would recommend students work in ability groups of three to four students when completing their information sheet. Less-able students are assigned to 'abnormal levels of neurotransmitters' as the area has already been covered, in part, through discussing genetic influences. More-able students are assigned 'abnormal brain circuits'. This gives students the chance to check with understanding with each other and ensure consolidation of understanding before leaving the group to teach another.

TOPIC: The biological approach to explaining OCD

Construct a commentary

Ask your students to answer each question to form developed evaluations for the biological explanation of OCD, focusing specifically on genetic explanations. *'What is meant by the term..?'* boxes encourage students to use specialist terminology in their answers as well as reinforcing important points relating to research evidence i.e. the amount of DNA shared between relatives and the function of OFC (sends signals to thalamus about things that are worrying us). The second text boxes include questions designed to develop students' thinking in terms of the role of nurture in the development of OCD and real-life applications (brain scans might be used as a diagnostic tool, MRI scanners enable researchers to see areas of the brain).

You could then challenge students to apply the two-step model (studied in behavioural explanations for and treatment of phobias) to the development of OCD. This could be used as an evaluation paragraph suggesting that if OCD can be explained and treated psychologically then the biological approach might not be the only explanation for OCD. This activity provides a useful revision opportunity of the two-step model. However, to ensure comments are seen as evaluation by the examiner, students must consider why the two-step model may be better than the biological explanation rather than simply outlining the two-step model.

HANDOUT 92

P **H** S G **T**

The first question text boxes are less challenging: simply asking students to define key terms which are important when discussing research into the biological explanation of OCD. The second questions are more challenging, requiring students to consider the nature/nurture debate and making links to the diathesis stress model.

Students who are really struggling with this topic may benefit from being provided with a set of answers they are able to cut and stick into the relevant text boxes allowing time to discuss each answer with you.

TOPIC: The biological approach to treating OCD

Understanding mode of action

Challenge your students to create a passage of information regarding the three main drug therapies for OCD: SSRIs, Tricyclics and BZs (this passage can be created using information from the *Complete Companion* p114, as well as their own internet research). This could be set as a homework task where time is given to consider all three drug therapies or students work in groups of three taking the responsibility for researching one drug therapy each.

Using a range of highlighters students are asked to colour code the text based on the following criteria:

1. Commercial names for each drug type e.g. Prozac.

2. Effect of drug on specific neurotransmitters, e.g. increases levels of serotonin.

3. How the drug creates this effect (mode of action), e.g. blocks reabsorption of serotonin.

Students may then wish to transfer this coded information into a table of the same headings to create a revision chart for all three drugs.

Drawing the action of the drug at the synapse is a helpful activity for students to visualise the mode of action of each drug. In addition, students could draw three diagrams (one for each drug type) and label how each drug impacts on neurotransmitters.

In my experience a number of students who study psychology have also chosen biology. These students could take on the role of 'lead learners' for this topic. Place students in groups of four with one biology student in each group. Other students direct their questions to these students first, rather than turning immediately to you.

TOPIC: The biological approach to treating OCD

Six hats analysis

After students have developed an understanding of drug therapy as a treatment for OCD, you can use this activity to consider its appropriateness and effectiveness. Assign students to a hat. Students with the same hat sit and work together to complete their section. Once they have finished their section they then form new groups (three students of different hats for two sessions seems to work better than a single session with a group of six) to share their ideas.

In addition, following the six hats activity draw a continuum on the board (shown below).

CBT..Drug therapy.

Give each student a Post-it® note to record their ideas. Students are asked to consider which treatment they feel should be provided to OCD patients. The stronger their decision the closer toward CBT or drug therapy they place their Post-it®. For example, if they are unsure or feel it should be the patient's choice then they place their note in the middle. If they feel CBT should be used first and then if needed, drugs offered later, they then would move along the left side of the continuum. Students have to apply their knowledge of CBT from their study of depression (offering an opportunity to revise this treatment).

The red and the white hat should be accessible to most students, whereas the green hat and blue hat require higher-order thinking.

References

DeBono, E. (1985). *Six Thinking Hats*. Little, Brown and Company.

TOPIC: End of Psychopathology topic summary

Confidence ratings

The confidence rating handout could be annotated in a number of different ways. You may wish to set a percentage in each cell (25%, 50%, 75%, 100%) for students to colour code as they revisit each area as part of their revision. An alternative method could be to colour code a cell (red: cannot achieve this; amber: can achieve with some support; white: feel comfortable; green: feel confident).

Again as topics are revisited through revision cells above the original colour can be highlighted to correspond with current confidence levels.

The checklist could be used to form targeted revision groups and allow students to sign up to sessions that cover the areas they are least confident in.

Students may wish to reflect on their own progress through the unit as an individual or as part of a peer discussion. Alternatively the checklist could form part of a one-to-one discussion with a student who is of particular concern.

TOPIC: Origins of psychology

What is science?

If students are studying in their first year of AS/A Levels, it is likely that they have studied science subjects for the previous 12 years of their schooling. And yet, ask those students to outline what 'science' is and they usually struggle. My (MG) students usually cannot go beyond 'biology, chemistry and physics' or 'how the world works'.

This activity is designed to help students use their previous knowledge to construct their own definitions of science.

Display the following words on the board:

- Knowledge
- Evidence
- Hypothesis
- Experiment.

Using a collaborative learning structure such as group statements (see page 6), ask the students to define these words. In addition, ask them to come up with a sentence or two that uses all of the words. Essentially, you are encouraging them to look at the connections between those words. The sentences the students produce are usually basic definitions of the scientific process, e.g. 'You gain knowledge through experiments which test hypotheses. The experiments provide evidence which support knowledge.'

As long as the sentences are not woefully inaccurate, I usually respond to them by saying 'You have just defined science' and encourage the students from this point forward to think of science as a verb (a doing word) rather than a noun (a name of the subjects they do at school). After this activity, you can start to explore how psychology conducts itself as a scientific subject.

NO HANDOUT

P · H · S · G · T

You could add extra words for more-able students to tackle, e.g. 'causation', 'theory', 'objective' etc.

Using collaborative learning structures (see page 5) can also ensure that your higher-ability students are stretched and that your lower-ability students are supported.

TOPIC: Origins of psychology

The object game

How can we introduce the concept of 'the approaches in psychology' to students?

The basic concept that students need to understand is that the same behaviour can be interpreted and explained on different levels.

A fun topic starter to introduce this idea is the 'object game'. Give groups of students random objects, e.g. balloon, plant pot, wooden plank etc. Ask them, within two minutes, to brainstorm as many uses for that object as they possibly can. It is fair to say that this activity is not rigorously academic, but it can be a good way to introduce the idea that the same behaviour can be interpreted and explain in different ways – just like the random object. You can call it the psychology of approaches...!

NO HANDOUT

P · H · S · G · T

Using collaborative learning structures (see page 5) can also ensure that your higher-ability students are stretched and that your lower-ability students are supported.

TOPIC: Origins of psychology

The blind men and the elephant

Find the 'Blind men and the elephant' parable through an internet search engine; it is an ideal way to introduce the approaches in psychology.

The parable is essentially about six blind men who stumble across an elephant and feel different areas of its body. Depending on the part of the body they feel, their interpretation of what the elephant is like changes. For example, the blind man who feels the elephant's trunk likens the elephant to a snake and the blind man who feels the knee likens the elephant to a tree trunk. The last paragraph of the parable finishes with the conclusion that each of the blind men were partly right, but also partly wrong; that is, they were not necessarily looking at the whole picture.

The lessons for psychology and the approaches are easy to spot; each approach is partly right but also partly wrong because they do not necessarily make connections with each other and look at the big picture.

Read this parable to your students and discuss the moral of the story and the implications it might have for psychology.

NO HANDOUT

P · H · S · G · T

This activity is fairly flexible. You could create a handout to scaffold the students' analysis of the parable and what it might mean for psychology.

Equally, the use of collaborative learning structures (see page 5) can also ensure that your higher-ability students are stretched and that your lower-ability students are supported.

You can also target questions that develop higher-order thinking skills to more able students, e.g. 'How might this parable be relevant to psychology?'

TOPIC: Origins of psychology

Key words are good for you!

Some students have an aversion to key words, partly because they are intimidated by them and partly because they do not see the point of them.

One way to bring them around on both points is to show them that using key words actually reduces the amount they have to write! **Handout 96** contains an introduction to the ideas of Wundt and introspection. The words in bold and brackets can be replaced by just one or two key words. The job of the students is to use their knowledge and understanding to work out which key word(s) should be used. Options are included at the bottom of the page.

A follow-up activity could be to give the students the key words and ask them to write their own definitions; hopefully this activity would have given them some ideas.

HANDOUT 96

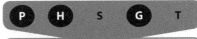

More-able students could be instructed to cover the possible answers to make the activity more challenging

TOPIC: Origins of psychology

Connect 5

The 'origins of psychology' topic has the potential to be very difficult for students. It involves a number of abstract concepts which are intimidating. In addition, although students may come to understand some of those concepts, it is even more tricky for them to see the connections between them and to comprehend the 'bigger picture'.

Handout 97 is an activity which aims to encourage students to link the different elements together.

In the grey shaded areas, students should articulate their understanding of the principles, i.e. empiricism, introspection, scientific methods, hypotheses, determinism. They could do this using their textbooks (in the *Complete Companion*, the relevant pages are 124 and 125).

In between the grey shaded areas, students should try and explain how the key scientific concepts link together.

If you and your students are feeling especially creative, you could even run this activity with different coloured strips of paper in order to make a paper chain!

The end result is hopefully that students have a more holistic understanding of the origins of psychology, and they are encouraged to use higher-order thinking skills.

Suggested links

Introspection/Empiricism: Empiricism, using observation and experience, was used by Wundt to systematically measure internal processes such as memory and thought.

Empiricism/Scientific Methods: Objective and replicable methods such as experiments are used to fulfil the requirements of empiricism.

Scientific Methods/Hypotheses: Scientific methods often seek to test at least one prediction/explanation about human behaviour.

Hypotheses/Determinism: Making predictions about human behaviour assumes that behaviour is determined and caused by internal and external factors. There can be no free will if human behaviour can be entirely predicted.

HANDOUT 97

The instruction to define key terms is a lower-order thinking skill which requires knowledge and understanding.

The instruction to 'link' elements of the origins of psychology together constitutes a high-order thinking skill which some of the students may find more difficult.

As such, you could group students in mixed-ability pairs and give the students different roles to complete the activity, i.e. less-able students complete the definitions, more-able students complete the links. Crucially however, in the whole-class feedback session, reverse the roles so that you ask less-able students about the links and more-able students about the definitions. This will ensure that all students are accountable for all aspects of the work and the students work collaboratively to understand all aspects.

TOPIC: Learning approaches: Classical and operant

Pavlov's Dog Game

Have a look at the following web page: http://www.nobelprize.org/educational/medicine/pavlov/pavlov.html.

This game has been on that website for a number of years and was still working at the time of writing. It poses the very simple question: 'Can you make a dog drool on demand?'

Of course, this game is based on the famous Pavlov's dogs study. Pose your students the same question in groups and ask for their ideas. Most students know exactly how to make the dog drool on demand so the next question to ask is, 'why would that work?' At this point, you could ask the students to try and incorporate certain words into their answers, e.g. association.

This a simple topic starter for introducing the basic concepts of the behaviourist approach.

NO HANDOUT

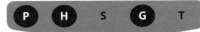

The use of collaborative learning structures (see page 5) could ensure that your higher-ability students are stretched and that your lower-ability students are supported.

In addition, you could ask more-able students to try and incorporate more key terms into their 'why would that work?' answers. For example, 'stimulus' and 'response'.

TOPIC: Learning approaches: Classical and operant

Being cruel to be kind using classical conditioning

Some of you may remember 'Jedward', the Irish pop duo, considered irritating by many, that featured on the X Factor (you could do some research on YouTube if you dare...).

When teaching the principles of classical conditioning one year, I decided to ask students to create an equation to describe a method that could be used to ensure that children would cry when Jedward came on the television. This was done under the guise of being 'cruel to be kind' for the children, that is, ensuring that they do not grow to think

that Jedward's pop act is acceptable! The ethics of this type of activity are questionable, but good fun all the same...! Lots of students came up with the method of taking away the children's favourite toys (UCS) whenever Jedward started to sing (NS) which helped the students to consolidate their understanding of the classical conditioning equation.

You could try bringing this activity up to date with a similar act currently offending you on TV.

NO HANDOUT

P **H** S **G** T

The use of collaborative learning structures (see page 5) could ensure that your higher-ability students are stretched and that your lower-ability students are supported.

TOPIC: Learning approaches: Classical and operant

Explaining with classical conditioning

The student activity on **Handout 98** is fairly self-explanatory. The students must identify the UCS, UCR, NS, CS and CR in each of the six examples and then construct a classical conditioning equation to explain how the behaviour was learnt.

This is a good activity to use once you have gone through a couple of worked examples and you want to test and consolidate the students' understanding.

HANDOUT 98

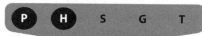

P **H** S G T

For more-able students, you might consider asking them to complete four of the examples and then writing two examples of their own instead, as this is a more challenging activity.

TOPIC: Learning approaches: Classical and operant

Operant conditioning: Reinforcements and punishments

Like the activity in **Handout 98**, the student activity on **Handout 99** is fairly self-explanatory. The students must identify the type of reinforcement or punishment that is illustrated in each of the examples. This is actually quite hard and I remember initially getting very confused when these concepts were introduced to me at degree level!

Again, this is a good activity to use once you have gone through a couple of worked examples and you want to test and consolidate the students' understanding.

Just in case you are not sure of the answers yourself... here they are!

1. Negative reinforcement
2. Positive reinforcement
3. Positive punishment
4. Negative punishment
5. Negative punishment
6. Negative reinforcement
7. Positive punishment
8. Positive reinforcement
9. Negative reinforcement
10. Positive reinforcement
11. Negative punishment
12. Positive punishment
13. Negative reinforcement

HANDOUT 99

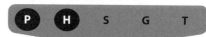

P **H** S G T

For more-able students, you might consider asking them to complete a few of the examples and then writing two examples of their own instead, as this is a more challenging activity.

TOPIC: Learning approaches: Social learning

Social learning theory: Applying key concepts

An important but difficult skill for students to develop during this topic is that of application. Not only do the students need to understand the different approaches and be able to explain them, they also need to be able to apply them to new concepts.

A good way to do this is to display some of the key concepts of an approach and to then have the students connect these to some stimulus material. On **Handout 100**, the students must write

brief definitions of the key concepts in the boxes and then draw connections to relevant material in the example. For example, direct reinforcement can be connected to Lucy's friends commenting that her recent weight loss means she 'looks good'.

This worksheet can then be used to help students complete an exam-style question on the same stimulus material.

HANDOUT 100

The handout provides scaffolding for weaker students so that they can feel more confidence in attempting the exam-style question.

If appropriate, you could provide even more support by drawing the connect lines for the students.

TOPIC: Learning approaches: Social learning

Bandura et al.'s (1961) research: Study deconstruction

Research methods is embedded throughout the examination papers; in fact, research methods questions are worth 25% of all marks. As such, research methods teaching and learning should be embedded throughout the course.

One way to encourage this is to ask your students to deconstruct psychological studies into their constituent parts. **Handout 101** provides students with a framework to do this and to consider the potential weaknesses of the study.

Encourage students to contextualise the criticisms because it is easy to just write the generic statements.

References

Bandura, A., Ross, D. and Ross, S. A. (1961). Transmission of aggression through imitation of aggressive models. *Journal of Abnormal Social Psychology*, *63*, 575–82.

HANDOUT 101

For less-able students, you could provide them with definitions of the keys terms (i.e. independent variable, dependent variable etc).

In the feedback and progress-checking session, ensure that you target the highest-order questions to the most able (i.e. potential problems).

For the highest ability, you could offer a completely different pathway, by not offering them the handout. Instead, ask them to identify key research methods concepts just from the description of the study (it would help if they had already completed a deconstruction-style worksheet before this activity so that they know what might be expected).

TOPIC: The cognitive approach

Chinese whispers

An interesting way to demonstrate the power of schemas is to play Chinese whispers with your students.

Arrange the students into groups of around six to eight people. The groups should be large enough so that mistakes might be made.

If you are unfamiliar with Chinese whispers, the basic premise is that you give the first person in the group a statement to pass on in whisper form to the next person, who whispers it to the next person, and so on. The last person in the group writes down the statement

which can then be shared with the class and compared with the original statement.

For the purposes of demonstrating schemas, something like the following statement is good:

- If somebody is feeling sleepy, they should get out of bed.

The statement obviously doesn't make sense. You would, in fact, expect someone to get in bed if they were sleepy. When your students whisper this statement to each other, one of your students may change this statement in

NO HANDOUT

This is more of a demonstration than an activity, but when discussing the causes of the change in statements, try and ask more challenging questions to more-able students.

line with their schemas so that it makes more sense to them.

You can try this with a few statements like this to see whether, in ambiguous circumstances, where students are not sure about what they have heard, their schemas influence them to change the details.

TOPIC: The cognitive approach

Cognitive approach: Evaluation and elaboration

| P | H | S | G | **T** |

Handout 102 is designed to illustrate to students the level of depth required to achieve top AO3 marks.

Students should start by reading the boxes on the far left-hand side of the page, which outline simple evaluation points. Ask them to highlight (or shade in) each of the boxes in that column with a different colour.

The students should then read the boxes in the next column. Each represents further explanation/elaboration of one of the evaluation points, but they are not in the same order. Students should highlight (or shade in) those boxes with the correct, corresponding colour.

They should repeat this until all boxes in all columns are shaded in. This will require some thought from the students.

The purpose of this activity is to show students that the more they can elaborate their original evaluation points (e.g. 'A strength of the cognitive approach is that it has many applications'), the more AO2 marks they are likely to get. This is denoted at the top of the worksheet. The evaluation comments start at 'Level 1', and then increase in marks the further they are elaborated, through 'Level 2', 'Level 3' and 'Level 4'. These are loosely based on the AQA essay mark schemes.

The correct answers are as follows:

"A strength of the cognitive approach is that it has many applications"

- For example, the cognitive approach to psychopathology has been able to explain dysfunctional behaviour in terms of faulty thinking processes.

- This has led to the development of treatments for illnesses such as depression with cognitive-based therapies.

- These treatments, which aims to change dysfunctional ways of thinking, have been shown to be successful in some mental disorders which suggests that the emphasis on mental processes for explaining mental disorders is valid.

"Another strength of the cognitive approach is that it can be considered a scientific approach"

- Although cognitive psychologists create theories and models of behaviour, they do this as a result of experimentation with human participants.

- This means that their conclusions are based on far more than common sense and introspection, which can give a misleading picture.

- As such, the approach can be seen as a systematic, objective and rigorous way for reaching accurate conclusions about how the mind works.

"One major limitation of this approach is the use of computer models"

- For example, the approach uses terms such as 'encoding' and 'storage' for the mind which are borrowed from this field.

- However, there are important differences between the human mind and computer programmes.

- For example, human minds make mistakes, can forget, and are able to ignore available information when necessary. These are all fundamental differences.

To challenge your more able, you could decide to cut out the sixteen boxes and instruct the students to match them up to make four evaluation points. Once they have cut out the boxes, they should mess them up so it is no longer clear which boxes belonged to which columns. This is a more difficult activity because the students must decide on the order of the elaboration as well.

"A further problem is that the cognitive approach appears to ignore important factors"

- Although the cognitive approach tells us *how* cognitive processes take place, it doesn't tell us *why* they take place. The roles of emotion and motivation are largely ignored.

- This may be a result of the computer analogy and the over-dependence of this approach on information-processing analogies.

- Humans possess motivation and emotion, whereas information-processing machines do not.

TOPIC: The biological approach

True/False

| **P** | H | S | G | T |

Handouts 103, 104 and **105** provide another activity designed to encourage students to read textbook content carefully and a way to ensure that students are more likely to retain and understand that knowledge.

Various statements are included on the handouts and mirror the content from pages 132 and 133 in the *Complete Companion*. Students need to decide whether they think that statement is true or false. If the statement is true, they should develop that point with

more detail. If the statement is false, the students should correct the statement.

Answers

1. True, 2. False, 3. True, 4. False, 5. True, 6. False, 7. True, 8. False, 9. True, 10. False, 11. True, 12. True, 13. True, 14. True, 15. False, 16. True

This activity does not lend itself too easily to differentiation; students are more likely to differentiate themselves by the level of detail they include in their extensions and corrections.

However, you could separate the students into two groups: those that complete the activity with their textbook, and those that complete the activity after reading the relevant textbook page once only.

TOPIC: The psychodynamic approach

Seeing the bigger picture

P **H** S G **T**

Freud and the psychodynamic approach are really fun to teach but it can be tempting to go off on too many tangents because you know your students will want to hear about it!

Students tend to hold on to the 'shocking' elements they hear about in the psychodynamic approach but do not always fully engage with the psychodynamic approach in the holistic way that it requires.

Freud was the first person to put forward an integrated and comprehensive explanation of all human behaviour. It could be argued that he is the only person to have done this.

Consequently, it is important that students see Freud's approach for what it is: a jigsaw of interrelated parts.

The activity on **Handout 106** is designed to help students to do this.

Ask your students to cut out the grey shapes on the handout. Then, using their notes or their textbook (page 134 and 135 in *Complete Companion*), ask them to define the terms and concepts, i.e. repression, displacement, unconscious mind etc.

Then provide students with some A3 poster paper. This could be done using mixed-ability groups. Ask the groups to stick the grey shapes onto their paper in a pattern which they feel reflects the links between the terms and concepts (this could literally be in any order, such is the interrelatedness of Freud, so reassure them this is a subjective activity).

Once they have arranged their shapes, they should then draw a series of arrows/lines to illustrate the links between them. On those arrows/lines they should write explanations of how/why these elements are linked.

If your students have done this properly, their poster should look like a web of messy associations between various elements of Freud's psychodynamic approach.

This hopefully will give students a better feel for the holistic nature of the psychodynamic approach, and reinforce the interrelated nature.

If you feel that some of your students will struggle with this activity, provide them with a sheet which suggests some of the concepts that they should attempt to connect. For example, the 'cheat sheet' could suggest that 'defence mechanisms' and 'displacement' should be connected. This could be accompanied by prompt clues such as 'one of these is an example of the other'.

TOPIC: The psychodynamic approach

Freud appreciation society

P **H** S G T

Undoubtedly the best part about teaching Freud is the opportunity to inform the lads that they have repressed the desire to sleep with their mothers (through fear of castration from their father), and the girls that they have repressed envy of their father's penis. God bless the Oedipus complex and the idea of 'penis envy'!

However in highlighting these 'interesting' elements of psychoanalysis, we do tend to take away from some of the genuine achievements of Freud. Students always dismiss psychoanalysis as 'that weird mother-love sexual stuff' and Freud as 'the perverted one'!

This of course is a little unbalanced! Whilst some of Freud's ideas now seem a little 'wacky', other elements still pervade the way we think of the mind and behaviour today.

Redressing the balance!

So, consider setting your students this homework. Tell them to look again at the psychodynamic approach and identify three good positive evaluations. They may wish to research this in their textbooks or on the internet. In what way are Freud's ideas still influential today? Which elements of his approach have received empirical support?

At the start of the next lesson, brainstorm these positive evaluations on the board.

Then inform students that their task will be to set up a 'Freud appreciation society'. This will entail devising a campaign to re-educate the nation on the brilliance of Freud. Students could create advertising slogans, posters, record radio or TV interviews (if your school has the necessary equipment).

For more-able students, set them the task of researching areas of the brain and whether they correspond with functions of the id, ego or superego.

Alternatively, give your more-able students this article: http://cogns.northwestern.edu/cbmg/PsychoNeuro2012.pdf.

Using the evidence from the article, they should write a PEE paragraph or 'burger' (see page 8) which supports the psychodynamic approach.

Make sure that you set clear objectives for them to follow, and share tangible outcomes that they must show evidence of at the end of the activity.

TOPIC: The psychodynamic approach

Dominoes

A good 'Dominoes' activity is a great way to help students review key terms, concepts, studies and evaluation points. However, I rarely do this activity with my students because it is quite labour intensive to set up and construct the cards.

Here are some I prepared earlier so you don't have to!

Students should match the key terms etc with their relevant definitions until all cards are matched.

You will actually find that the dominoes are already in order for your reference i.e. the definition for 'unconscious mind' is directly beneath that domino, the definition for 'conscious mind' is directly beneath that... and so on. My students have NEVER noticed this! Once they cut them out, they'll have no idea they were already in order!

HANDOUTS 107 and 108

| P | H | S | G | T |

This activity is difficult to differentiate because it is largely designed to assess students' understanding. However, you may wish to keep an eye on your weaker students and provide them with support, clues and prompts where necessary.

TOPIC: The humanistic approach

Goals and motivation: Hierarchy of needs

Handout 109 is designed to help make the hierarchy of needs, as proposed by the humanistic approach, more tangible. It should also help students think about how they might tackle application questions in this topic.

In the first part of the worksheet, the students simply have to state which level of need each statement is related to:

1. Self-actualisation
2. Self-esteem
3. Safety
4. Love/belonging
5. Physiological.

Then, the students should identify a long-term goal that they have, for example, to train to be a teacher (perish the thought!). In addition, they should note their motivations and which level of need they relate to, for example:

- To earn money to live (safety/physiological)
- To help other people (love and belonging)
- To be part of a respectable profession (well, that one is subjective!) (self-esteem)
- To fulfil my potential (self-actualisation).

HANDOUT 109

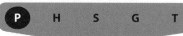

The first activity on this handout is relatively straightforward, and therefore you could instruct your more-able students to miss this part out. Instead, they could be instructed to make sure that their 'five reasons' which motivate the achievement of their goal, reflect each level of the hierarchy of needs.

TOPIC: The humanistic approach

Spot the deliberate mistakes

Once you have taught the humanistic approach to your students, you could test their knowledge and understanding by asking them to spot the 14 deliberate mistakes on **Handout 110**. The correct version is shown below:

Free will: Unlike most other approaches, humanistic theories emphasise that people have full <u>conscious</u> control over their own destiny, i.e. they have free will. However, we are also subject to many other forces, including biological and societal influences.

Maslow's theory: Maslow's hierarchy of needs emphasised the importance of personal growth and fulfilment. The most basic, physiological needs are represented at the bottom of the hierarchy and the most advanced needs at the top. Each level must be fulfilled before a person can move up to a higher need.

1. ***Physiological*** needs are essential for survival and include basic necessities such as air, food, and water.

2. ***Safety*** needs include feeling physiologically safe and economically secure.

3. ***Love and belonging*** needs include emotional needs such as the need for love, friendship and intimacy.

4. ***Esteem*** needs represent the need for social recognition and respect.

5. ***Self-actualisation*** needs represent the highest level of human achievement and include personal growth, highly developed morality, and creativity.

Focus on the self: The self (or self-concept) refers to how we perceive ourselves as a person. Feelings of self-worth develop in <u>childhood</u> and through further interactions with significant others (friends, spouse etc.). The closer our self-concept and our ideal-self are to each other, the greater our feelings of self-worth and the <u>greater</u> our psychological health.

Congruence: When there is similarity between a person's ideal self and how they perceive themselves to be in real-life, a state of <u>congruence</u> exists. The closer our self-image and ideal-self are to each other, the greater the congruence and the higher our feelings of self-worth.

Conditions of worth: The love and acceptance given by others may be <u>unconditional</u> (<u>unconditional</u> positive regard), when a person is accepted for who they are or what they do. Or, acceptance may be <u>conditional</u>, when they are accepted only if they do what others want them to do. When people experience conditional positive regard they develop conditions of worth. These are the conditions that they perceive others (e.g. parents or a spouse) put upon them, and which they believe have to be in place if they are to be accepted by others. For example, a person may apply to study at university to please their parents, not because he or she wants to. Failure to meet these conditions of worth, claimed Rogers, results in incongruence and distress.

The influence on counselling psychology: Rogers (1959) claimed that an individual's psychological problems

HANDOUT 110

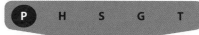

It might be necessary, for your less-able students, to give them more instruction as to where the mistakes might be. You could do this by highlighting the sentences where the mistakes are located.

were a direct result of their conditions of worth and the conditional positive regard they receive from <u>other people</u>. He believed that, with counselling, people would be able to solve their own problems in constructive ways, and move toward becoming a more fully functioning person.

Therapists provide empathy and <u>unconditional</u> positive regard, expressing their acceptance and understanding, regardless of the feelings and attitudes the client expresses. This results in the client moving toward being more authentic and more true to self, rather than the person others want them to be.

References

Rogers, C. (1959). A theory of therapy, personality and interpersonal relationships as developed in the client-centered framework. In S. Koch (ed.) *Psychology: A Study of a Science. Vol. 3: Formations of the Person and the Social Context*. New York: McGraw Hill

---

TOPIC: Humanistic approach

Venn diagram congruence

Congruence is about how similar a person's ideal self is to how they perceive themselves to be in real-life (their actual self).

Exploring the concept of congruence could lead to an interesting introspective activity for students.

You could ask the students to write a series of bullet points which list what they perceive to be their ideal self, and, what they perceive to be actual self. Then, using a Venn diagram like the one displayed below, they can consider how

close they are to a state of 'congruence'. It would be best to encourage your students to do this on their own and anonymously.

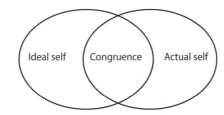

NO HANDOUT

This is a relatively personal activity that isn't necessarily appropriate for differentiation. Perhaps, if your less-able students struggle to complete the activity, you could display a worked example on the board so that they have some ideas that could trigger their own introspection.

TOPIC: Comparison of approaches

Do you know your approaches?

The activity of **Handout 111** is fairly self-explanatory: the students have to match the approach with the correct explanation. However, the psychodynamic and humanistic approaches are not part of the AS Level qualification so make sure that students following the AS Level pathway are aware of this.

HANDOUT 111

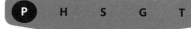

If students are following the AS qualification, you could ask the students to delete the humanistic and psychodynamic explanations to make it easier for your less-able students. Alternatively, you could leave them in to make the activity that little bit harder.

For more-able A Level students, a good follow-up activity would be for them to reproduce the table from memory.

TOPIC: Comparison of approaches

Comparing the approaches

One mistake that students make when trying to compare two concepts is that they do not always compare those concepts on the same criteria. For example, they might write something akin to this:

'One difference between Manchester City and Manchester United is that one plays in blue and the other plays at Old Trafford.'

Both statements are of course true, but they are not related to each other.

Handout 112 aims to provide students with a scaffolded writing frame which helps them to plan and structure their comparison answers. The students must select the two approaches they are comparing and the similarity/difference they will write about. The worked example should help them to do this and to write well-focused paragraphs.

HANDOUT 112

The scaffolding and worked example should allow less-able students to access this activity. However, you could write a list of comparison points that less-able students could use to practise this technique. In contrast, more-able students would be expected to identify their own similarity/difference points to explain.

TOPIC: Comparison of approaches

Cool Wall

This is very much a 'Top Gear' inspired idea. On the BBC programme for petrol heads, the presenters sort different brands and models of car onto their 'Cool Wall' display. There are four sections on the display: Seriously Uncool, Uncool, Cool and Sub Zero. A photo of each car is put onto the display (magnetic board) and the reasons for its placement are justified.

This could be a good activity to do throughout the approaches topic or as a topic summary. A picture/symbol for each approach can be used and the students must place each approach on the 'Cool Wall' and must justify their reasons. You could give them criteria to think about as well, for example: evidence, explanatory power etc.

You could go to town with this and create an amazing display for your classroom!

NO HANDOUT

It would be best to use collaborative learning structures for this activity (see page 5). This could ensure that your higher-ability students are stretched and that your lower-ability students are supported.

TOPIC: End of Approaches topic summary

Confidence ratings

The confidence rating handout could be annotated in a number of different ways. You may wish to set a percentage in each cell (25%, 50%, 75%, 100%) for students to colour code as they revisit each area as part of their revision. An alternative method could be to colour code a cell (red: cannot achieve this; amber: can achieve with some support; white: feel comfortable; green: feel confident).

Again as topics are revisited through revision, cells can be highlighted to correspond with current confidence levels.

The checklist could be used to form targeted revision groups and allow students to sign up to sessions that cover the areas they are least confident in.

HANDOUTS 113 and 114

Students may wish to reflect on their own progress through the unit as an individual or as part of a peer discussion. Alternatively the checklist could form part of a one-to-one discussion with a student who is of particular concern.

TOPIC: The nervous system

Hierarchies: The nervous system

This activity can either be used as a starter activity (if you feel your students will have retained good GCSE Biology knowledge) or a consolidation activity.

You need enough laminated copies of **Handout 115** for the class. Then, the statements on **Handout 116** need to be cut out and placed into envelopes; there should be enough envelope 'sets' for each member of the class.

In essence, this is a very simple sorting exercise. The students then have to sort all of the other statements into their correct places in the nervous system hierarchy; to start them off, you may wish to tell them that 'nervous system' goes at the top. The grey boxes are for definitions of the white boxes; for

example, 'nervous system' should be in the white box at the top of the hierarchy and then 'Network of nerve cells and fibres. Helps all parts of the body communicate with each other' should be in the grey box below it.

The smaller grey boxes on **Handout 116** can be used as an extension activity. These do not fit onto the hierarchy on **Handout 115** but can be placed in relevant areas on the hierarchy to show that the student understands their role/relevance. There are several options for where each box could be placed, but students must justify their choices. For example, 'Sensory receptors, e.g. eyes, ears, skin etc.' could be placed near the brain because it must receive information from these areas.

HANDOUTS 115 and 116

P H **S** G T

You could use this activity to provide structure and scaffolding for an exam answer on the 'divisions of the nervous system'.

The activity is also differentiated with extension boxes (see lesson notes). If you feel your more-able students already know the divisions of the nervous system hierarchy, they could go straight onto placing the definitions and the extension boxes.

TOPIC: The structure and function of neurons

Knowing the synapse

In the Biopsychology topic, the more diagrams the better I (MG) suspect. Students get intimidated by the terminology in textbook prose so allowing them to 'see' the terminology helps.

On **Handout 117**, the students have to label the synapse diagram; the correct labels are included at the top of the handout. In the grey expansion boxes, the students must explain the role and function of that label. They could do this using their textbooks or from memory.

Following the completion of this handout, I think it is important that the students do the exercise again, but this time from memory. That is, they should have to draw the synapse, label it and explain it. I'm sure they won't get everything right first time, but the more times they repeat the exercise, the more likely it is that they will feel confident and familiar with the synapse.

HANDOUT 117

P H S G T

For more-able students you could insist that they cover the labels at the top of the handout and use their memory instead. Similarly, you could ask them to read the textbook and then complete the activity, rather than completing the activity with the textbook.

TOPIC: The endocrine system

Multiple choice: Endocrine system

I went on a course delivered by Dylan Williams (author of *Inside the Black Box*, an early proponent on assessment-for-learning) and came away feeling the value of multiple-choice questions.

Multiple-choice questions seem like a fairly basic activity, but with well-written questions, they have the potential to really get your students thinking and to test their understanding. **Handout 118** has nine multiple-choice questions about the endocrine system designed to do just that; the choices of answers cannot be guessed through common sense, only knowledge and understanding.

In the feedback session, I would ask the students to raise A, B, C or D cards depending on their answers so that you can get a good sense of what the students understand and what they are confused about. As a teacher, this will then allow you to spend time on the parts they are less sure of; this is genuine assessment-for-learning.

Answers

1. B
2. D
3. C
4. D
5. A
6. B and C
7. B
8. C
9. C

HANDOUT 118

P H S **G** T

This activity is difficult to differentiate because it is mainly designed to be used as an assessment tool.

However, as an alternative, you could set this up as a group activity using the 'random numbers' technique (see page 5). This will ensure your less-able students are supported and your more-able students are given the responsibility for teaching.

TOPIC: The endocrine system

Blue label

NO HANDOUT

Although this activity has been placed in 'The endocrine system' section, it can be useful throughout the Biopsychology topic.

Project a large image of the endocrine system or draw one on the whiteboard. Students should then be given cards with the names of different parts/keywords/processes/definitions that belong to that diagram. Students then take it in turns to come out and stick on their labels (with Blue-Tack ®, hence 'blue label') in the correct place on the diagram. This could be done with the use of an interactive whiteboard instead.

If you have a large group and not enough parts to the diagram, you could always run this as a race between two sides of the room who both have to complete the same diagram.

The best way to differentiate this activity is to target who you give the cards to; that is, give the easier cards to less-able students and more difficult cards to more-able students.

TOPIC: The fight or flight response

Key concepts: Fight or flight response

HANDOUT 119

The instructions for this activity are included on **Handout 119**. It is a very structured activity and has the potential to take the majority of a lesson. It is also a very independent student activity which should help them to be more confident about describing the biology that underlies the fight or flight response; in the Biopsychology topic, student confidence is very important.

The end outcome should be that students produce a flow diagram which describes how the body responds to acute and chronic stressors. The diagram should also state how the various 'key concepts' are connected to each other.

Once the task is completed, the students could also use their diagrams to answer an examination-style question which requires them to describe the fight or flight response.

More-able students are likely to finish this activity much faster than less-able students. As such, an evaluation extension activity has been included for those students to complete.

Less-able students are likely to find the activity difficult in places. It is important that you identify the students that are likely to need support and help them through the activity. The independent nature of the task should mean you have the flexibility to do this.

TOPIC: Localisation of function

| P | H | S | **G** | T |

Plasticine brain modelling

It is difficult for students (and teachers!) to understand brain diagrams in textbooks because of their 2D nature. Again, there is a lot of potential for students to lose confidence in the Biopsychology topic so we should try and think of as many ways as possible to increase student familiarity with the key terms.

Plasticine is perfect for this! Give students enough plasticine so that they can create a model brain and use that as a basis to help them understand the different areas and functions. Instead of listing just one activity, here are some ideas that might be helpful in your lessons depending on the context.

Ideas for plasticine brains

- Use this activity to teach students about brain and neuroanatomical directional terms such as ventral, medial, lateral etc. If they are confident with these terms, they will realise that 'medial' isn't another term they have to learn, it simply means 'towards the middle' and it will actually help them remember the names of brain areas because it gives those terms meaning (semantic processing!). See the diagram below for ideas.

- Give students different colours to create the six different brain lobes. Again, this will help them to navigate the brain better and talk more confidently about locations in the brain. See below for ideas.

- Use plasticine brains to create classroom displays, e.g. cocktail sticks with labels.

- Use plasticine brains and scalpels to 'deconstruct' the brain or to create 'lesions'. By instructing students to create 'lesions' in certain areas of the brain, you can test them on what behavioural changes they think might occur.

Plasticine brains could also be used to aid in the understanding of split-brain patients (see page 212).

You could put students into pairs or threes for this activity based on ability. Ask students about their confidence in this activity and then appoint student 'leaders' to each pair/group. The leader's responsibility is to guide the other students through the activity, but crucially, never actually leading the creation of the plasticine brains... this should be done by the less-able students.

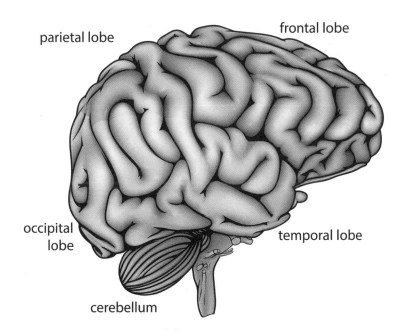

TOPIC: Localisation of function

Brain function revision cards

Examination questions in Biopsychology may require students to pinpoint the location of certain brain areas, identify their function or describe their function.

As such, the revision cards on **Handouts 120** and **121** should be a very useful learning tool for students. For each brain area named in the specification, they require students to shade the correct location on the brain, describe that location and identify the

function. In addition, the students can use the reverse side to add more bullet points of detail which they could use in an exam answer.

The students can then use these cards to test themselves and each other.

You could make it clear that students with different target grades have different expectations in terms of the details they add on the back of the revision cards. For example:

- Students with E–D target grades must include at least one 'detail' bullet point on the back of each card.

- Students with C–B target grades must include at least three 'detail' bullet points on the back of each card.

  Students with A–A* target grades must include at least five 'detail' bullet points on the back of each card.

TOPIC: Localisation of function

Pictionary®

I'm sure most of you are familiar with the game Pictionary®. It is usually a game played in teams. One of the team members will be given a term/action to draw and the other team members must guess what they are drawing.

It strikes me that this game is perfect for this topic. As the teacher, you can give

the students brain areas to draw, e.g. Broca's areas. The students would then need to draw this area for the rest of their team mates to guess, for example, by drawing the actual area in the brain or the function that it plays.

You could ensure mixed-ability teams are used for this activity and give the 'drawing' role to the most able if you feel that the others might struggle.

You could also ensure that the areas/terms get progressively more difficult so that the most-able groups are stretched as the activity progresses.

TOPIC: Lateralisation and split-brain research

Create your own split-brain patient!

This activity builds on the idea of plasticine brains, but also introduces a potato and scalpel! Also, a handout with a list of words and a set of pictures used in the Sperry experiment will be needed.

Students make a pair of eyes (e.g. out of sewing pins) and stick them on the potato so that it looks like a face (add a nose, mouth, hair (at front) and a mouth as well!). The students should then create a brain on the back of that head that has two basic hemispheres and a rudimentary corpus callosum. You should draw the parts on the board as you go to help the students.

At this point, explain to students that the right brain processes pictures and the left brain processes words. The middle part, corpus callosum, allows the two to talk to each other so that words and

pictures are processed no matter by what side they are seen.

Get students to read the Sperry words and name the pictures:

- with both eyes
- with the left eye covered
- with the right eye covered.

Then ask them to cut the corpus callosum of their participant (i.e. the potato) and imagine that they are the 'participant'. The teacher should present the words/pictures randomly to the students who should decide whether they can 'see' them or not with a split brain. There should be two conditions:

- With the right eye of the 'participant' covered (*the students should read the words but not the pictures*)

It is probably best that this activity is completed in mixed-ability pairs, with more-able students supporting less-able ones.

Alternatively, you should identify students that will need support with the activity and ensure that you are on hand to give clues and prompts.

- With the left eye of the 'participant' covered (*the students should identify the pictures but not the words*).

It might be best to follow this activity with some sort of consolidation worksheet, **Handout 122** for example.

TOPIC: Lateralisation and split-brain research

Choose the right word!

Handout 122 includes a very simple activity to consolidate students' learning on hemispheric lateralisation and Sperry and Gazzaniga's split-brain research.

The text on the handout is taken from page 158 of the *Complete Companion*. Where they are given the choice, the students must choose the correct words from the ones given in bold. Students can easily get themselves in a tangle during this topic and confuse their lefts/rights/areas of the brain, so this is designed to help them think that through and increase their confidence in the understanding of the research.

HANDOUT 122

P   H   S   G   **T**

This is another activity that is difficult to differentiate other than by outcome. However, less-able students are likely to struggle in some areas so you should be on hand to support. This might be done by drawing diagrams when students get stuck to guide them towards the correct answer (rather than giving them the correct answer).

TOPIC: Lateralisation and split-brain research

Experiment: Left brain right brain

Handout 123 briefly describes an experiment that students can conduct that is relevant to the split-brain topic.

Essentially the experiment involves students presenting two words on a screen to participants, one on the left side of the screen and one on the right. They should then ask their participants to recall one of the words. What they should find is that the participants should show a preference for recalling the word on the right because the left brain is responsible for processing speech and language, and information from the right visual field goes to the left hemisphere.

Students can also repeat the experiment by presenting two pictures, again, one on the left and one on the right. This time, the participants should show a preference for recalling the picture on the left because the right brain specialises in processing visual information, and information from the left visual field goes to the right hemisphere.

Running experiments like this is also a perfect opportunity for reinforcing research methods concepts. **Handout 123** includes a table for students to identify key aspects of the study.

HANDOUT 123

      S   T

Preparing for and conducting this experiment may be challenging for some less-able students so it might be wise to pair more and less confident students. In this scenario it is also wise to be clear about the roles; for example, the less-able students must complete the research methods summary sheet under the guidance of the more-confident student.

There are plenty of extension activities and questions that could also be given to the more-able students if you would prefer the students to conduct this experiment independently. For example:

- Write a standardised instructions sheet and debrief script.

- Identify potential ethical issues and how they can be dealt with.

- Calculate whether the results are statistically significant.

TOPIC: Lateralisation and split-brain research

Stepping stones

It will be hard for students to keep track of the hemisphere specialisms, the visual fields they process and the hands they operate… never mind analyse the results of split-brain research and explain the findings. In all honesty, this is a challenging topic on the course.

The 'stepping stones' activity on **Handout 124** is designed to help the students walk through the various elements of this topic and to help them put together everything they know.

Essentially, the activity simply involves students answering the questions on the handout. However, there are some rules; students should NOT 'skip' a question level. For example, they should NOT attempt question 5 before they have successfully answered questions 4a and 4b.

The reason for this is that the order of questions has been designed very carefully to build students' confidence in their understanding of the topic. The arrows on the handout indicate where previous answers might help or be relevant to answering other questions. In addition, the questions tend to get harder. For example, questions 1a and 1b require students to state 'left' or 'right'; whereas, questions 7a and 7b require more detailed analysis and use of key terms. The point of the handout is that most students would find 7a and 7b very difficult if they had to tackle those first, but having progressed through the others, they should have a better chance of articulating and analysing the split-brain research.

HANDOUT 124

  S   T

This handout provides scaffolding for all students to be able to explain and analyse the results of the split-brain research.

The handout is challenging, so it will be important to identify students in your class at risk of making mistakes and to provide them support throughout the activity.

To increase independence, you could give students a 'cheat sheet' which they can refer to if they are struggling. This 'cheat sheet' would provide prompts to help the students answer the questions. For example:

1a. Cat or dog?
1b. Cat or dog?
2a. Left or right? Look at the diagram to see how information in each field is processed.
2b. Left or right? Look at the diagram to see how information in each field is processed.
3. Use the word 'function' and/or 'specialisms' in your answer.
4a. Language/speech or Visual/Spatial?
…etc.

TOPIC: Lateralisation and split-brain research

Split-brain internet games

There are some excellent split-brain illusions, games and experiments to be found on the internet which could be worked into your lessons.

For example: http://www.nobelprize.org/educational/medicine/split-brain

In addition, typing 'split brain test', 'left brain right brain experiment' and other such variations into YouTube will lead you to some excellent potential lesson material.

NO HANDOUT

P H S G T

This activity is not differentiated.

TOPIC: Plasticity and functionary recovery of the brain

Finish these sentences

The activity on **Handout 125** is fairly self-explanatory. The students should 'finish the sentences'! This activity could be used in a variety of ways.

You could go through the various content with the students on PowerPoint or with the help of a textbook (*Complete Companion*, page 160) and then the students can complete this activity immediately afterwards to consolidate what they have learnt. Going through complex ideas like these demands some sort of consolidation activity as the majority of students will not retain this information without active processing.

The sentence starters are designed to act as memory triggers and cues for students' retained knowledge so that they recall more information than they might have done if they had been asked to free recall.

The activity could also be used as a plenary activity and/or a starter activity for the lesson following the one where the content was taught.

The questions are roughly categorised into the type of thinking skill required, (e.g. the definition sentence starters are classed as knowledge recall). In reality the classifications are possibly slightly crude but they may serve as a useful differentiation tool…

Less-able students would be expected to at least recall the 'knowledge' sentences (i.e. the main topic idea) and some of the 'understanding' sentences which focus on the processes involved in plasticity.

More-able students would be expected to attempt as many of the sentences as possible, especially the application sentences at the end of each box.

TOPIC: Ways of studying the brain

Studying the brain: Summaries

Handout 126 would be a good activity to use once you have gone through the various ways of studying the brain (post-mortem examinations, fMRIs, EEGs and ERPs). Alternatively, you could give the information on the four techniques (e.g. page 162 of the *Complete Companion*) and ask the students to complete the activity by reading the information.

The students must sort the 16 numbered statements into four groups using the worksheet (i.e. group A, B, C and D). Once they have done this, they should name the four groups. The 16 numbered statements have been written in such a way that the most obvious way to sort them is in terms of their relevance to a way of studying the brain. So, the group names should be 'post-mortem examination', 'fMRIs', 'EEGs', and 'ERPs'… or very similar.

Once the students have grouped the statements, they should then write a brief summary of each brain study technique by using the statements as part of the summary

Answers

Group name: Post-mortem examinations
Numbers: 1, 2, 7, 15
Group name: fMRIs
Numbers: 4, 6, 13, 16
Group name: EEGs
Numbers: 3, 5, 10, 11
Group name: ERPs
Numbers: 8, 9, 12, 14

(You could also argue that numbers 6 and 11 could also be placed in the ERP group, but through process of elimination, hopefully the students will come to this 'best-fit' classification of the numbers. If students do question this, it is best to reassure them that they didn't get the activity 'wrong'.)

For less-able students it would be advisable to give them the group names before starting the activity as they may need this support to sort the statements into groups.

TOPIC: Ultradian and infradian rhythms

Ultradian rhythm homework: Sleep stages

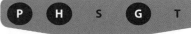

The instructions for the activity on **Handout 127** are included at the top. I use this as a homework research task, but there is no reason why it could not be adapted for a lesson if you feel that would work better with your students. Most of the information on the sheet is taken from the *Complete Companion*, page 166.

The homework I set is for the students to research 'sleep stages' at home on the internet or at the library (if they take the *Complete Companion* home, you may wish to take it off them because the task will be too easy!). The students must cut out each box and arrange the concepts on A3 paper (or similar) in a way that makes sense to them; they should add annotations and explanations so that it is also clear to anyone who looks at their 'concept organiser'.

The task requires students to look at various different websites and sources of information to organise the boxes in

a structured way which makes sense. For example, the most obvious (and probably only) way to set about this is for the students to use 'stage one', 'stage two', 'stage three', 'stage four' and 'stage five' boxes as category/table titles and then structure the other concepts around those.

However, I give students minimal input and advice for this homework so the task is not as easy as it first seems. The rationale behind this activity is that it requires students to be independent and to construct their own understanding of the sleep stages rather than it being given to them. If students are given the opportunity to work out the sleep stages for themselves using various sources on the internet, they are more likely to remember them.

In the feedback lesson, you can then compare their work to page 166 of the *Complete Companion* and discuss any misconceptions or inaccuracies.

The grey boxes can be used as extension research for more-able students or those motivated to learn more about this topic.

For less-able students, the unstructured nature of the activity (i.e. it is their job to structure it!) may be too challenging. If you feel it is appropriate, you could tell some of the students how you think it should be roughly organised, i.e. use the 'stage' boxes as headings from which to work under.

Please note, the information in the grey boxes is NOT included in the *Complete Companion* but is included as a possible extension/enrichment activity. If you decide you do not want to 'over teach', just tell the students to ignore these.

TOPIC: Biological rhythms: Summary

Knowing your biological rhythms!

Handout 128 is a simple exercise but it should also be an effective topic summariser. It is also designed to help students build up the level of detail in their answers.

There are four sections to the handout: key words, definitions, examples and details.

Firstly, the students should match the key words to the definitions. They can do this either by cutting up the boxes

or using three coloured highlighters. Then they should match these to the examples, and finally to the details. I would advise against them drawing lines to complete these activities because the handout will end up looking like a bowl of messy spaghetti.

Students can then use this scaffolding handout as a way to answer the following question: '*Outline two or more biological rhythms.*' (8 marks)

The completed handout should provide scaffolding for less-able students to answer relevant exam questions.

More-able students could also be asked to add extra details to the end section.

TOPIC: Endogenous pacemakers and exogenous zeitgebers

Cut and paste – Pacemakers and Zeitgebers

The first section of **Handout 129** illustrates what the exam board requires students to know and breaks down the terms 'endogenous pacemaker' and 'exogenous zeitgeber' to help students' understanding.

Students should then be provided with the challenge card from **Handout 130**. They use this to create a flow diagram of the interaction between exogenous zeitgeber (light) and the endogenous

pacemaker (the SCN). Images contained on the handout are to be cut out and pasted onto paper to produce this diagram. The challenge card does not explain the process in a direct order yet many students' initial attempts will simply represent the images in the order they appear on the challenge card. Students should be encouraged to think about what they are reading to create an accurate diagram.

Less-able students could use the check card instead of the challenge card while those more able can be given the check card to assess the accuracy of their completed diagram.

TOPIC: Endogenous pacemakers and exogenous zeitgebers

Stepping stones 2

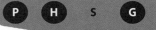

The 'stepping stones' activity was described on page 74 and is used here again as an effective way to help students develop their understanding of 'entrainment' and the interaction between the endogenous pacemaker (the SCN) and the exogenous zeitgeber (light) in the control of the sleep-wake cycle.

> The handout is challenging in places, so it will be important to identify students in your class at risk of making mistakes and to provide them with support throughout the activity.

TOPIC: End of Biopsychology topic summary

Confidence ratings

HANDOUTS 132 and 133

The confidence rating handout could be annotated in a number of different ways. You may wish to set a percentage in each cell (25%, 50%, 75%, 100%) for students to colour code as they revisit each area as part of their revision. An alternative method could be to colour code a cell (red: cannot achieve this; amber: can achieve with some support; white: feel comfortable; green: feel confident).

Again as topics are revisited through revision, cells can be highlighted to correspond with current confidence levels.

The checklist could be used to form targeted revision groups and allow students to sign up to sessions that cover the areas they are least confident in.

> Students may wish to reflect on their own progress through the unit as an individual or as part of a peer discussion. Alternatively the checklist could form part of a one-to-one discussion with a student who is of particular concern.

TOPIC: The experimental method

The experimental method

This activity provides a summary of the key features of the experimental method as well as giving students the opportunity to practise their noticing skills. Students are required to identify these key features in the scenario presented, an AO2 application skill.

You may wish to carry out this experiment with the class (half recall images, half words) to support them in identifying the key features of the method. In my (RG) experience the more practical experience students have of being involved in studies, even little ones such as that in **Handout 134**, the better their understanding of the research process. By actually experiencing the procedure they are able to identify potential extraneous variables and how they were controlled for as well as spotting any confounding variables.

HANDOUT 134

| P | **H** | S | G | T |

Questions contained in the thought bubbles offer an extension activity to more-able students who can use their textbook to read ahead and consider, for example, the key features of science such as replicability (importance of standardised procedure and operationalised IV/DV).

Extension question: why did the students match the images in condition 2 to the words in condition 1?

TOPIC: The experimental method

Operationalisation

For some students, spotting the IV and DV in a scenario is a challenging task and repeated opportunities are needed for them to practise this skill. For others, they are quickly able to spot the variables but lose marks when asked to, '*Identify the independent variable*' (2 marks), as they do not state the variable in a testable form. This activity encourages students to firstly identify the IV and DV then record them in the level of detail required for the exam.

In addition, depending on what aspects of research methods have already been taught, the following questions could be asked for each scenario:

1. Identify the research design used.
2. Write either a directional or non-directional hypothesis.

3. Identify any confounding variables that might have impacted the DV.

When introducing operationalisation, I have found it helps to give students everyday examples before applying this concept to research. For example, '*It takes a long time to get to school*' is not operationalised; '*It takes 45 minutes to travel to school*' is operationalised. Students can play this game in pairs to describe themselves, what they did yesterday etc. to highlight the requirement to give a full explanation.

HANDOUT 135

| **P** | H | S | G | T |

With each scenario, clues as to the IV and DV are gradually withdrawn. Scenario one models how to operationalise both variables, scenario two identifies the IV and DV but they are not operationalised, the final scenario requires students to identify and operationalise the variables.

You may wish to remove all clues for more-able students for all scenarios. They could then check their ideas with students who had a little more support.

TOPIC: Control of variables

Validity and Reliability: The tea challenge

This activity aims to highlight the difference between reliability and validity: concepts students often confuse or use interchangeably in their written work.

With them working in small groups, challenge your students to write a recipe for the perfect cup of tea in five minutes. Remind the class the recipe needs to be specific to ensure the instructions can be followed by others.

Groups are now set the following tasks:

1. Change one thing about your recipe that would increase reliability (in my experience students often miss specifics, e.g. stating '*add milk*' without giving an amount).

2. Change one thing about the recipe that would decrease reliability, (e.g. '*add something sweet*'; this could be honey, sugar, sweetener).

3. Change one thing about the recipe that would decrease validity, (e.g. '*add coffee to cup*' rather than tea bag).

As an additional activity, you could present the scenarios shown below to students and ask them to identify whether they demonstrate a problem with validity or reliability.

• There is a study on obedience conducted in the morning and in the afternoon. The results in the morning were significantly different in the afternoon.

NO HANDOUT

| P | H | S | **G** | T |

Mixed-ability groups work well for this activity. Writing a recipe for a cup of tea should be accessible to all students. When asking to manipulate validity and reliability, more-able students are able to lead their group.

• A study on maths ability is conducted using a maths test written in English. The sample in the study was American and French students.

• Criticisms have been made of observations of attachment because the infants and caregivers may have acted differently (i.e. more sensitively) because they knew they were being observed.

TOPIC: Control of variables

Speak like a psychologist

Psychology can be challenging for many students because not only are they learning about new research and theories, they are simultaneously learning a new language. Keeping a log of key terms will help students understand text, decode exam questions and improve the quality of their written work. Completion of **Handout 136** provides students with a glossary of key terms. Devote lesson time to find definitions for the key terms shown or set this activity as homework (*Complete Companion pages* 180, 181). Another

option would be to refer to the glossary across a series of lessons with students filling in relevant terms as they meet them. The flow-chart style helps students see the links between associated terms.

Once completed, a range of word games can be played as simple starters, process checks or literacy revision across the topic. For example, Taboo; a student describes the key term for the class to guess. This could be conducted as a team challenge with the winning team being the first to correctly guess all words on the sheet.

HANDOUT 136

| P | H | S | G | T |

Differentiation may vary depending on how this activity is presented to the class. If set in lessons, then mixed-ability groups would work well. However, if set for homework, less-able students may need some support to guard against them simply copying text into boxes without understanding what they have read. Spending time in class to provide real-life examples helps students understand abstract concepts (such as the tea challenge discussed above).

TOPIC: Control of variables

Critical continuum

Students form small groups of three to four students (this could be self-selected or assigned by you based on ability). Each group is given a study from a different area of the specification. They are asked to consider where they would place the study on the continuum displayed on the board (see below):

Control .... Realism

In deciding where to place their study the group needs to consider a range of

factors, for example; realism of the task participants completed, population validity, whether the behaviour recorded was influenced by the era, researchers' ability to control extraneous variables.

This activity introduces studies, or acts as a revision of previously learnt studies, both of which encourage the formation of more lasting memories in preparation for the linear exams.

NO HANDOUT

| P | H | S | G | T |

Once each group has placed their study on the continuum and explained their decision to the class, a question and answer session could be carried out with everyone. Lower-order thinking questions such as 'What is meant by the term…?' could be targeted at less-able students, while questions that require higher-order thinking such as, 'How could the study be changed to increase control over…?' would be suitable for more-able students.

TOPIC: Return to hypotheses and other things

Class research project 1 and project 1 materials

Carrying out research is an effective way for students to develop their understanding of key concepts and provides an opportunity to apply their understanding to a specific scenario (AO2 application skill).

Split the class into two (how you do this could lead to a discussion of random allocation).

Group A are provided with 15 words (**Handout 138**) to learn right side up.

Group B are provided with the same 15 words but need to hold their sheet upside down as they learn them. Be sure each group is clear of these instructions before the test begins then allow 2 minutes to learn the 15 words.

Students then complete the name matching task to prevent them rehearsing the words. Group feedback for this task also adds to the delay between learning and recall. All materials can be found on **Handout 138.**

Students are then asked to write down any words they can recall from the list (free recall).

Following this activity, share the aim with the class, 'to investigate whether greater mental effort (learning words upside down) leads to greater recall'. Students then complete the previous **Handout 137.**

Mark scheme.

Aim, IV, DV – 2 marks for operationalised variables and full detail in aim.

Directional hypothesis – 2 marks if IV (both levels) and DV are clearly stated and direction is given.

Research design – 1 mark for stating 'independent measures'

Pilot study – 3 marks for identifying any aspects researchers may wish to check, e.g. length of word list, clarity of 'read upside down' instructions. Only 1 mark if term 'pilot study' is defined but not applied to the questions.

HANDOUTS 137 and 138

| P | H | S | G | T |

Placing students in ability groups enables you to sit with students who might struggle with identifying concepts within research such as operationalising variables and stating the research design employed. More-able groups can be provided with textbooks to support their completion of the sheet as well as using class notes from previous lessons.

Name matching task – 2 marks for stating 'a distraction task', 'to prevent rehearsal of words'

Conclusions – 2 marks for link made back to hypothesis.

TOPIC: Experimental design

Experimental design

HANDOUT 139

| P | **H** | S | G | T |

Handout 139 takes an opportunity to model to students how to apply knowledge to a scenario (AO2). This is a skill I have found students take time to develop and need repeated reminders and examples of how to make detailed reference to the question stem. Students are required to read the scenario and associated commentary then apply their understanding of research design.

As an extra activity, you could play *Bingo taboo*. Students are asked to think of nine words they would expect to hear in a spoken summary of research design, (e.g. independent measures, counterbalancing, participant variables, order effects). You (or a nominated student) summarise research design as a topic to the class but without using any key terms. As they listen, students tick off the key terms they think the speaker has referred to. Prizes can be awarded for lines and a full house!

Once completed, students could be challenged to explain how the limitation of one research design is a strength of another. For example, independent measures design is at risk of participant variables while repeated measures design overcomes this problem. Students may wish to work together to create a revision table that can be photocopied for the rest of the class:

Design	Strength	Limitation

TOPIC: Types of experiments (Laboratory, Field, Natural, Quasi)

Types of experiments

HANDOUT 140

| P | H | S | G | **T** |

This activity encourages students to focus on the aspects of an investigation that might lead to it being labelled a certain type of experiment. Students may find it helpful to identify the IV and DV, then explain the experiment classification. This is a tricky task and it should be remembered that classifications are not set in stone.

Studies are taken from other areas of the specification to support revision of topics throughout the course. Once students have recorded the key features they are then asked to identify the strengths and limitations of this type of experiment which links to the earlier topic of control verses realism (see **Handout 136**, 'Speak like a psychologist').

Students are asked to identify the difference between field and natural experiments as less-able students will often give the same definition for these two types, *'an investigation that takes place in a more natural environment'.* Teacher note: natural experiments often do not take place in a natural environment; it is the IV not the environment or DV that is 'naturally' occurring. In a field experiment the IV is manipulated by the experimenter so is not considered 'natural'.

Decide – debate- deliberate. In this additional activity, students are set the question *'What makes a 'good' experiment?'* Working alone or in pairs

students reach their conclusion. 'Good' is deliberately ambiguous to allow for debate in the second phase of this activity. The class now shares ideas and a discussion develops. This is likely to focus on what students deem more important; control over variables or increased realism. However, links can also be drawn to replicability and testing reliability (easier the more control you have over the situation). Following this discussion, students return to their original conclusion to deliberate: based on what they have just heard do they want to change their answer or has the discussion cemented their original response?

Students are encouraged to work independently using their resourcefulness to complete the activity. This could mean using class notes, textbooks, internet research, and group discussions to find the answers. This enables you to sit with less-able students who need more focused support when using resources to find answers.

References

Johnson, C. and Scott, B. (1976). Eyewitness testimony and suspect identification as a function of arousal, sex of witness, and scheduling interrogation. Paper presented at American Psychological Association Annual Meeting. Washington D.C.

Peterson, L.R and Peterson, M.J. (1959). Short-term retention of individual verbal items. *Journal of Experimental Psychology*, *58*, 193–8.

Sheridan, C.L. and King K.G. (1972). Obedience to authority with an authentic victim. *Proceedings of the 80th Annual Convention of the American Psychological Association*, *7*, 165–6.

TOPIC: Types of experiments (Laboratory, Field, Natural, Quasi)

Evaluating natural and quasi-experiments

HANDOUT 141

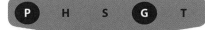

This activity provides another opportunity to model PEEL evaluation structure while recapping limitations of natural and quasi-experiments resulting from the lack of control over variables. A stretch activity is also included for students who find they are able to quickly identify the various components of the paragraph. The information contained on **Handout 141** can also be useful when evaluating research into the effects of institutionalisation on attachment and later development (Romanian orphan studies).

Why not challenge your students by asking

them to visit the British Psychological Society's research digest web page http://digest.bps.org.uk/ to find an experiment that interests them and decide whether it was a laboratory, field, natural or quasi-experiment. (Tip: always identify the IV to be clear about what kind of experiment it is; and identify the DV to be sure that it is an experiment.) You could create a wall display in your classroom of recent research or encourage students to contribute to the school newspaper by producing their own summary of the research they read.

> Students may find working together on this task helpful to check understanding of PEEL structure and evaluative comments. An extension task would be to challenge students to create their own PEEL such as, *'the unique characteristics of the sample may result in low population validity'.*

TOPIC: More problems with experiments

Demand characteristics, investigator effects, participant effects, and participant and situational variables

NO HANDOUT

> Placing students in ability groups allows the most-able students to focus on demand characteristics (participant effects) and single bind design, and investigator effects and double bind design, while less-able students can consider participant and/or situational variables allowing them to recap prior learning.

Two minute talk is an activity requiring students to produce a short speech on a given topic (in this case either demand characteristics, investigator effects, participant effects and participant variables or situational variables). Students are given time in lessons to prepare their talk and may benefit from a checklist to ensure their talk is useful to the rest of the class. For example, define the term 'demand characteristics' in your own words; give an example of when demand characteristics may appear in a study; explain how demand characteristics may be reduced. The

group then presents their talk to the class with a designated time keeper (mobile phones often have a stop watch function), keeping a record of the length of their talk. Prizes can be awarded to those whose talks were closest to two minutes and most informative. Groups should write up their talks so copies can be made for the rest of the class.

As an additional activity, once talks have been typed up they can be used in a variety of ways when revising:

Taboo – ask a student to explain the concept but forbid them for using

certain words in their explanation. The rest of the class have to guess the concept they are describing.

Cloze exercise – blank out key words in the talk and ask students to fill in these blanks.

TOPIC: Sampling

Sampling methods

HANDOUT 142

> Less-able students may find a list of the answers helpful, allowing them to match the key word to the clue before entering them into the grid.

Crossword answers for **Handout 142**

Across: 4: opportunity. 6: selfselected. 8: systematic. 9: generalisation. 10: random. 11: stratified.

Down: 1: sample. 2: lotterymethod. 3: population. 5: volunteer. 6: strata. 7: bias.

Modelling these sampling methods is a helpful way for students to visualise each method. Create an additional but simple and fun task that students will be keen to get involved in. For example, the participant stands with their back to the researchers. On a given signal the

participant turns to face the researcher who, on giving the signal has thrown (underarm!) a bean bag or soft ball to the participant. The aim is to catch the item and the class records out of five goes how many catches are made. Different sampling techniques can be used to select volunteers, e.g. every 5th person on the register (systematic sampling), names drawn out of a hat (random sampling). Leave volunteer sampling till last so any student who has not yet been selected has an opportunity to take part. After each type of sampling the class can

discuss the strengths and limitations of the method. A useful exam tip would be that if students wish to say a certain method is quick they should make a comparison to another method and explain why it takes less time to collect the sample.

TOPIC: Ethical issues

Ethical issues bingo

Bingo is an excellent way to review key terms for any theory or topic that you have been covering. Give students one of the 3 x 3 bingo grids provided on **Handouts 143** and **144**. Alternatively, you could make your own. Read out various definitions, questions or descriptions of the terms in those grids. Students can then mark them off if they think one of the terms on their grid corresponds to your definition/ question. Once they have crossed off all their squares they can call 'bingo' and win the game (as long as they haven't made any mistakes). Guidance for the terms on the handouts is provided in the table below.

HANDOUTS 143 and 144

P   H   S   G   **T**

The first grid on **Handout 143** contains more common key terms relating to ethics, such as the issues themselves, while other grids contain more subtle references to ethics or research examples.

As an additional activity, this table can be used as a match up activity (match the key term to the definition) or form the basis of paired discussions into the importance of ethical issues: one student takes the role of the participant, the other the role of the researcher.

References

Baumrind, D. (1985). Research using intentional deception: Ethical issues revisited. *American Psychologist, 40(2)*, 165–74.

Epstein, L.C. and Lasagna, L. (1969). Obtaining informed consent: Form or substance. *Archives of Internal Medicine, 123*, 682–8.

Haney, C., Banks, W.C. and Zimbardo, P.G. (1973). Study of prisoners and guards in a simulated prison, *Naval Research Reviews, 9*, 1–17. Washington, DC: Office of Naval Research

Confidentiality	The Data Protection Act makes the trust that personal information will be protected a legal right.
Anonymity	A researcher's guarantee to withhold participants' names to protect their identity.
Privacy	A person's right to control the flow of information about themselves, for example people do not expect to be observed in their own home.
Deception	Withholding information from participants (reasonably acceptable) or deliberately providing false information (less acceptable).
Baumrind (1985)	Argues deception is morally wrong as it goes against basic ethical rules of right to informed consent, protection of participant welfare and responsibility of researchers to be trustworthy.
Informed consent	Telling participants what is going to happen in a study so they can decide whether they wish to take part.
Epstein & Lasagna (1969)	Researchers who found only a third of participants volunteering for an experiment really understood what they had agreed to take part in.
Right to withdraw	People can stop participating in a study if they feel uncomfortable in any way. This is especially important in cases where full informed consent has not been given.
Protection from harm	Nothing negative should happen to a participant that they could not expect to experience in ordinary life, and participants must be in the same state after the study as they were before.
Zimbardo (1973)	This researcher's prison experiment took great care to gain informed consent but participants did not know the amount of psychological distress that would be caused by participating.
Code of ethics	Standards that concern a group of professional people such as psychologists, advising what is expected of them in terms of right and wrong in their job.
Respect	One of the four ethical principles proposed by the British Psychological society, it refers to the dignity and worth of all persons and includes standards of privacy, confidentiality and informed consent.
Competence	One of the four ethical principles proposed by the British Psychological society, it states psychologists should maintain high standards in their professional work.
Responsibility	One of the four ethical principles proposed by the British Psychological society, it highlights the requirement for psychologists to protect their participants from harm and debrief them at the end of the study.
Integrity	One of the four ethical principles proposed by the British Psychological society, it demands that psychologists are honest and accurate when reporting their findings and acknowledging possible limitations.

TOPIC: Dealing with ethical issues

Class ethics committee

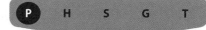

> More-able students take the role of researcher which requires imagination and problem solving. Less-able students act as the ethical committee which provides an opportunity to revise their understanding of ethical issues and ways of dealing with such issues.

Task 1: planning

Students acting as researchers are challenged with designing a study (this could be taken from another topic within the specification). Students are to identify the aim, hypothesis, procedure of their proposed study in detail and are requested not to consider ethical issues.

Students forming the ethical committee first familiarise themselves with the various ethical issues they may face when researchers present their ideas. They may find it helpful to create an ethics checklist in preparation for the next task.

Task 2: presenting

Researchers and ethical committee members meet (this could be on a one-to-one basis) to discuss the proposed research. Researchers present their study plans for the ethical committee member to identify potential ethical issues.

Task 3: perfecting

Working in pairs the researcher and committee member re-design the study to ensure ethical issues are reduced or dealt with.

Extension – students could be challenged to consider the limitations of the solutions they have put in place and score their effectiveness in reducing the ethical issue in question on a scale of 1–10.

Once concepts are introduced and understood, students could be set a homework challenge to identify studies from other areas of the specification that contain potential ethical issues. They

can present their revision to the class highlighting potential issues and how the researchers attempted to deal with those identified. This encourages revision of previously learnt topics as well as providing AO3 evaluation commentary.

TOPIC: Observational techniques

Improve the answers

> Students can work in pairs allowing you time to support students with literacy needs. Modelling the first 2 mark question may help such students understand how to approach this task:
>
> 1. Identify the key term in the question.
> 2. Use textbook (*Complete Companion* p198) to find extra details.
> 3. Add improvements to **Handout 145**.

This activity presents students with a set of answers that, while correct, lack the detail needed to score full marks. This activity models the level of detail needed for exam answers; something students often struggle to understand and often need repeated reminders and examples.

'Explain what is meant by participant observation.' (2 marks) The answer shown on **Handout 145** re-uses terms from the question and does not elaborate so is unlikely to score 2 marks.

Improvements would include re-wording the sentence: *'The researcher who is carrying out the observation is also taking part in the activity being observed. For example, if observing behaviour of crowds at a football match the researcher may also join fans in the stands.'*

'Explain the difference between a naturalistic observation and a controlled observation.' (4 marks) The answer shown on the handout does not make a direct comparison between the two types of observation and only considers one difference that can be drawn. The answer would not score 4 marks. Students should aim to include words that highlight a comparison is being drawn.

Improvements would include making a direct comparison on more than one point: *'**One difference** would be the situation in which the observation is conducted. In a naturalistic observation the participant is studied in a natural*

*situation where everything has been left as normal. **However**, in a controlled observation the situation has been regulated in some way by the researcher which reduces the naturalness of the situation.*

***A second difference** would be how easy it is to record observations without raising suspicions of the participants, especially in covert observation. In a natural observation participants may notice if someone is recording information and changes their behaviour. However, in a controlled observation one-way mirrors could be used to reduce the influence of an observer on participant's behaviour.'*

'Identify and explain one ethical issue related to cover observations.' (2 marks) Again, this answer only contains one comment so would be unlikely to score full marks. In my experience this is an exam skill less-able students need repeat reminders of throughout the course. Another common error is giving two points when the answer clearly states only one is required.

Improvements would include adding further detail to the answer and focusing on only one issue: *'One issue would be lack of informed consent as the participant is unaware they are being watched as part of an observational study. This results in deception and on learning they had been involved in a study they may feel taken advantage of.'*

'Over to you: Give one limitation and one strength of using non-participant observation as a method of collecting data.' (2 marks + 2 marks) Students now apply the exam technique identified from the above questions. For example, giving only one limitation and one strength. Ensuring the point is identified and elaborated upon to gain the second mark.

In addition, students could keep an exam tips record. Similar to a glossary, every time an exam tip is modelled in class or mentioned in feedback students could add this to a record sheet to form part of their revision. This record could be placed on their desk during in-class assessments to remind students of how to apply their understanding in exam questions.

TOPIC: Observational design

Conducting observations

NO HANDOUT

P H S **G** T

> Placing students in mixed-ability groups helps facilitate conversation when comparing unstructured and structured observations.

One of the great things about teaching research methods is the opportunity to carry out mini versions of the methods. Using the method helps students understand the process as well as giving first-hand experience of the strengths and limitations associated with the chosen method. In this activity students will conduct two different observations: unstructured and structured.

You first need to decide what you wish your students to observe. Ideally this would be a real-life situation for example, in the school/college dining hall at lunchtime. However, you could use a video clip, unless you would like to reserve this for doing content analysis as part of the A Level specification.

Once you have chosen the focus for the observation, split the class into two groups: those who will carry out an unstructured observation (simply recording everything they see) and those who will conduct a structured observation (supply these students with a coding system listing a range of behavioural categories they are likely

to see in the chosen observational situation).

Once students have completed the observation, they form groups of four (two students from each observational design) to compare their findings. Students can consider the following questions to encourage them to compare the two methods:

- What comparisons can be made between findings from each type of observation?

- What conclusions can be drawn from the observation you carried out?

- What were the strengths of the observational design you carried out?

- What problems did you experience when carrying out the observation?

- Considering the strengths and limitations you have identified what comments can be made about the validity of the data collected?

- Which observational design would you recommend to other people interested in conducting an observation?

An extra activity is *Key word flash cards*. There are a lot of key terms associated with observations and so methods of rehearsing terminology are useful during these lessons and for rapid-revision sessions (5–10 minute slots in lessons or lunch/break time). Students create flash cards showing the key word on one side and the definition on the other for the following words; behavioural categories, operationalisation, event sampling, time sampling, structured observations, unstructured observations, covert, overt, participant observation, non-participant observation, naturalistic observation, controlled observation. These cards can be used to test recall, in a game of taboo or to play snap (one student places cards definition face up, the other plays with the key word face up).

TOPIC: Self-report techniques

Select a method

HANDOUT 146

P **H** S G T

> Some students may benefit from a writing frame:
> 1. The method I recommend is…
> 2. This method is appropriate because…
> 3. One problem may be…
> 4. This can be overcome/reduced by…

To complete the activity, students need to select from questionnaires, structured and unstructured interviews to recommend a suitable self-report technique for each research scenario. As there is not one correct answer, students could share their answers with each other and decide which is best.

Attitudes to drug use: a questionnaire would allow a large sample and offer anonymity if delivered online or in a student newspaper which may encourage more responses for this sensitive topic. Using closed questions would allow for easier analysis as quantitative data can be collected which reduces time taken to analyse data collected from such a large sample.

Recall of various film clips: a structured interview would be suitable as the same questions could be asked for each anxiety level in a pre-determined

order to allow comparisons to be made between the different clips. Questions could include, 'What colour were the two cars?' and 'Did you see any witnesses on the pavement?' However, interviewers would have to be trained to ensure they use the same wording for each question and conduct the interview in the same manner to reduce the risk of interviewer bias.

An extra activity is *Question and answers*. Split students into teams of four. Give the groups time to create five questions, with an answer sheet and marks, based on the topic of self-report techniques. The groups then swap their question sheets and answer the questions they receive. Following this the groups receive the questions they created along with their peers' answers to mark and provide feedback.

TOPIC: Self-report design

Questionnaire project

Working in small groups, students select a suitable topic from the specification to create a questionnaire, for example, fear of different animals (phobias). You need to confirm the topic choice to ensure it is appropriate and will not cause offence or harm to the respondents. It goes without saying that no questionnaires should try to diagnose mental illness or attachment disorders but our students may need reminding of this!

When designing their questionnaire students need to consider:

- What filler questions will they include?
- How will they sequence the questions?
- What kind of data do they wish to collect (qualitative from open questions, quantitative from closed questions) and how they will analyse it?
- How to word the questions to ensure they are clearly phrased and not leading?
- How long will the questionnaire be?
- How to maintain confidentiality?
- What sampling technique will be used and what will be the size of the sampling?

Once data has been collected students can present their findings to the class.

As an additional activity, a range of questionnaires, from online sites, magazines etc. could be given to the class for them to identify various features specific to questionnaire formation (see list above).

TOPIC: Correlations

Similarities and differences

Handout 147 provides a useful reflection of the main differences between experiments and correlations. From experience as a teacher and exam marker I have found students often confuse concepts from these two methods, e.g. stating correlations have an IV of saying they are looking for a difference. This activity helps to clarify thinking and allows the teacher to spot any misconceptions students still hold.

The answers

Experiments: 1, 5, 6, 10, 13, 16

Both: 2, 3, 4, 8, 9, 11, 15

Correlations: 7, 12, 14.

Tip: in an experiment you may be looking for a relationship between an IV and DV; that's why 'you can easily see a relationship' is not a unique strength of a correlation and so is not credited when asked to give strengths of the correlational method.

Tip: Matched pairs can be used in a correlational study as each participant has a matched equivalent in the other condition.

The stretch question at the bottom of the handout is included to allow students to apply their understanding of the similarities and differences to evaluate the two methods. It is also helpful to highlight to students a common error when discussing the strengths of correlations: students are often tempted to state 'one strength of a correlation is that you can easily see a relationship'. This is not creditworthy. A more appropriate answer would be, 'correlations are useful when it would be unethical or impractical to use an experiment. For example, you could not ask a parent to deliberately act in an insensitive manner towards their child for an extended period of time just to determine the effect on the quality of attachment. Instead you would rate the parent on sensitivity (1-10) and rate the security of attachment (1-10) to identify whether a relationship between the two variables exists.'

For an additional activity, prior to completing **Handout 147** students may benefit from running a few class correlations and plotting them on a

scattergram to illustrate the key concepts relating to the correlational methods. For example:

- Length of left foot and length of left arm in centimetres (positive correlation).
- Time spent completing AS work/revising last night and time spent on social media last night (most likely a negative correlation!).
- Amount of money you have at the moment and time taken to travel to school/college (probably no correlation found due to bus or train passes).

TOPIC: Other research methods

Research Methods glossary

As the course progresses it is likely that students will meet different research methods through topics such as Memory, Attachment, Social Influence and Psychopathology. As research studies are understood and evaluated, students can keep a research methods glossary to record these studies in which they outline the procedure with associated strengths and limitations. Alternatively, you can set the formation of a glossary as a homework, providing students with the names of key studies to outline and evaluate the procedure. This activity helps revise content from other topics as well as reinforcing research methods.

For example, *Complete Companion* p208 mentions the following methods which students may wish to research and add to their glossary. You may wish to challenge your students to find further research methods in other areas of the specification.

Case study (A Level route only) – Memory: Scoville and Milner (1957) HM.

Content analysis (A Level route only) – Memory: Riniolo (2003) Titanic survivors' testimonies.

Controlled observation/role play – Social Psychology: Haney et al. (1973) Stanford Prison experiment.

Longitudinal study – Attachment: Zeanah (2005) Romanian orphanages.

Meta-analysis – Attachment: Van Ijzendoorn and Kroonenberg (1988) Cross cultural research.

Memory: Köhnken et al. (1999) Cognitive interviews.

Systematic review – Memory: Cowan (2001) review of capacity of STM studies.

Remember that many studies are a mixture, for example, a lab experiment using a questionnaire to assess the IV.

An additional activity is *Market place*. Split the class into groups and assign one method per group: systematic review, meta-analysis, longitudinal studies, comparison methods (cross-cultural, cross-sectional), case study (if following A Level route), content analysis (if following A Level route). Each group has to produce a poster explaining the procedure and strengths/limitations. Students then visit the various market stalls to complete their research methods glossary.

References

Cowan, N. (2001). The magical number 4 in short-term memory: A reconsideration of mental storage capacity. *Behavioral and Brain Sciences*, *24*, 1, 87–114.

Haney, C., Banks, W.C. and Zimbardo, P.G. (1973). Study of prisoners and guards in a simulated prison, *Naval Research Reviews*, *9*, 1–17. Washington, DC: Office of Naval Research

Riniolo, T. (2003). An archival study of eyewitness memory of the Titanic's final plunge. Heldref Publications.

Scoville, W.B. and Milner, B. (1957). Loss of recent memory after bilateral hippocampal lesions. *Journal of Neurology, Neurosurgery, and Psychiatry*, *20*, 11–21.

Van IJzendoorn, M.H. and Kroonenberg, P.M. (1988). Cross–cultural patterns of attachment: A meta–analysis of the Strange Situation. *Child Development*, *59*, 147–56.

Zeanah, C.H., Smyke, A.T., Koga, S.F.M., Carlson, E. and The BEIP Core Group (2005). Attachment in institutionalized and non-institutionalized Romanian children. *Child Development*, *76*, 1015–28.

TOPIC: Mathematical skills

Mathematical skills audit

Before beginning to teach the mathematic skills, or at the start of the course, ask students to complete the skills audit. This provides an indication of the skill level of your class to allow for differentiated activities and can help when grouping students for different mathematical activities. For example, students who feel confident in using measures of central tendency make useful group leaders. The audit also acts as a revision checklist for students when preparing for the exams. It may be helpful to highlight which skills may require a calculator to reinforce the need to bring one to the exam.

To complete the audit, students simply tick their level of performance for each skill. Skills found in the shaded cells relate to the A Level route only. As the course progresses, students can re-visit the audit to indicate whether their performance level has improved. This could be by dating when they felt they had moved to a new level.

Most of the mathematical skills in the new specification were already seen in the old AQA qualification, for example, types of data, graphical displays, descriptive statistics and, at A Level, inferential statistics. In the new specification, the mathematical content is only 10% of the overall qualification, so bear this in mind when planning teaching time. The AQA specification includes a useful list of mathematical requirements and exemplifications to support planning for this section of the

course. AQA advise that students should be able to calculate mean, median, mode, range and percentages, fractions, decimals, ratios and the sign test (add up pluses and minus and S = smallest value). At A Level they will not be expected to calculate any other inferential statistics.

Repeated revisits: I would advise teaching mathematical skills early in the course then revisiting them as mini tasks at the start or end of lessons as well as adding mathematical questions to other activities.

TOPIC: Mathematical skills

Back to basics

The answers:

Calculating fractions.

The lowest common denominator for 32 (the numerator) and 80 (the denominator) is 16.

$32 \div 16 = 2, 80 \div 16 = 5$, so the fraction is 2/5.

Calculating percentages – changing a fraction to a percentage.

$45 \div 75 = 0.6, 0.6 \times 100 = 60\%$

Calculating ratios.

The ratio can be expressed as the fraction 27:63. The lowest common denominator is 9, meaning the lowest form of the fraction is 3:7. Three men to every 7 women returned the questionnaire.

Students may find it helpful to create flash cards of the basic mathematical skills (*Complete Companion*, p210). Students write the key skill on one side of the card, then on the reverse

HANDOUT 149

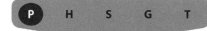

Students who are competent in calculating fractions and percentages could be assigned the role of lead learners for this activity, working with students who need more support.

record the explanation. These can be used to text recall in class or at home by presenting the cards to a willing volunteer who will hold up cards one at a time for the student to explain.

TOPIC: Measures of central tendency and dispersion

Data analysis

The activity offers students the chance to revisit prior learning (IV, DV and hypothesis writing) as well as applying newly gained knowledge of measures of central tendency and dispersion.

The answers:

IV = Age: either Year 7 (11–12 years) or teachers (over 25)

DV = Level of conformity as measured on a scale of 1–50 (50 = high conformity)

Non-directional hypothesis = The conformity scores of teachers over 25 and Year 7 students (aged 11–12 years) are different.

HANDOUT 150

Less-able students may find a hint sheet beneficial. If they have been keeping a research methods glossary throughout the course they could use this to remind them of the key concepts covered in **Handout 150.**

Data	Year 7	Teachers	**Problems:** no mode for teachers so comparison cannot be made to Year 7 data. Mean takes into account all data so any anomalies (score of 6 in Year 7 group) will distort mean, so it is unrepresentative of most people tested.
Mean	27.8	33.5	
Median	32.5	34	
Mode	34	None	
S.D	10.80	8.39	

Standard deviations = The larger standard deviation seen by Year 7 suggests there is more dispersion around the mean than is seen by the Teacher's data. This implies there was more variety in conformity scores for Year 7 students, some showed low conformity, others showed higher conformity. Teachers scored more similarly to each other.

However, the anomaly (6) may have moved the S.D calculated higher in the Year 7 data.

Conclusions = The mean suggests teachers are slightly more conforming than Year 7 students. The median, which is not affected by anomalies, also suggests teachers are more conforming.

Students could be given the following extension questions:

1. Use graph paper to plot the data using an appropriate graph. Clearly label the X and Y axis and give a suitable title.

2. Why might social desirability bias be a problem in this study?

3. What problems might occur by asking participants to complete the questionnaire in a classroom during break time?

4. Why do you think the researchers decided not to use interviews to research levels of conformity?

5. What ethical issues might researchers need to address in this study?

TOPIC: Display of quantitative data and data distributions

Graphical match up

The activity requires students to match the type of graph/distribution to the correct image and explanation. Students may wish to cut out each cell and stick them in groups on an A3 sheet of paper or use colour coding to group the key term, image and description. This can be used to introduce graphs and act as a check of prior knowledge if your class is competent in maths, or can form a revision activity once the section has been taught.

As an additional activity, when conducting mini research studies in class, ask students to draw and label the appropriate graph to display the data. For example, a class correlation on arm and foot length in centimetres provides students with the opportunity to create scattergrams.

HANDOUT 151

P H S G T

Students can be challenged to answer the following questions:

1. Explain the difference between bar charts and histograms.

2. Why can correlations only be represented by scattergrams?

3. In a negatively skewed distribution is the mean higher or lower than the median and mode?

4. How is the concept of normal distribution related to the statistical deviation definition of abnormality?

TOPIC: Types of data

Word games

NO HANDOUT

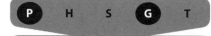

The activities listed below can be used to familiarise students with key terms and associated words relating to types of data. Key terms include: quantitative data, qualitative data, primary data, secondary data. Associated words: open questions, closed questions.

> More-able students can be given the role of game leader for the word games shown below. Mixed-ability groupings may support less-able students.

Listening bingo

Provide students with a blank 3x3 bingo grid and ask them to write down any words or phrases they would expect to hear in a short lecture about types of data. Obvious words include data, qualitative, quantitative, open questions, closed questions, numbers/numerical. Less obvious may be methods that gather different data such as experiment, unstructured interview as well as evaluative comments like low detail, in-depth, simple/brief, graphical representation. Students may find it challenging to think of nine words or phrases so this activity could be set as a group task.

Dice roll

In small groups students are given a set of cards containing key words relating to types of data and a dice. One at a time students pick a card and roll the dice. They have to explain the key term in the number of words shown on the dice face. For example, card states 'closed question' and the dice roll showed 5: 'fixed choice e.g. yes no'.

Team taboo

Position two to four chairs (depending on the size of your class) at the front of the class. Split the class into groups who then nominate one team member to sit in one of the chairs facing the class. This person has to guess the key word displayed on the whiteboard behind them. Teams have to describe this key word without actually using any of the words from the term shown. The first person seated in the chair who guesses correctly earns their team a point. This games can be made harder by banning certain words, e.g. if key term shown is 'quantitative' ban the word 'numbers'.

TOPIC: Introduction to statistical testing

Research project: aim & procedure materials, recording & analysing data, reaching a conclusion

HANDOUTS 152, 153 and 154

Handouts 152, 153 and **154** form a series of activities which enable students to carry out a mini research project on their friends/family or can be used by you with the class as participants.

> Less-able students may need one-to-one support the first time they carry out the sign test (**Handout 153**: recording & analysing data models how to complete the data table).
>
> More-able students could be challenged to create a further research project suitable for use with the sign test.

Aim and procedure materials

The project aims to compare people's attitude towards the value of psychology before and after exposure to an information passage. This passage is related to another area of the research methods topic: psychology and the economy, so it is useful for students to familiarise themselves with this area.

As this is a repeated measures design, participants need to be tested twice, completing the rating scale before reading the passage and again after reading. Therefore, an interval between each condition is needed. If using the class as participants condition 1 (before reading) could be completed a few lessons before asking students to read the passage and give a second rating. If students are acting as researchers then they need to choose a person they will be able to meet again to complete condition 2 (read the passage and give second rating).

Depending on class size students can test one or two people to compile a class set of data.

Recording and analysing data

Once data are collected they are transferred to the table on **Handout 153**. Students follow the steps listed to carry out the sign test leading to the calculation of the S value.

Reaching a conclusion

With the S value calculated, students then identify the critical value from the table shown to determine whether the data collected are significant (the passage changed attitudes) or simply due to chance. Students then consider the strengths and limitations of the procedure. For example, was there a suitable interval between condition 1 and 2? Did the passage contain enough information? Could the presence of the students effect participants' responses (the participant may give a higher rating if they know the student is studying psychology, so as not to offend them)?

TOPIC: The scientific process and peer review

Triplets

The words and phrases shown at the start of the **Handout 155** all relate to the scientific process and peer review. For each set, students choose three words or phrases that link together in some way. The lines to the right of each set give students the opportunity to explain the connection between the selected words. There is no right or wrong answer as long as a connection can be made.

For example, 1. Refereeing, 12. Assessment, 18. Experts. Explanation – Refereeing is another term for peer review. It is the assessment of scientific work by experts in the same field.

Why not hold a class debate as an additional activity? Students could form two opposing teams, one for the use of peer review, another against. These groups may choose to nominate one or two speakers for their stance. You may wish to nominate one student to chair the discussion in which they invite people to speak, control the debate and using questioning to move the discussion forward. Another group of students could act as note-keepers who have the responsibility of recording the key points raised.

HANDOUT 155

P   H   **S**   G   T

A helpful hint for less-able students would be to take one word of phrase from column one, a second from middle column and the third words/phrase from the end column. Triplets for a range of aspects of peer review and the scientific process can be formed by following this method.

TOPIC: Psychology and the economy

Reading record

Completing the reading record provides students with the opportunity to practise making notes in their own words from text (*Complete Companion* page 222, 'Psychology and the Economy'). You should stress the importance of reading, understanding and writing in their own words to your class as a useful skill. The first text box on **Handout 156**, 'five sentence summary' models this process and could be completed as a class before students move on to recording specific examples from a textbook and finding their own examples from their class notes or own research. 'Soft paternalism' refers to attempts to influence people to make choices that lead to better outcomes for themselves. Much like a parent guides a child to make the right choice rather than dictating what they should or shouldn't do. In the case of junk food, influence occurs by placing such food out of shoppers immediate gaze rather than banning purchase of these items.

For an extra activity, rather than working individually to complete the handout, groups of students could be given a specific example of psychology's contribution to the economy to present to the class.

Suitable topics include:

Social Psychology: The process of social change for example, health campaigns.

Cognitive Psychology: The cognitive interview.

Developmental Psychology: Attachment and childcare settings.

Approaches in Psychology: Mental Health.

Biopsychology: Neuroscience and artificial intelligence.

This activity also provides an opportunity to revise previous topics. Each group could be challenged to present in a certain medium (you could ask them to draw a method out of a hat), for example, role play, poem, PowerPoint, short film.

HANDOUT 156

P   H   S   G   T

More-able students can be challenged to find their own examples of where psychology might contribute to the economy from previous sections of the course. Less-able students may benefit from topic areas to help their search such as, Improving memory (cognitive interview), Attachment (childcare settings). Students who really struggle with finding their own examples can be directed to their textbook (*Complete Companion*, page 223, 'Applying the topics in this book').

References

Thaler, R.H. and Sunstein, C.R. (2008). Nudge: Improving decisions about health, wealth and happiness. New Haven, CT: Yale University Press.

Confidence ratings

Compared to confidence rating handouts for other topics the headings used here refer to students' understanding of concept, whether this be outlining or evaluating, and their ability to apply their knowledge to question stems. The first column, 'I have a basic awareness' suggests students can give a simple explanation of the concept/ method but would struggle to identify the finer points. The second column, 'I have a secure understanding' means students have gone beyond awareness and can now give a full explanation, highlighting key features in detail, and where appropriate, give extended evaluative comments. The final column, 'I can apply this concept/ method to novel scenarios' relates to students' ability to apply their understanding to question stems.

The confidence rating handout could be annotated in a number of different ways. You may wish to set a percentage in each cell (33%, 66%, 100%) for students to colour code as they revisit each area as part of their revision. An alternative method could be to colour code a cell (red: cannot achieve this; amber: can achieve with some support; white: feel comfortable; green: feel confident). Again as topics are revisited through revision, cells can be highlighted to correspond with current confidence levels.

HANDOUTS 157, 158 and 159

P　　H　　S　　**G**　　**T**

Students may wish to reflect on their own progress through the unit as an individual or as part of a peer discussion. Alternatively the checklist could form part of a one-to-one discussion with a student who is of particular concern.

Additional activities

The checklist could be used to form targeted revision groups and allow students to sign up to sessions that cover the areas they are least confident in.

Refer to the appropriate skills for the question set

MARKING GRID
6–8 MARK QUESTION

Question:

Skill ↻	AO1: Knowledge & understanding	AO2: Application to the question stem	AO3: Evaluation	Structure and specialist terminology
Level 4 **7–8 marks**	Knowledge is accurate and generally well detailed. Minor detail and/or expansion of argument sometimes lacking.	Appropriate application and links made between research and question stem. Clear and effective comments.	Discussion is thorough and effective. Minor detail and/or expression of argument are rare.	Answer is clear, coherent and explicitly focused on the question. Effective use of a range of specialist terminology.
Level 3 **5–6 marks**	Knowledge is accurate and generally well detailed.	Appropriate application and links made between research and question stem. Most comments are clear and effective.	Discussion is thorough and effective. Minor detail and/or expression of argument sometimes lacking.	Answer is clear, coherent and focused on the question. Effective use of specialist terminology.
Level 2 **3–4 marks**	Knowledge is of the concept/research is evident.	Some effective application seen but research (theory/study) links to stem not always explained.	Evaluation is apparent and mostly effective though there may be occasional inaccuracies.	Answer is mostly clear and organised but may lack focus in places. Specialist terminology mostly used appropriately.
Level 1 **1–2 marks**	Knowledge is limited. Answer is mainly description focused.	Application to the question stem is absent or inappropriate.	Evaluative comments have limited effectiveness.	The whole answer lacks clarity, accuracy and organisation in places. Specialist terminology used inappropriately or is absent from the answer.

Markers' comments:

Author's next steps:

▶ Lesson notes p. 1

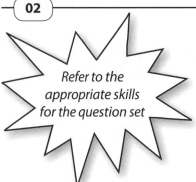

Refer to the appropriate skills for the question set

EXTENDED ANSWER MARKING GRID

Question:

Skill ⤵	AO1: Knowledge & understanding	AO2: Application to the question stem	AO3: Evaluation	Structure and specialist terminology
Level 4 AS 10–12 marks / A 13–16 marks	Knowledge is accurate and generally well detailed.	Appropriate application and links made between research and question stem.	Discussion is thorough and effective. Minor detail and/or expression of argument sometimes lacking.	Answer is clear, coherent and focused on the question. Effective use of specialist terminology
Level 3 AS 7–9 marks / A 9–12 marks	Knowledge of the concept/research is evident. There may be occasional inaccuracies.	Appropriate application but research (theory/study) links to stem not always explained.	Evaluation is apparent and mostly effective though there may be occasional inaccuracies.	Answer is mostly clear and organised but may lack focus in places. Specialist terminology mostly used effectively.
Level 2 AS 4–6 marks / A 5–8 marks	Knowledge is vague and/or inaccurate or partial performance in relation to question*. Answer is mainly description focused.	Only partial application is seen.	Only partially effective.	Answer lacks clarity, accuracy and organisation in places. Specialist terminology used appropriately on occasion.
Level 1 AS 1–3 marks / A 1–4 marks	Knowledge is limited and/or or partial performance in relation to question*.	Application to question stem is limited or absent.	Evaluation is limited, poorly focused or absent.	The whole answer lacks clarity, shows many inaccuracies and is poorly organised. Specialist terminology is either absent or inappropriately used.

* partial performance e.g. questions states, 'discuss two explanations' and answer only considers one.
If only one explanation (or study) outlined at level 3 or 4 then candidate cannot score above level 2.
If only one explanation (or study) outlined at level 2 then candidate cannot score above level 1.

Markers' comments:

Author's next steps:

▶ Lesson notes p. 1

EXPERIMENT PLANNING

Idea to be investigated

Aim – what do you want out?	IV – what are you manipulating?
Hypothesis – what do you think you will find out? (directional/non-directional) *do not use 'I'	DV – what are you manipulating?

Sourcing and sorting participants

Sampling method and reasons for choice – random, systematic, stratified, opportunity and volunteer	Experimental design and reasons for choice – independent measures, repeated measures, matched pairs
Sample and reasons for choice – number of participants, age, gender etc.	

Planning the procedure

What do participants have to do? Condition 1, condition 2.	Ethical issues – Informed consent Deception Protection from harm	Dealing with issues – Right to withdraw Confidentiality Debrief
Type of data collected		

▶ Lesson notes p. 1

EXPERIMENT ANALYSIS

Analysis of the findings

Data gathered from each condition.	Measures of central tendency
	_____ _____ Mean (total/number of participants)
	_____ _____ Median (the middle value in the data)
	_____ _____ Mode (the most common occurring number)
	Measures of dispersion
	_____ _____ Range (the difference between the highest and lowest score)
	_____ _____ Standard deviation (the spread of data around the mean)

Conclusion

Evaluating the procedure

What went well?	What needed to be improved?
Internal validity – did you measure what you set out to measure?	External validity – can your findings be applied to other situations (ecological) and people (population)?

▶ Lesson notes p. 1

REVISION RECORD

| TOPIC: | SECTION: | PAPER: |

Six sentence summary:

1.

2.

3.

4.

5.

6.

Topic glossary (including definitions):

PEEL Evaluation: Strength

PEEL Evaluation: Limitation

PEEL Evaluation: Strength

PEEL Evaluation: Limitation

▶ Lesson notes p. 2

ASSESSMENT:
FEEDBACK AND FEEDFORWARD

Date: [   ]

Type of question: [Knowledge / Evaluation / Essay / Application / How Science Works / Maths]

Total Marks: [   ]   out of [   ]   Grade Equivalent: [   ]   Over Target
On Target
Under Target

Improvements/Amendments/Responses:

A:

B:

C:

Improved mark if resubmitted:

▶ Lesson notes p. 3

PEER ASSESSMENT GRID

Write down four key words that the student has used. **Suggest one key word that they could have used but didn't.**	
Write down the best sentence/quote from their piece of work and explain why you chose that, i.e. what is good about it?	
Write down one sentence/ quote which doesn't make sense to you, i.e. it lacks clarity, or accuracy, isn't fully explained.	
Add one complete sentence which improves the essay. **On the essay, write *1 to show where the sentence should go.**	*1 –

▶ Lesson notes p. 5

AO2: APPLICATION OF KNOWLEDGE AN EXAMPLE

Helena works in a busy florists, she finds it really difficult to read customer orders submitted by email when talking to her colleagues. However, she is able to look through photographs of floral displays while listening to the radio.

Explain the key components of the working memory model making reference to Helena's ability to perform different tasks simultaneously.

Stem sentence	Concept/research	Application
Helena is trying to complete two tasks at the same time.	Central Executive.	The Central Executive is seen as being in charge of Working Memory as it allocates information to be processed to the different salve systems. When Helena tries to complete two tasks at the same time the Central Executive assigns tasks to the relevant slave system. This component also directs attention and can prioritize different tasks so Helena may find she performs one of the tasks well at the expense of the other.
Really difficult to read customer orders on email when talking to colleagues.	Phonological Loop, Limited capacity.	The Phonological Loop is responsible for spoken and written material and so Helena would need to use this component to process both emails and spoken words. The Loop consists of the Phonological Store (speech perception) and Articulatory Control Process (speech production). To understand the email and listen to her colleagues Helena needs to use her Phonological Store but as this has limited capacity, both tasks cannot be performed well at the same time.
She is able to look through photographs of floral displays while listening to the radio.	Phonological Store. Visuo-Spatial Sketchpad. Two separate components.	The Phonological Store would be responsible for processing spoken word heard on the radio, however, she would be using her Visuo-Spatial Sketchpad to view the photographs of the flowers as this component deals with visual information as well as spatial information and navigation in a space. Although both components have limited capacity they are dealing with different types of information so both tasks can be performed well simultaneously.
Helena understands the information she is processing.	Episodic Buffer Links to LTM.	A final component of the Working Memory Model is the Episodic Buffer. This was added in (2000) by Baddeley to further explain the function of Working Memory. When reading the emails, listening to colleagues or the radio and viewing photographs Helena needs to have access to her LTM to actually make sense of the information being processed. The Episodic buffer communicates with LTM by feeding information to LTM and retrieving information from LTM.

▶ Lesson notes p. 6

AO2: APPLICATION OF KNOWLEDGE

Stem sentence	Concept/research	Application

▶ Lesson notes p. 6

ELABORATION LADDERS

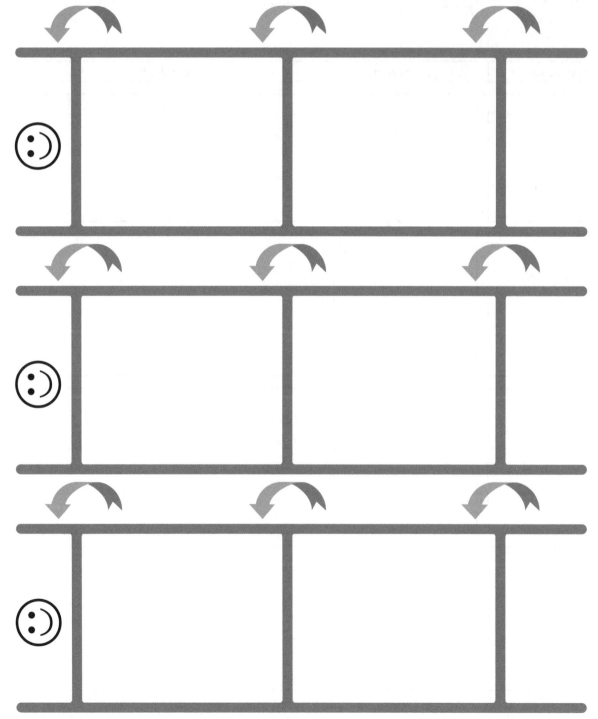

Why does that matter?
—
How would that affect the results/validity?
—
Can I explain my point with an example?
—
Have I got evidence?
—
How could it be improved?
—
Have I got a counter argument?
—
How does this affect the main argument?

Use the prompts above to help you **elaborate** the evaluative arguments on the bottom rung of the ladders.

The more you elaborate your points (without repeating yourself), the more marks you get – hence the smiley face at the top!

▶ Lesson notes p. 7

BURGER EVALUATION SKILLS

A study that supports/undermines the [insert name of theory/explanation here] is...

Describe procedure and findings of a relevant study.

This supports/undermines the [insert name of theory/explanation here] theory because...

The 'burger technique' is a way for you to structure an evaluation paragraph where you use a study to support or undermine a theory/explanation. The most important point of the process is the bottom of the burger where you explain how and why that study is relevant. This is where you can really demonstrate your understanding of a) what the theory/explanation would predict, and b) whether or not we should accept that theory based on the research evidence.

Example

A study that undermines the learning theory explanation of attachment is Harlow's (1959) study of rhesus monkeys.

Harlow separated rhesus monkeys from their mothers at birth and placed them in a cage with a wire monkey with a feeding bottle attached and a wire monkey wrapped in soft cloth. The monkeys spent most of their time clinging to the cloth monkey, especially in times of distress.

This undermines the learning theory view of attachment because, according to the explanation, the young monkeys should have attached to the wire monkey which dispensed food because they would associate it with a sense of pleasure and the reduction of their hunger drive. However, the infants tended to cling more to a mother which offered them comfort.

▶ Lesson notes p. 8

BURGER EVALUATION SKILLS

Which type of conformity?

Read these examples of conformity, and decide what type of conformity they illustrate and the motivation behind the conformity.

Example of conformity	Type of conformity (Compliance/ Internalisation/ Identification)	Motivation underlying the conformity (Wanting to gain approval under pressure/ Fear of rejection/ Wanting to validate our behaviours and beliefs by comparing them to others/ Wanting to be associated with another person or group/ Conforming to the expectations of a particular social role)
Despite knowing the dangers, Lisa tried a cigarette because her friends pressured her into trying one.		
Brian meets some church-goers at his local gym. After discussing religion with them for a few hours, he decides there is a God and that he should start attending church.		
There are a group of football supporters known as 'casuals' who wear designer clothes and do not wear the colours of the teams playing at football matches. John makes the decision to follow this fashion because he wants to be part of that group.		
Sheema was sitting in the doctor's surgery full of people and noticed smoke billowing in from the next room. No one else around her raised the alarm, so neither did Sheema. She assumed it couldn't have been an emergency.		
Everyone in the sixth form used to think that having to wear a smart uniform was a bad idea. However, the head boy Liam, and head girl Steph managed to convince most people that it would help them to be more productive in their lessons.		
Brett is not really interested in politics but most of the people at his University are left-wing. Brett often tells people he supports left-wing views.		

▶ Lesson notes p. 12

Conformity Table Mats

Informational Social Influence

Human basic need:	How this basic need leads to conformity:	Type of conformity it leads to:	Why it leads to this type of conformity:	Example:	Important factors

Normative Social Influence

Human basic need:	How this basic need leads to conformity:	Type of conformity it leads to:	Why it leads to this type of conformity:	Example:	Important factors

▶ Lesson notes p. 12

Conformity Table Mats

As a social species, humans have a fundamental need for social companionship and a fear of rejection.

Public AND private conformity.

When we are unsure and not confident of how to behave, or not confident in our opinions, we may seek other people's opinions or observe their behaviours.

To gain approval and acceptance by others we may conform to the *behaviour* of those groups or say that we agree with their viewpoint.

Humans have a need to feel confident that their opinions, beliefs and perceptions are correct.

We must believe that they are **under surveillance** by the group, i.e. that their behaviour and opinions are being judged by the people around them.

Going to a posh restaurant is an unfamiliar experience. We may observe others' behaviour, particularly those who have been to the restaurant before, so we use the correct cutlery in the right order.

Internalisation.

We may conform to a group publicly (e.g. in order to gain acceptance by them), without actually accepting their point of view privately.

Public conformity but NOT private conformity.

We evaluate our behaviours and opinions against others. On occasion we conform to others because we genuinely believe them to be right.

Compliance.

To avoid rejection and disapproval by others we may conform because we do not wish to go against the group's behaviours or opinions.

A group of students is making fun of one of their 'bad' teachers. One student is joining in with the jokes despite believing that the teacher is actually very good.

Most likely to occur when the situation is **ambiguous** and the right course of action is unclear. Also, where we believe others to be **experts** who know more than us in that situation.

Once we're convinced that someone else's behaviour or opinion is correct, we conform privately in our attitudes, and then also conform in our public attitudes and behaviour.

▶ Lesson notes p. 12

Asch's numbers quiz

The number of male American undergraduates tested in Asch's (1956) original research.	
The number of lines the students were asked to look at (excluding the comparison line).	
The number of confederates used in the original research.	
The number of trials each participant took part in.	
The number of critical trials each participant took part in.	
The total number of critical trials in Asch's original research (hint, you'll probably need a calculator for this).	
The percentage of the total critical trials where the participants conformed (the overall conformity rate).	
The percentage of participants who never conformed.	
The percentage of participants who conformed at least once.	
The percentage of mistakes made by participants in the control trials, where no confederates were present.	
The percentage conformity rate when the real participant was given the support of a confederate who had been given instructions to give the right answers throughout.	
The percentage conformity rate, when a lone 'dissenter' (confederate) gave an answer that was different from the majority *and* different from the true answer.	

If your teacher instructs you to, cover these possible answers with your textbook or folder:

9%, 1%, 123, 18, 5, 75%, 33%, 12, 5.5%, 3, 1476, 25%.

▶ Lesson notes p. 14

Asch evaluation ladders

Why does that matter?

How would that affect the results/validity?

Can I explain my point with an example?

Have I got evidence?

How could it be improved?

Have I got a counter argument?

How does this affect the main argument?

Use the prompts above to help you **elaborate** the evaluative arguments on the bottom rung of the ladders.

The more you elaborate your points (without repeating yourself), the more marks you get – hence the smiley face at the top!

It could be argued that Asch's experimental paradigm is ethically questionable.

A further weakness of Asch's research is that it would have been difficult for the confederates to act convincingly.

One of the problems with Asch's conformity research is that the results may have been unique to one culture and one era – a 'child of its time.' – due to McCarthyism.

▶ Lesson notes p. 14

Asch evaluation ladders

Why does that matter?

How would that affect the results/validity?

Can I explain my point with an example?

Have I got evidence?

How could it be improved?

Have I got a counter argument?

How does this affect the main argument?

Use the prompts above to help you **elaborate** the evaluative arguments on the bottom rung of the ladders.

The more you elaborate your points (without repeating yourself), the more marks you get – hence the smiley face at the top!

Hint: Explain why it matters that these ethical issues arise, e.g. trust in psychologists, fairness etc.

Hint: Explain what ethical issues may arise and WHY. e.g. choose one of protection from harm (embarrassment), deception, etc.

It could be argued that Asch's experimental paradigm is ethically questionable.

Hint: Explain how and why this may have affected the validity of the study. Use key terms! Show that you understand what validity means.

Hint: Explain why this would have been difficult.

A further weakness of Asch's research is that it would have been difficult for the confederates to act convincingly.

Hint: Clearly explain how and why this might have affected the results of Asch's study.

Hint: Explain what McCarthyism is, and how it is relevant to the time and culture in which the study took place.

One of the problems with Asch's conformity research is that the results may have been unique to one culture and one era – a 'child of its time.' – due to McCarthyism.

▶ Lesson notes p. 14

Dimension Line – Conformity to Social Roles?

Strong evidence for

Strong evidence against

Evidence A: Even when the participants in the SPE were unaware that they were being watched, their behaviour still conformed to their 'guard' or 'prisoner' role. One prisoner even asked for 'parole' rather than asking to withdraw from the study.

Evidence B: In the BBC study, prisoners were given the possibility of 'promotion' after 3 days from the prisoners group to the guards group. As a result, the prisoners offered no challenge to the guards in the first few days.

Evidence C: In Abu Ghraib, a military prison in Iraq, the Iraqi prisoners were abused and tortured by American soldiers. Situational factors such as lack of training, boredom, and a lack of accountability were present in both Abu Ghraib and the SPE.

Evidence D: The male participants in the SPE were psychologically and physically screened and the 24 most 'normal' and 'stable' were used in the study and randomly assigned to play the roles of 'prisoner' or 'guard'.

Evidence E: Over the first few days of the SPE, the guards grew increasingly tyrannical and abusive towards the prisoners. They woke prisoners day and night and forced them to clean the toilets.

Evidence F: Banuazizi and Movahedi (1975) presented some of the details of the SPE experimental procedure to a large sample of students who had never heard of the study. The vast majority of the students guessed that the purpose of the study was to show that ordinary people assigned the role of prisoner or guard would act like a prisoner or guard.

Evidence G: Haslam (2012) suggests that Zimbardo gave his guards a general sense of how he expected them to behave. This suggests that the 'behavioural scripts associated with the roles' were not the sole source of guidance.

▶ Lesson notes p. 16

Milgram Obedience Barometer

In Milgram's original study, there were two confederates: an experimenter (the authority figure), and a 47 year-old accountant, who played the part of the 'learner'. Milgram found that 65% of 'teacher' participants delivered a maximum 450 volts to the confederate 'learner' when asked to by the experimenter.

Percentage (%) of Milgram's participants administering maximum shock (450 volts)

Task instructions:

1. Read about variations of Milgram's research in the boxes below.
2. Estimate the percentage of participants you think gave the maximum 450 volts in that variation of the study.
3. Add the estimation to the barometer above using the name of the variation.
4. Briefly explain why you think the obedience levels decreased/increased from the original 65%.
5. Use textbooks, the internet and/or your teacher to find the actual results and compare with your own.

Touch-proximity variation: The teacher was required to force the learner's hand onto a shock plate.

Teacher's discretion variation: The level of shock delivered to the learner was left to the participants' discretion.

Different location variation: The experiment was conducted in a run-down office block in the town centre, rather than the prestigious Yale University lab.

Proximity variation: The teacher and learner were seated in the same room. As a result, the teacher was able to see the reactions of the learner.

Experimenter-absent variation: After giving instructions the experimenter left the room and gave subsequent orders over the telephone.

Two peers rebel variation: Three participants (two confederates and one real participant) shared the task of teaching the learner. At a certain point in the experiment, the two bogus teachers refused to carry on.

▶ Lesson notes p. 18

Discussing Milgram's internal validity

KEY CONCEPTS...

Internal validity: When a study measures what it intended to measure.

Milgram's study: Intended to measure the willingness of people to obey, even if that obedience resulted in harming another person.

Demand characteristics: When a participant becomes aware of what the experimenter might expect, which then influences their behaviour in the study.

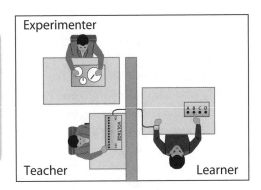

Experimenter

Teacher   Learner

Orne and Holland (1968) have argued that Milgram's research lacks internal validity. They argued that the participants may have guessed that the 'victim' was not really suffering because the experimenter remained cool and distant, despite the fact that the learner was crying out with pain. This affects the internal validity because ....

....

....

....

[Show off that you understand what validity means, refer to all of the key concepts above.]

To counter the argument that his participants did not believe the deception, Milgram could point out that ....

....

....

....

[Think about the behaviour of the anxious participants during the study, does this show validity of measurement?]

However, Perry (2012) discovered that many of Milgram's participants had doubted whether the shocks were real. One of Milgram's researchers, Taketo Murata, found that the participants who had believed that the shocks were real were more likely to disobey the experimenter and give lower intensity shocks. This evidence suggests that the internal validity was low because

....

....

....

....

► Lesson notes p. 18

Discussing Milgram's external validity

KEY CONCEPTS...

External validity: The ability to generalize the results and conclusions of a study to different populations, settings and/or situations outside of the study.

Milgram's results and conclusions: Milgram concluded that his study demonstrated that normal people are capable of inflicting awful harm on others simply through their obedience to malign authority figures.

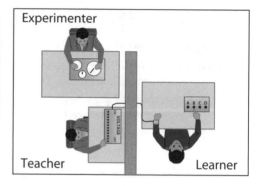

Experimenter

Teacher   Learner

Mandel (1998) argued that Milgram's conclusions lacked external validity and should not be applied to events such as the Holocaust. He felt that there were several key differences between Milgram's study and the historical events in the Holocaust, for example, ...

....

....

....

....

[Think about the willingness of the participants compared to the Holocaust perpetrators, think about the fact that Milgram's participants were told the procedure was not harmful and compare that to the Holocaust.]

These arguments challenge the external validity because ....

....

....

....

[Refer to the key concepts to show off your understanding of what external validity means.]

It might be tempting to also criticize Milgram's external validity because the original research was conducted with males only. However, he replicated the study with females and found exactly the same rates of obedience. In addition, Blass (1999) found there were no gender differences observed in eight out of nine Milgram replications. This provides evidence for Milgram's research having external validity because ....

....

....

....

....

▶ Lesson notes p. 19

The case of Sandor Képírió

Sandor Képírió was a Hungarian military police officer ('gendarmerie') during World War II. He was tried in court for war crimes in 2011 as a result of a pro-Nazi raid by the Hungarian forces in Serbia.

The raid in the Serbian city of Novi Sad, in January 1942, resulted in the rounding up of thousands of Jews and Serbs who were then killed. Sandor Képírió was accused of being involved in the raids that resulted in their deaths.

A documentary programme called 'Nazi Hunters' tracked down Képírió and interviewed him. The video can be found here and is well worth a watch: https://www.youtube.com/watch?v=vCJpd6_RGfU

- Watch the video and use this handout to write notes on how Képírió defends his actions and tries to excuse himself from responsibility.
- Alternatively, you can research this case by searching the internet for 'Sandor Képírió' and 'Novi Sad raid'.
- In particular, listen to/research what Képírió has to say about the 'written commands'.
- Use your notes to complete the question at the bottom.

Video/internet research:

Using your knowledge of obedience, explain why Sandor Képírió may have completed his orders, despite the consequences that those actions may have had.

Try and mention the following concepts in your answer:
- Agentic state
- Autonomous state
- Responsibility
- Obedience
- Legitimate authority
- Self-image
- Evaluative concern
- Institutional structure.

▶ Lesson notes p. 19

Questionnaire 1

Tick your reaction for each statement in the questionnaire using the following scale:

1   Disagree strongly
2   Disagree mostly
3   Disagree somewhat
4   Agree somewhat
5   Agree mostly
6   Agree strongly

	1	2	3	4	5	6
1. Obedience and respect for authority are the most important virtues children should learn.						
2. A person who has bad manners and habits can hardly expect to get along with decent people.						
3. If people would talk less and work more, everybody would be better off.						
4. Young people sometimes get rebellious ideas, but as they grow up they ought to get over them and settle down.						
5. No sane, normal, decent person could ever think of hurting a close friend or relative.						
6. Nobody ever learned anything really important except through suffering.						
7. What the youth needs most is strict discipline, rugged determination, and the will to work and fight for family and country.						
8. Sex crimes, such as rapes and attacks on children, deserve more than mere imprisonment, such as painful physical punishments, or worse.						
9. A person who does not feel great love or gratitude or respect for their parents is the lowest type of person.						
10. When a person has a problem or worry, it is best for him not to think about it, but to keep busy with more cheerful things.						
11. People can be divided into two distinct classes: the weak and the strong.						
12. Most people don't realise how much of our lives are controlled by plots hatched in secret places.						
13. With human nature being what it is, there will always be war and conflict.						
14. Most of our social problems would disappear if we could get rid of immoral, crooked, and weak-minded people.						
15. Nowadays when so many different kinds of people move around and mix together so much, a person has to protect himself.						
16. A businessman and a manufacturer are much more important to society than an artist and a professor.						

Adapted from Adorno et al. (1950). *The Authoritarian Personality*. New York: Harper and Brothers.

▶ Lesson notes p. 20

Questionnaire 2

Tick your reaction for each statement in the questionnaire using the following scale:

-4 Very strongly disagree
-3 Strongly disagree
-2 Moderately disagree
-1 Slightly disagree
 0 Neutral
 1 Slightly agree
 2 Moderately agree
 3 Strongly agree
 4 Very strongly agree

	-4	-3	-2	-1	0	1	2	3	4
1. Authorities and people in charge generally turn out to be right. Protestors and radicals are usually just 'loud mouths' who do not know what they are talking about.									
2. Women should have to promise to obey their husbands when they get married.									
3. People who do not believe in God and rebel against the established religions are usually every bit as good as those who go to church (or similar) regularly. *									
4. There is nothing wrong with nudist camps. *									
5. Our country needs free thinkers who are brave enough to go against the usual ways of doing things – even if that upsets people. *									
6. The 'old-fashioned ways' and the 'old-fashioned values' are still the best ways for us to live.									
7. Everyone should be free to have their own lifestyle, religious beliefs and sexual preferences – even though they may be different from everyone else. *									
8. People who bravely challenge the law and the majority's view by protesting for animal rights, euthanasia and abortion rights should be admired. *									
9. Our country needs a strong and determined leader who will crush evil and take us back to our true path.									
10. Some of the best people in the country are those who challenge the government, argue against religious beliefs, and ignore the 'normal way things are done'. *									
11. There are many radical and immoral people in this country who are trying to ruin it for their own selfish purposes.									
12. There is no one right way to live, everybody has to live life in their own way.									
13. Homosexuals and feminists should be praised for being brave enough to defy 'traditional family values'.									
14. This country would be much better and work better if certain troublemakers and protestors would just shut up and accept the traditions of our society.									

Adapted from Altemeyer,B.(2006) *The Authoritarians*. Page 10–15. (http://members.shaw.ca/jeanaltemeyer/drbob/ TheAuthoritarians.pdf)

► Lesson notes p. 20

Questionnaire 3

	Agree very much	Agree somewhat	Agree slightly	Disagree slightly	Disagree somewhat	Disagree very much
1. Sometimes I don't feel that I have enough control over the direction my life is taking.						
2. By taking an active part in political and social affairs people can control world events.						
3. It is impossible for me to believe that chance or luck plays an important role in my life.						
4. Many times I feel that I have little influence over the things that happen to me.						
5. Getting people to do the right things depends upon ability; luck has little or nothing to do with it.						
6. Unfortunately, an individual's worth often passes unrecognized no matter how hard he tries.						
7. Capable people who fail to become leaders have not taken advantage of their opportunities.						
8. This world is run by a few people in power, and there is not much the little guy can do.						
9. What happens to me is my own doing.						
10. Most people don't realize the extent to which their lives are controlled by accidental happenings.						
11. People's misfortunes result from the mistakes they make.						
12. There is really no such thing as 'luck'.						
13. The average citizen can have an influence on government decisions.						
14. In the long run people get the respect they deserve in the world.						
15. In my case getting what I want has little or nothing to do with luck.						
16. With enough effort we can wipe out political corruption.						
17. Who gets to be the boss often depends on who was lucky enough to be in the right place first.						
18. Many of the unhappy things in people's lives are partly due to bad luck.						
19. It is difficult for people to have much control over things politicians do in office.						
20. People are lonely because they don't try to be friendly.						

From: McIlveen, R., Higgins, L. and Wadeley, A. (1992). *BPS Manual of Psychology practicals*. BPS Books.

▶ Lesson notes p. 22

Application skills:
The two-sentence technique

- Students often find application questions difficult to answer and do not receive full marks. When attempting to answer these types of questions, you should remember that the examiner is actually looking for two elements:

  - Selection of appropriate KNOWLEDGE
  - That the knowledge has been **APPLIED** appropriately

- One way to ensure that you include both elements, is to write your answer using the 'two-sentence' technique.
- This means writing one KNOWLEDGE sentence from your textbook or revision that you feel is relevant to the question...
- And then, writing one APPLIED sentence where you explain how that knowledge is relevant to the question.
- You can do this several times until you think you have fully answered the question.

Example application question:

Simon did not enjoy smoking cigarettes but often felt pressured to smoke when his group of friends teased him for not being as 'cool' as them. Then, one of the friends in the group, Paul, decided not to smoke again even if that meant he would get teased. Now, when Simon and Paul are with the group, Simon is able to resist the pressure and the teasing and refuses to smoke.

'Explain the change in Simon's behaviour using your knowledge of resistance to social influence.' (4 marks)

Example application answer:

KNOWLEDGE	It is easier to resist conformity when there is at least one other ally and/or 'dissenter' in the group.
APPLIED	In this situation, Simon is at first on his own trying to resist the pressure to smoke, but he then finds an ally in Paul who also wants to resist the group of friends.
KNOWLEDGE	It is easier to resist conformity when we have an ally because they offer us social support – that is, when we believe we have the assistance of other people.
APPLIED	In this situation, Simon has social support in Paul and believes that if he tries to resist smoking, Paul will be able to help him and defend him from the teasing.

► Lesson notes p. 23

Application skills:
The two-sentence technique

Use **Handout 27** to help you complete this application examination-style question.

Sarah and Amelia have just joined a local hockey sports team. Sarah believes that if she practises and trains well, she will improve her skills and will then get selected for matches. Amelia thinks that whether she gets selected for matches will depend on whether the coach likes her and whether she gets the right luck during the training sessions.

'Identify the type of locus of control shown by Sarah.' (1 mark)

'Identify the type of locus of control shown by Amelia.' (1 mark)

Sarah	
Amelia	

The coach asks the team not to shake hands with the opposition to try and intimidate them before the next match. Both Sarah and Amelia think that the instruction from the coach is unsporting and wrong.

'Which one of these players, Sarah or Amelia, is most likely to disobey the coach? Use your knowledge of psychology in your explanation.' (4 marks)

KNOWLEDGE	
APPLIED	
KNOWLEDGE	
APPLIED	

▶ Lesson notes p. 23

Maximising your outline marks

Imagine that you have been set the following examination question:

- 'Describe **one** study into the role of minority influence.' (6 marks)

The answer below is accurate but does not gain full marks because it lacks detail. Use the table below to make *small additions* to this answer that take it to a 'level 3' maximum mark answer. Sometimes it might just be a number!

Moscovici et al. (1969) studied social influence*¹. In each group, Moscovici placed some*² naïve participants*³ with a minority*⁴ of confederates*⁵.

They were all shown blue slides*⁶ and were asked to judge the colour of each slide. In the 'consistent' condition, the confederates called the blue slides 'green' on every trial. In the 'inconsistent' condition, the confederates sometimes*⁷ called the blue slides 'green', and sometimes*⁸ called the slides 'blue'.

They found that the naïve participants were more likely*⁹ to say 'green' on the consistent trials compared to the consistent*¹⁰ and control trials*¹¹.

After the experiment, participants were asked to sort blue/green chips into either 'blue' or 'green'. Participants in the 'consistent' and 'inconsistent' conditions judged the colour differently*¹². This shows that consistent minority influence was long-lasting*¹³.

*1	
*2	
*3	
*4	
*5	
*6	
*7	
*8	
*9	
*10	
*11	
*12	
*13	

► Lesson notes p. 23

Change the world!

Social change I would like to bring about:

Think of something about society you would like to change, it can be a very small change, or something more dramatic!

Using minority influence to cause 'conversion'

VS

You

1. Attention *(make a specific suggestion relevant to your context, suggest the purpose of this plan)*

2. Cognitive Conflict *(Explain what is meant by the term 'cognitive conflict' in this model. Then, fill out the conflict summary of cognitive positions.)*

Majority Position (the norm):	***Vs***	**Minority Position:**

▶ Lesson notes p. 24

Change the world! *part 2*

3. Consistency of position *(What is the consistent theme/message you will articulate for your campaign for social change? What is/are the reason(s) you want to promote it to the majority?)*

A)

B)

4. The augmentation principle

What is the augmentation principle?

How will you achieve this?

5. The snowball effect *(Explain how the snowball effect might work in the context of our example.)*

Conversion and social change has occurred!

You   **VS**

▶ Lesson notes p. 24

Confidence ratings

Social Psychology topic	I can identify key terminology in this topic.	I can give a detailed outline of research.	I can create effective evaluations of research.	I can apply my knowledge of this topic to novel scenarios.
Types of conformity: Internalisation, identification and compliance				
Explanations of conformity: Informational social influence and normative social influence				
Variables affecting conformity: Group size, unanimity, task difficulty				
Conformity to social roles as investigated by Zimbardo				
Explanations for obedience: Agentic state and legitimacy of authority				
Situational variables affecting obedience: Proximity, location and uniform				
Dispositional explanation for obedience: The Authoritarian Personality				
Explanations of resistance to social influence: Social support and locus of control				

▶ Lesson notes p. 25

Confidence ratings

Minority influence: Consistency, commitment and flexibility				
The role of social influence processes in social change				

- My strengths in relation to learning this topic were:

- Areas of my learning I need to develop during the next topic are:

▶ Lesson notes p. 25

The duration of STM

What are the limitations of using students attending university for this investigation?

Why did Peterson & Peterson use a distraction task (counting backwards) between the learning phase and recall in each trial?

Why do you think Peterson & Peterson tested recall using meaningless consonant syllables such as THX?

Lloyd and Margaret Peterson (1959) studied the duration of STM, using 24 students attending their university. Each participant was tested over eight trials. On each trial a participant was given a **consonant syllable** and a three-digit number (e.g. THX 512 or HJS 384). They were asked to recall the consonant syllable after a retention interval of 3, 6, 9, 12, 15 or 18 seconds. During the retention interval they had to count backwards from their three-digit number.

Participants, on average, were 90% correct over 3 seconds, 20% correct after 9 seconds and only 2% correct after 18 seconds. This suggests that STM has a very short duration, less than 18 seconds – as long as verbal rehearsal is prevented.

What are the limitations of using meaningless constant syllables such as THX?

Sketch a graph of the findings. Be sure to label each axis correctly and give a suitable title explaining what the graph represents.

Why might Peterson & Peterson's findings be said to show the effect of displacement rather than decay? What implication does this have on their conclusions regarding STM duration?

▶ Lesson notes p. 27

The duration of LTM

Read the exam responses carefully and decide what marks you would award, be sure to justify your decision. Consider what improvements might be made to increase the final mark.

> *'Briefly outline **and** evaluate the findings of any **one** study into the duration of long-term memory.'*
> *(4 marks)*

Candidate A

Bharick conducted a study to test the duration of LTM using participants' recall of yearbook photos. 15 years after graduation, recall of school friends and acquaintances showed 90% accuracy when asked to identify faces, but this dropped to 70% after 48 years.

However, the validity of the results may be questioned as the procedure may not have tested LTM correctly.

Marker's comments:

Suggested improvements:

Candidate B

A photo-recognition task in which participants were asked to identify faces showed 90% recall accuracy after 15 years but declined to 70% after 48 years. In a free-recall task requiring participants to list names of classmates they could recall, accuracy was 60% at 15 years but dropped to 30% after 48 years.

Marker's comments:

Suggested improvements:

Candidate C

Recall using a cue, such as photo-recognition from yearbook photos, showed 90% accuracy after 15 years but only 70% accuracy after 48 years. When asked to list names of people participants went to school with, free-recall accuracy after 15 years was 60% which dropped dramatically to 30% after 48 years.

The validity of these LTMs could be questioned as participants may have regularly looked through their yearbook or even have continued contact with school friends so would regularly rehearse their memories.

Marker's comments:

Suggested improvements:

Mark scheme

Level 2 3–4 marks	AO1: findings are clearly outlined and accurately reported. AO3: Evaluation/analysis is effective, explicitly linked to the findings outlined.
Level 1 1–2 marks	AO1: Findings are clearly outlined but no evaluation is given. OR, findings and evaluation (AO3) are incomplete and may have some inaccuracies.
0 marks	No relevant content is given.

► Lesson notes p. 27

Describing the MSM

1. Replace the words in bold with psychological terminology.
2. Colour code each textbox to identify whether the comments refer to the structure of memory or the process in which memory moves through the system.

Things in the environment enter the **first memory store.**	
This store can handle **lots of different types of information** but cannot cope with a **lot of information at once or for a very long time.**	
Information can be lost from this store by **fading away.**	

If **noticed** information moves to the **second memory store.**	
This store can **only hold a few items** for **a few seconds.** It **holds information in the form of sounds.**	
Information is lost by **fading away** or **being pushed out by other items.**	
However, **repeating the items again and again** can maintain the memory in this store.	

Adding meaning to the information can move it to the **final store.**	
Here **a lot of items can be held for a long time. Information is meaningful.**	
Information is lost by **fading away or becoming muddled with other items.**	

Information **flows along a line** in the model and each store is **one single block.**	

▶ Lesson notes p. 27

MSM essay practice

'Outline and evaluate the multi-store model (MSM).' (8 marks)

> Outline – AO1
> Evaluate – AO3

Highlight any AO1 comments.

In a second colour highlight AO3 comments.

...According to this model, information reaches the brain from the senses (sound, sight etc.). This information enters the sensory register. The information that receives our attention is transferred to our short-term memory (STM) for further processing.

The MSM presents the STM as a simple concept; it is often drawn as a box in diagrams. This may be a limitation of the model as some argue STM is much more complex and contains different components that attend to different types of information.

The STM is seen as very limited by the model and information must be constantly rehearsed for it to be held in STM for longer than 30 seconds...

To reach the higher levels of the mark scheme your answer needs to show a good level of detail for AO1 outline of the structures and processes of the MSM. For example, rather than stating limited duration, the extract above identifies duration as 30 seconds. To access the higher levels at AO3 your evaluative comments need to be developed and relate specifically to the MSM as an explanation of memory.

A study that supports the MSM is Glanzer and Cunitz's Serial Position Curve. They tested people using a list of words which must be recalled. Their study found that the words at the start of the list (the primary information) was remembered well due to maintenance rehearsal moving it to LTM; also the words towards the end of the list (recency information) were remembered as they were still in STM. Words in the middle had been either displaced or decayed. In a later variation, they made participants count backwards in 3s before recalling and the graph showed that more of the recency words were forgotten as they were lost due to lack of rehearsal. These findings support the MSM explanation of memory as they suggest STM and LTM are two separate stores and that rehearsal is the process used to transfer information as the model suggested.

Annotate this paragraph to illustrate how to structure an evaluative comment.

Point – are you supporting or criticizing the MSM?

Evidence – explain relevant research evidence.

Expansion – Add further detail such as another research finding.

Link – relate back to the MSM: does this evidence increase the validity of the model?

Can you apply the PEEL structure to improve the evaluation comment given in the first extract on this handout?

▶ Lesson notes p. 28

Baddeley et al. (1975a)

Get evaluating!
What are the strengths and limitations of using a laboratory experiment to investigate the working memory model?

Evidence for the phonological loop and articulatory control process

---

Aim: to investigate the existence of a phonological loop in STM.

Procedure: Participants saw everyday words displayed very quickly one after the other. They were then asked to write the words seen in serial order (the same order as on the list).

Condition 1 – the list contained five one-syllable English words e.g. tree, once, pain.

Condition 2 – the list contained five polysyllabic (many syllables) English words e.g. university, recommendation, establishment.

Identify the operationalised IV in this experiment?

Identify the operationalised DV in this experiment?

Write a directional hypothesis for this experiment.

Findings: From analysing several trials Baddeley found participants recalled the shorter, one-syllable words much better than the polysyllabic words. He called this the **word length effect.**

Conclusions: The phonological loop has a role in the capacity of STM. The amount you can hold in your STM is determined by the length of time it takes to say the words NOT the number of items. It seems that the phonological loop holds the amount of information that you can say in 2 seconds.

Making links: How can Baddeley's findings be used to criticize Miller's 'Magic number 7' view of STM capacity?

What might Baddeley's research suggest about the size of chunks when trying to increase the capacity of STM?

Making predictions: What do you think happened when participants were given an articulatory suppression task such as chanting 'the, the, the, the' while viewing the word lists?

▶ Lesson notes p. 28

Baddeley et al. (1975b)

Aim: to investigate the existence of the visuo-spatial sketchpad in STM.

Procedure: Participants were asked to visualise a letter and describe the angles at each point of that letter at the same time as completing a visual tracking task.

Task 1 – Imagine a letter. As you move round the letter, if an angle falls on the top or bottom line then say 'YES' aloud, if the angle falls anywhere else say 'NO'.

Task 2 – Track the movement of a dot of light with a pointer.

Evidence for the visuo-spatial sketchpad.

Task 1.

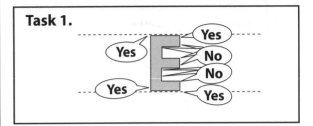

Task 2.

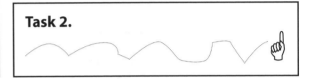

Findings:

Why did participants found it really hard to complete the two tasks simultaneously?

When asked to perform Task 2 while carrying out a verbal task such as saying 'the, the, the', rather than another visual task, participants performed much better. Why?

Conclusions: This investigation could be said to support the existence of separate stores in STM because…

Making links: Which method do you feel is a more successful exploration of working memory model; laboratory investigations such as those by Baddeley et al. (1975a/b) or case studies such as KF (Warrington 1970)?

▶ Lesson notes p. 29

Types of LTM

Colour-code each brick depending on whether the key term relates to episodic, semantic or procedural LTM.

Personal knowledge	Knowledge of skills	e.g. knowing Paris is the capital city of France	Shared knowledge	Automatic
Acquired through practice	Concrete facts	Hippocampus	Emotional tone	Abstract knowledge
Temporal lobe	e.g. remembering your school prom	Cerebellum	e.g. being able to drive a car	Context of event

Deepen your thinking.

- Which types of LTM are labelled explicit (declarative)?

- Can you explain the difference between 'knowing that' and 'knowing how'?

- How has brain imaging research been used to support the suggestion than LTM is comprised of different types of memories?

- What impact does brain imaging research have on our acceptance of the multi-store model as a complete explanation of the structure and process of memory?

Can you create definitions for each type of LTM from these key terms and examples?

▶ Lesson notes p. 30

Making links

Link the point to the conclusion using your knowledge of research into the different types of LTMs.

Brain scanning techniques show different areas of the brain are active when different kinds of LTM are active.		This might explain some cases of memory loss when only some types of LTM are lost but others remain intact.
The case of HM suggests a distinction can be made between procedural and declarative memories.		This showed HM had procedural memory but had no recollection of learning which implies no episodic or semantic LTMs.
Research with Alzheimer's patients has helped psychologists look for double dissociations between memory functions.		Data suggests episodic memories may be a gateway to semantic memory but it is possible for semantic memories to form separately.
Research has often been conducted on living patients or through post mortem analysis of the brain. Both methods may be problematic.		Therefore, research data gathered from samples of patients with brain damage should be treated with caution.

▶ Lesson notes p. 30

Explanations for forgetting

Proactive or retroactive interference?

For each example identify whether the forgetting experienced is due to PI or RI.

Molly recently changed her mobile phone provider but when a friend asks for her new number she found herself reciting her old one.

Ajay spent five years catching the same bus to his secondary school. Now he is attending college he catches a different bus from a different bus stop near his home. When his secondary school asked him to visit them to share his experiences of college life he found he could not remember which bus he needed to catch to get there.

Sam is a keen netball player who recently took part in a four week basketball course. When she next played netball she kept fouling by travelling while in possession of the ball.

Dylan recently visited America for a holiday. He found it hard to adjust to using the currency; he continually thought $5 was the same value as £5.

Researching interference.

Use your knowledge of forgetting and wider understanding of research methods to address the questions below.

Howe (1995) researched interference in four and six year-old children. In the control condition children were given a list of eight pictures to learn while the children undergoing the experimental condition had to learn two picture lists, one after the other. Following an interval of 24 hours children were asked to recall either:

- items from the picture list they had learned (the control group)
- items from only the first picture list they had learnt (half the experimental group)
- items from both of the picture lists they had learnt (half the experimental group).

Results indicated that participants who learned both lists experienced interference during storage of the lists which resulted in the unlearning of the first picture list they had been asked to learn.

| Identify the research design employed in this research study. | Why do you think the researcher chose to use pictures rather than word lists? | What type of interference was demonstrated in this research study? |

Stretch yourself: how would you modify this study if you were researching interference in adults?

Apply your understanding

Apply your knowledge of forgetting to this situation. Aim to use research evidence to develop your answer.

Year six students at a local primary school were taking part in a languages activity day. In the morning they learnt French and were given a short list of French words to learn. In the afternoon they took part in a Spanish lesson. When tested the next day many students recalled Spanish words in the French test.

Use your knowledge of forgetting to explain why the students performed poorly in their test. Include relevant research in your answer.

▶ Lesson notes p. 31

Research into interference

'State the aim of this natural experiment.' (1 mark)

'Identify the levels of the independent variable.' (2 marks)

'Identify the dependent variable.' (2 marks)

'Write a non-directional hypothesis for this experiment.' (3 marks)

Baddeley and Hitch (1977) investigated interference effects in an everyday setting of rugby players recalling the names of the teams they had played against over a rugby season. Some players played in all of the games in the season whereas others missed some games because of injury. The time interval from start to end of the season was the same for all players but the number of intervening games was different for each player because of missed games.

If decay theory is correct then all players should recall a similar percentage of the games played because time alone should cause forgetting.

If interference theory is correct then those players who played most games should forget proportionately more because of interference.

'Explain why this study is a natural experiment.' (3 marks)

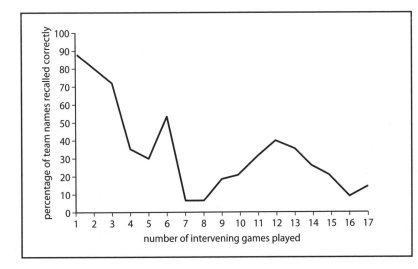

'Explain why the data collected can be seen as support for interference theory.' (3 marks)

Lesson notes p. 31

Investigating cued recall

AIM: to investigate the impact of exposure to cues on recall of items.

RESEARCH DESIGN:

independent measures design

Why was independent measures design chosen for this study?

How will participants be assigned to each group?

PROCEDURE:

Firstly, assign participants to either the control group (free recall condition) or the experimental group (cued recall condition.

Next, give participants time to learn a list of 48 words belonging to 12 categories e.g. fruit – orange, fruit – pear, sport – football, sport – tennis.

Now ask participants to recall the 48 words. Participants in the control condition should be provided with a blank piece of paper for this. Participants in the experimental group should be provided with a recall sheet showing the 12 categories (to cue recall of the words).

State the operationalised independent variable.

How long will you give participants to learn and later recall words?

Why is it important to standardize the procedure?

FINDINGS: compile data from the two groups to determine who has recalled more of the words. Create a graph to display your findings and calculate measure of central tendency.

State the operationalised dependent variable.

CONCLUSION: What conclusions can you draw from your data? Can you relate your findings to previous research into retrieval failure?

▶ Lesson notes p. 31

Investigating cued recall – research materials

Items to be recalled.

Fruit – orange	Pet – dog	Drink – tea	ICT – computer
Fruit – pear	Pet – cat	Drink – coffee	ICT – printer
Fruit – banana	Pet – hamster	Drink – milk	ICT – mouse
Fruit – apple	Pet – rabbit	Drink – water	ICT – monitor
Sport – football	Food – pizza	Country – France	Veg – peas
Sport – tennis	Food – sandwich	Country – India	Veg – carrot
Sport – rugby	Food – salad	Country – America	Veg – mushroom
Sport – badminton	Food – curry	Country – Greece	Veg – celery
Toy – teddy	Zoo – lion	Home – bathroom	Flower – daisy
Toy – dolly	Zoo – penguin	Home – kitchen	Flower – rose
Toy – jigsaw	Zoo – monkey	Home – bedroom	Flower – tulip
Toy – ball	Zoo – elephant	Home – dining room	Flower – buttercup

Recall sheet for participants in the experimental group.

Fruit –	Pet –	Drink –	ICT –
Fruit –	Pet –	Drink –	ICT –
Fruit –	Pet –	Drink –	ICT –
Fruit –	Pet –	Drink –	ICT –
Sport –	Food –	Country –	Veg –
Sport –	Food –	Country –	Veg –
Sport –	Food –	Country –	Veg –
Sport –	Food –	Country –	Veg –
Toy –	Zoo –	Home –	Flower –
Toy –	Zoo –	Home –	Flower –
Toy –	Zoo –	Home –	Flower –
Toy –	Zoo –	Home –	Flower –

▶ Lesson notes p. 31

Evaluating research into retrieval failure

There are a number of points to consider when evaluating research into retrieval failure. Complete the diagram shown below to revise the central evaluative points as well as those extra details that add depth to your critique.

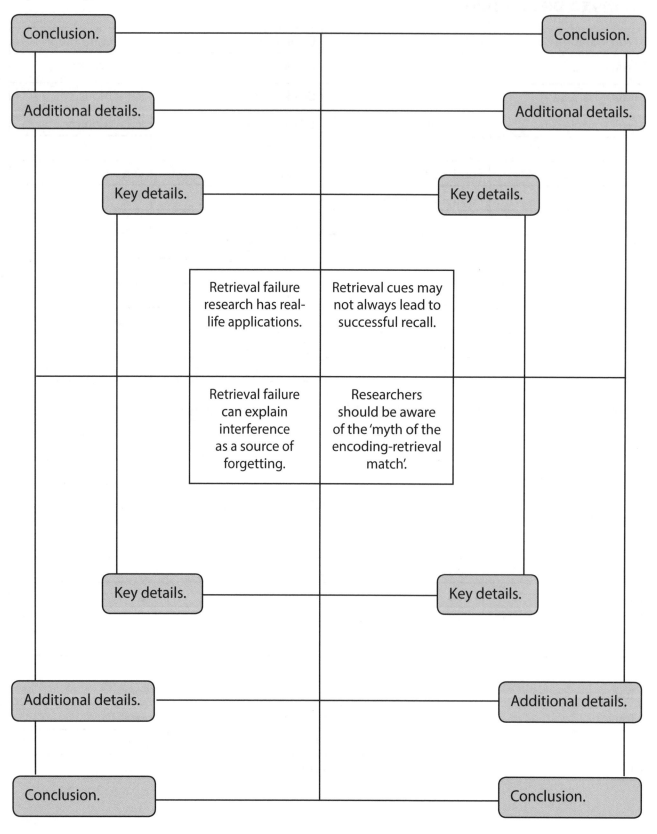

Conclusion.

Additional details.

Key details.

Retrieval failure research has real-life applications.	Retrieval cues may not always lead to successful recall.
Retrieval failure can explain interference as a source of forgetting.	Researchers should be aware of the 'myth of the encoding-retrieval match'.

Key details.

Additional details.

Conclusion.

▶ Lesson notes p. 32

Loftus and Palmer (1974) –
The broken glass study

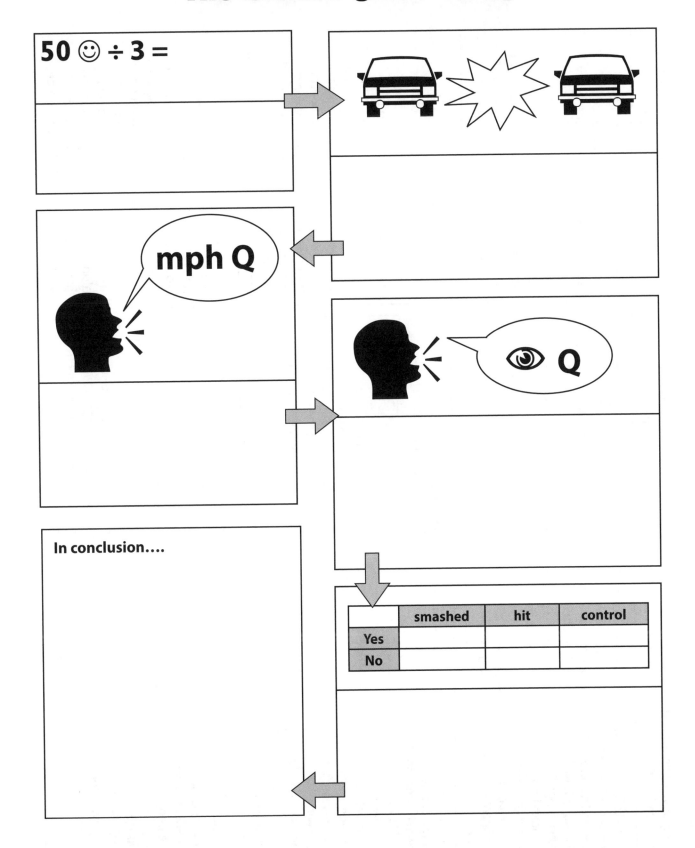

50 ☺ ÷ 3 =

mph Q

In conclusion....

	smashed	hit	control
Yes			
No			

▶ Lesson notes p. 32

Evaluating research into misleading information

Creating developed evaluations that are specific to the topic you are discussing is vital if you wish to access the higher levels of the mark scheme. Match each Point to the relevant Evidence and Expansion, then corresponding Link comment, to form effective evaluation paragraphs.

Link – This might have implications for research into EWT conducted in laboratory settings. If researchers only target student populations then we may not gain an accurate understanding of the effect of misleading information for wider age ranges. For example, do children also find it difficult to monitor the source of their information about an event?

Link – This study shows how misleading information can create an inaccurate memory which is similar to the false memory of broken glass that Loftus created in some participants using the verb 'smashed'. However, the Disneyland study could be considered an improvement on the previous procedure as it demonstrated the power of misleading information on a meaningful memory from childhood rather than memory of a film clip.

Link – From these studies it seems research conducted with participants who have experienced real-life crimes do provide accurate eyewitness testimony. Could it be that the importance placed on the events they are witnessing strengthens their memory for the event and so the memory is more resistant to misleading information? This research also suggests that we could treat the findings of laboratory studies of EWT with caution.

Evidence – Foster et al (1994) found that if participants thought they were watching a real-life robbery, and also thought that their responses would influence the trial, then their identification of the robber was more accurate.

Expansion – Furthermore, Yuille and Cutshall (1986) found 13 witnesses of an actual armed robbery in Canada gave accurate details of the event when interviewed four months later. Their interview statements were compared to the detailed reports they gave at the time of witnessing the robbery.

Evidence – Lindsay (1990) states a witness acquires information about an event from two sources: what they observe and subsequent suggestions (misleading information).

Expansion – Research has found that compared to younger people, elderly witnesses have difficulty remembering the source of the information they can recall. Therefore, they become more vulnerable to the effect of misleading information when giving eyewitness testimony (Schacter 1991).

Evidence – In one study college students were asked to evaluate advertising material about Disneyland. Embedded in this material was misleading information about either Bugs Bunny (who is a Warner Bros. not Disney character) or Ariel from The Little Mermaid (this cartoon was not created during the participants' childhood). Participants were assigned to either the Bugs group, Ariel group or a control group with no misleading information. All participants had visited Disneyland previously. It was found that participants in the Bugs or Ariel group were more likely to have reported meeting these characters when they had visited Disneyland (Braun et al. (2002).

Point – Loftus' research, such as the five verbs study and the broken glass study, have been further supported by studies into the effect of misleading information on participants' recall of an event.

Point – Loftus' research suggested that EWT was generally inaccurate and therefore unreliable. However, not all researchers agree with conclusions derived from laboratory experiments.

Point – Individual differences may mean some people are more (or less) vulnerable to misleading information when giving eyewitness testimonies.

▶ Lesson notes p. 33

The effect of anxiety on the accuracy of EWT

What is meant by the term 'weapon focus effect'?

Describe research that suggests anxiety can have a negative effect on the petrol station staff's recall of the robbery.

Masked robbers stole cash from tills in dawn raid at local petrol station.

In the early hours of Saturday morning armed robbers, disguised in masks, burst into the local 24-hour petrol station and demanded cash from the tills and cigarettes stored behind the counter. Shocked staff had to endure a ten-minute encounter as the criminals pointed guns and shouted abuse as they filled bags with the money and cigarettes. As the gunmen fled staff called the police and statements were taken. When interviewed by our newspaper a few days later one worker, who wishes to remain anonymous, told us 'they seemed like big guys, I couldn't see their faces because of the masks but by their build and deep voices I guessed they were male. I think one might have had blonde hair and another had a scar on his left wrist. To be honest all I could look at was where their guns were pointing.

Describe research that suggests anxiety may have had a positive effect on the petrol station staff's recall of the robbery.

Why might some of the staff at the petrol station have a better recall of the robbery than other members of staff who also witnessed the crime?

▶ Lesson notes p. 33

The cognitive interview

Match the **cognitive interview component** to the **example** and rationale behind its use.

Mental reinstatement	Report everything	Change the order	Change the perspective

> Even little details may be important. Please try to recall as much as you can, even if it doesn't seem relevant to the event.

> Imagine you were watching events from the opposite side of the road. What do you think you would have seen if you were standing there?

> This may be difficult but try to report events in reverse order. Start at the last thing you remember seeing, then work backwards to the beginning.

> Think back to that day. What had you been doing? What was the weather like? How did you feel? Picture the scene in your mind.

Anderson & Pichert (1978) found when participants recalled a scene from the perspective of a house buyer and a burglar the kind of details they recalled varied depending on the character's perspective.

Recalling events backwards helps a person focus on the actual details they witnesses rather than following a pre-existing set of ideas about the situation or location where the event took place.

Memories are interconnected with one another. Recalling a small, insignificant detail may cue memory of an important item. In addition, little details can be pieced together from a number of witnesses to build a more complete version of events.

Asking witnesses to recall their emotions during the event and place themselves back into the scene can help make memories more accessible as the emotions and context act as cues for recall.

One goal of the cognitive interview is to overcome pre-existing schemes because…

Think a little deeper

Evaluating the effectiveness of the cognitive interview

There are three forms your evaluation of the cognitive interview technique could take:

- Consider the effectiveness
- Discuss the practical issues of using this technique
- Assess their value in real-life situations.

Stretch: use these ideas to make a final link (L) comment once each PEE has been formed.

Match the Point (e.g. The CI technique seems effective), to the evidence (e.g. Köhnken found a 34% increase in recall) and the expansion (e.g. This shows CI is a more effective method).

Point – Evidence – Explanation.

These findings suggest the CI technique could be used to develop a new approach in interviewing witnesses in Brazil. Hopefully, this will lead to a reduction in the amount of miscarriages of justice.

Point – Evidence – Explanation.

Thames Valley Police do not use the 'changing perspectives component' in their cognitive interviews, while others tend to use only 'reinstate context' and 'report everything'.

Point – Evidence – Explanation.

Kebbell & Wagstaff found many police officers did not use the CI technique in less serious crimes as they did not have the time to carry out this type of interview. Police often used strategies to deliberately limit an eyewitness report to the minimum amount of information deemed necessary by the officer.

Point – Evidence – Explanation.

Therefore, while CI may produce a vast amount of information, it may not always be practical or helpful in terms of allowing the police to efficiently investigate incidents, especially those seen as less serious.

Point – Evidence – Explanation.

Research into the effectiveness of the CI technique has been useful in improving the interview techniques in Brazil where police traditionally use interrogation, torture and ill treatment.

Point – Evidence – Explanation.

Stein & Memon showed university cleaning staff a video of an abduction. Compared to standard police interviews the CI showed an increased amount of correct recall. For example, detailed descriptions of the man holding the gun were obtained from the witnesses.

Point – Evidence – Explanation.

Not all police forces use the same procedure or components in their cognitive interviews.

Point – Evidence – Explanation.

The CI takes longer to complete than the traditional interview technique.

▶ Lesson notes p. 34

Confidence ratings

Memory topic	I can identify key terminology in this topic.	I can give a detailed outline of research.	I can create effective evaluations of research.	I can apply my knowledge of this topic to novel scenarios.
The multi-store model: Sensory register, STM and LTM				
The multi-store model: features of each store – coding, capacity and duration				
Types of LTM: Episodic, semantic, procedural				
The working memory model: central executive, phonological loop, visuo-spatial sketchpad and episodic buffer				
The working memory model: features of the model – coding and capacity.				
Explanations of forgetting: Proactive interference				
Explanations of forgetting: Retroactive interference				
Explanations of forgetting: Retrieval failure				

▶ Lesson notes p. 35

Confidence ratings

Memory topic	I can identify key terminology in this topic.	I can give a detailed outline of research.	I can create effective evaluations of research.	I can apply my knowledge of this topic to novel scenarios.
Accuracy of EWT: Misleading information – leading questions				
Accuracy of EWT: Misleading information – post event discussion				
Accuracy of EWT: Anxiety				
Improving the accuracy of EWT: The Cognitive Interview				

My strengths in relation to learning this topic were:

Areas of my learning I need to develop during the next topic are:

▶ Lesson notes p. 35

Caregiver-infant interaction crossword

ACROSS

1. When two people interact they tend to mirror what the other is doing in terms of facial and body movements (two words, 13,9). Fullstops missing

2. Meltzoff and Moore (1977) found that infants as young as 2-3 weeks _____ specific facial and hand gestures.

3. Infants demonstrating synchrony at three days old suggests that the behaviour is not learnt, instead, that the response is _____.

DOWN

1. Responding to the action of another with a similar action.

2. An emotional bond between two people.

3. The period of a child's life before speech.

4. Communication without words.

5. In a research study these would be examples: mouth opening, termination of mouth opening, tongue protrusion and termination of tongue protrusion (two words, 11,10). Fullstops missing.

▶ Lesson notes p. 36

Plenary questions

In two years, when your memory of this lesson has decayed, what fact are you most likely to remember?

What advice could you give to expectant parents as a result of this lesson?

What are the three most important key words from this lesson and what do they mean?

Define interactional synchrony in less than 16 words.

Bullet point three details of Meltzoff and Moore's (1977) procedure.

Summarise in one sentence why imitation behaviours are thought to be innate (not learnt).

Define reciprocity in less than 16 words.

What was the most difficult part of this lesson to understand? Why?

Pick one aspect of Meltzoff and Moore's (1977) study and explain how it helped to improve the validity of the study.

How does this lesson fit in the overall attachment topic?

▶ Lesson notes p. 36

Which stage of attachment?

Task:

Use highlighter pens or the boxes on the right to indicate which statements belong to which stage of attachment (there are four stages). Once you have grouped the stages of attachment, think about what each stage might be called.

Infants produce similar responses to all objects, whether animate or inanimate.	
At the end of this stage, infants begin to show a greater preference for social stimuli, such as a smiling face.	
Reciprocity and interactional synchrony are playing a role in establishing the infant's relationship with others.	
Infants start to become more social and enjoy being with people.	
Infants prefer human company to inanimate objects.	
Infants can distinguish between familiar and unfamiliar people.	
They are still relatively easily comforted by anyone and do not show stranger anxiety.	
Infants start to show separation anxiety, when one particular person puts them down.	
They show especial joy at reunion with their main caregiver and are most comforted by that person.	
At this point, infants are said to have formed a specific attachment to one person, their primary attachment figure.	
Stranger anxiety increases.	
The infant develops a wider circle of attachments depending on how many consistent relationships he or she has.	
The infants show separation anxiety in their secondary attachments.	

▶ Lesson notes p. 36

Maximising your outline marks

Imagine that you have been set the following examination question:

- **Outline the stages of attachment identified by Schaffer** *(6 marks)*

The answer below is accurate but may not gain full marks because it lacks detail. Use the table below to make *small additions* to this answer that take it to a 'level 3' maximum mark answer.

In stage 1*1, from birth to two months, infants produce similar responses to all objects*2. Towards the end of this period, infants are beginning to show a greater preference for smiling faces. Reciprocity*3 and interactional synchrony*4 are playing a role in establishing the infant's relationships with others.

In stage 2*5, infants become more social. They prefer human company to inanimate objects and can distinguish between familiar and unfamiliar people. However, they do not yet show stranger anxiety*6.

In stage 3*7, most infants at seven months begin to protest when one particular person puts them down*8. Equally, they show especial joy at reunion with that person. They are said to have formed a specific attachment to one person, their primary attachment figure*9. Around the same time, the infant also begins to display stranger anxiety. Shaffer and Emerson found primary attachments were not formed with the person who spent more time with the child*10.

In stage 4*11 the infant also develops a wider circle of attachments: with their other parent, to grandparents, siblings, other relatives, friends and/or neighbours*12.

---

*1	
*2	
*3	
*4	
*5	
*6	
*7	
*8	
*9	
*10	
*11	
*12	

▶ Lesson notes p. 37

The role of the father: True or False?

1. Fathers play the role of secondary attachment figure.	T F
Extension / correction (circle)	

2. The key factor in establishing the principle caregiver role is the amount of time spent with the infant.	T F
Extension / correction (circle)	

3. Most men may not be psychologically equipped to form an intense attachment.	T F
Extension / correction (circle)	

4. Biological factors may explain why men are less equipped.	T F
Extension / correction (circle)	

5. There are no longer sex-stereotypes that affect male behaviour, e.g. 'it is feminine to be sensitive to others'.	T F
Extension / correction (circle)	

▶ Lesson notes p. 37

The role of the father:
True or False? continued...

6. There is evidence which contradicts the idea that men are less sensitive than women.	T F
Extension / correction (circle)	

7. Research suggests that fathers are less playful, less active and less likely to provide challenging situations for their children.	T F
Extension / correction (circle)	

8. Mothers tend to play a more conventional parenting role.	T F
Extension / correction (circle)	

9. A lack of sensitivity in fathers could be seen as a positive.	T F
Extension / correction (circle)	

▶ Lesson notes p. 37

Brief summaries

Making notes on the **evaluations of animal studies on attachment** in these 'briefs' will force you to summarise the information. Use your textbook (e.g. pg. 00 of *Complete Companion*) to help you. Try and include the key words written beneath the 'briefs' in your summaries.

Lorenz's (1935) research

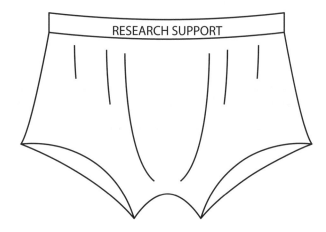

RESEARCH SUPPORT

Guiton (1966), predisposition, critical window

IMPRINTING SAME AS LEARNING?

Nervous system, 'plastic and forgiving', reverse

Harlow's (1959) research

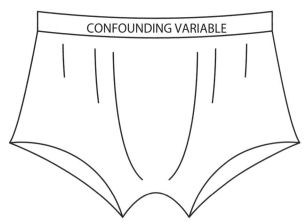

CONFOUNDING VARIABLE

Two heads, independent variable, validity

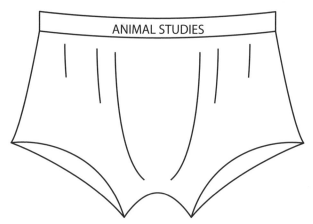

ANIMAL STUDIES

Generalise, conscious decisions, mirrored

▶ Lesson notes p. 37

Classical conditioning equation: What's missing?

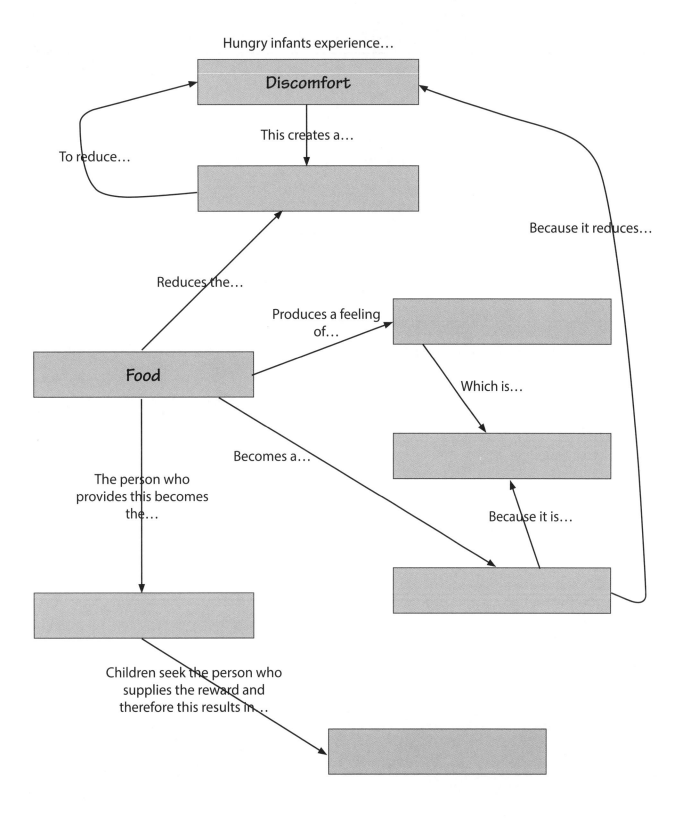

Hungry infants experience…

Discomfort

To reduce…

This creates a…

Reduces the…

Produces a feeling of…

Food

Which is…

Becomes a…

The person who provides this becomes the…

Because it is…

Because it reduces…

Children seek the person who supplies the reward and therefore this results in…

▶ Lesson notes p. 38

Bowlby — Connect 5

Social releasers...

Link…

Adaptive/Innate...

Link…

Critical Period...

Link…

Sensitivity/Reciprocity/Interactional synchrony...

Link…

Monotropy...

Burger evaluation skills

This technique ensures that you *use* research studies to evaluate Bowlby's theory, rather than just *describe* the research. Your job is to explain how and why the study supports or contradicts the theory.

Top of the burger: Here you write a simple sentence that introduces the evaluation to the examiner. Try and be specific about which element of Bowlby's theory you are evaluating, e.g. adaptive nature, social releasers, critical period, internal working model, continuity hypothesis, monotropy, the caregiver hypothesis etc.

Middle of the burger: Write a brief summary of the research. Only write what is necessary to your evaluation, procedural details can be left out if they are not required to make your general evaluative point. For example, the sampling technique may not be relevant to the evaluation point you want to make and so it is not necessary to include.

Bottom of the burger: Here is where you show off your understanding. How and why does this support Bowlby? What would Bowlby have predicted? Why? How do these results correspond with those predictions?

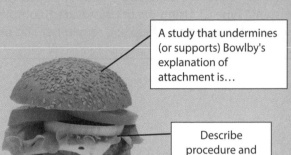

A study that undermines (or supports) Bowlby's explanation of attachment is…

Describe procedure and findings of study.

This undermines (or supports) Bowlby's explanation of attachment because…

Use these studies and Handout 62 to evaluate Bowlby's theory of attachment using the burger technique…

Sroufe et al. (2005)

The Minnesota parent-child study followed participants from infancy to late adolescence and found that individuals who were classified as securely attached in infancy were rated for social competence later in childhood and were found to be less isolated and more empathetic.

Belsky and Rovine (1987)

Belsky and Rovine (1987) found that infants aged between 1 and 3 days who had signs of behavioural instability (i.e. had a 'difficult' temperament) were later judged to be more likely to have developed an insecure attachment.

Rutter et al. (2010)

Rutter et al. (2010) followed orphaned Romanian children who were unable to form attachments due to the extremely poor conditions of their institutional care. They found that, even when adopted, the orphans found it very difficult to form attachments if they had failed to form an attachment before being 6 months of age.

Czech Twins

The Czech twins were 'discovered' at the age of 7. They had been locked up and isolated from the outside world and abused by their stepmother since birth. When discovered, they had no language ability at all. After loving care from two sisters, by the age of 14 the Czech twins showed normal social and intellectual functioning, and were able to form meaningful attachments.

► Lesson notes p. 39

Insecure attachments — spot the difference

Don't forget that there are **two** types of insecure attachment: Insecure-avoidant (Type A), and Insecure-resistant (Type C). Using the grids provided, complete this 'Spot the difference' page with simple drawings (e.g. use stick people) to help you remember and understand those differences!

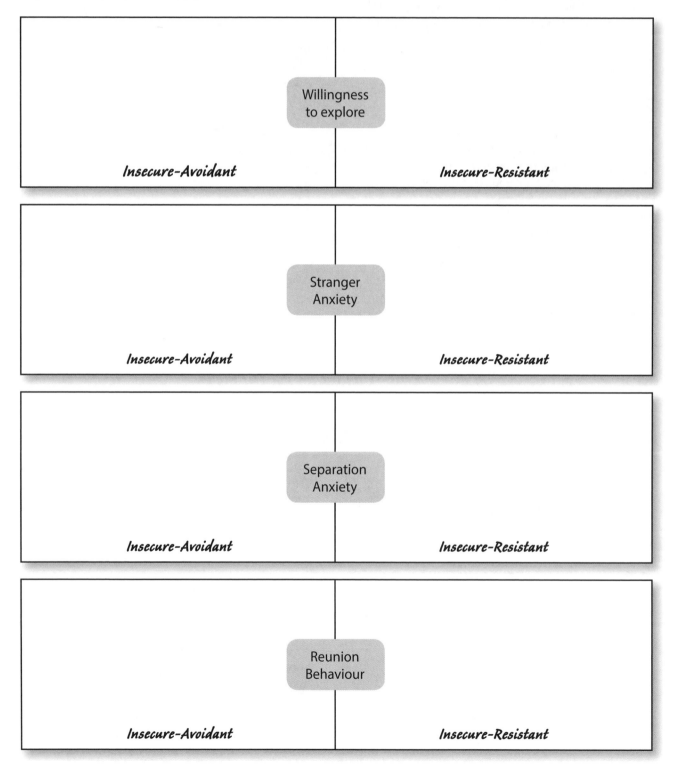

▶ Lesson notes p. 40

Attachment types: Table mats

Insecure-Resistant

General description:	Separation anxiety:	Reunion behaviour:	Stranger anxiety:	Exploration behaviour:	Percentage of infants:

Insecure-Avoidant

General description:	Separation anxiety:	Reunion behaviour:	Stranger anxiety:	Exploration behaviour:	Percentage of infants:

Secure Attachment

General description:	Separation anxiety:	Reunion behaviour:	Stranger anxiety:	Exploration behaviour:	Percentage of infants:

► Lesson notes p. 40

Attachment types: Table mats

May show some distress when the caregiver leaves the room, but unlikely to cry.	Happy to explore whether the caregiver is present or not.
Enthusiastically seek caregiver when they return.	Tend to avoid social interaction and intimacy with others.
Show some distress when with a stranger and caregiver is absent.	Tend to show intense distress when separated from their caregiver.
Show exploration behaviour when the caregiver is present, but unlikely to when caregiver is absent.	The child may show conflicting desires for and against seeking contact; they may seek the caregiver but angrily resist being picked up.
Harmonious and cooperative interactions with caregiver.	Tend to respond to strangers with intense distress and anxiety.
Show little reaction when caregiver leaves the room and they are separated.	Unlikely to explore whether the caregiver is present or not.
Do not seek caregiver when they return.	Both seek *and* resist intimacy and social interaction.
Show little anxiety towards strangers, whether the caregiver is present or not.	66%
12%	22%

▶ Lesson notes p. 40

Cultural variations in attachment

Japan

Japan is a collectivist country. Child-rearing appears to place a much larger value and emphasis on developing close family relationships. As such, Japanese mothers almost never leave their child with a stranger, and are rarely separated from their child. Mothers are generally highly responsive to their child's needs.

Germany

German cultures require distance between parents and the child.

The ideal is an independent, non-clingy infant who does not make demands on the parents but rather unquestionably obeys their commands.

German parents tend to value independence – they want self-reliant children who can 'stand on their own-two feet' and not make demands on them.

▶ Lesson notes p. 41

Cultural variations in attachment

It stands to reason that different cultures will place different emphasis on child-rearing values. The relationship between child and primary attachment figure will vary across cultures because of different beliefs about the qualities that should be nurtured in a child.

Based on the cultural values of these cultures, how do you think the 'average' infant will behave in the 'Strange Situation'? How will this affect the %s of each attachment type?

Country	SS Behavioural Categories	Justification
Japan	*Willingness to explore (circle):* Low / Medium / High *Separation anxiety (circle):* Low / Distress / Intense Distress *Stranger anxiety (circle):* Low / Medium / High *Reunion behaviour (circle):* Little / Enthusiastic / Mixed	
Country	**SS Behavioural Categories**	**Justification**
Germany	*Willingness to explore (circle):* Low / Medium / High *Separation anxiety (circle):* Low / Distress / Intense Distress *Stranger anxiety (circle):* Low / Medium / High *Reunion behaviour (circle):* Little / Enthusiastic / Mixed	
	Based on the above, what % of each attachment type do you think Germany will have? *Type A:* *Type B:* *Type C:* *Type D:*	

▶ Lesson notes p. 41

Developing your maternal deprivation evaluations

*Always make sure that you **elaborate** (explain and develop) your evaluation points. Match the evaluation point on the left to its development in the middle, and then further elaboration on the right. These evaluations for the maternal deprivation theory illustrate how to get your evaluation points into the higher mark bands.*

Evaluation Point

Development

Further development

1. One strength of Bowlby's ideas is that they had real-world applications.

This is because the term does not take into account whether the child's attachment bond had formed but been broken, or in fact had never formed in the first place. He argued that if the latter, the lack of emotional bond would have more serious consequences.

As such, he used the term 'privation' to refer to the failure to form attachment and 'deprivation' to refer to when one had formed but been lost.

2. Rutter (1981) argued that Bowlby's view of deprivation was too simplistic.

Bifulco et al. (1992) studied women who had experienced separation from their mothers at an early age because of maternal death or temporary separation of more than a year. Bifulco et al. found that about 25% later experienced depression or anxiety, compared to 15% in a control group. The effects were much greater when the separation occurred before the child was 6.

This supports the idea that maternal deprivation leads to a vulnerability in terms of negative outcomes later in life. It also supports Bowlby's notion of a critical period.

3. A further evaluation relates to the fact that there are individual differences in the reaction to separation.

In the past, children were separated from their parents when they spent time in hospital. Visiting was discouraged or even forbidden.

This suggests that the effects of maternal deprivation are not experienced in the same way and do not affect children in a uniform way.

4. Research studies do tend to support the idea that maternal deprivation can have long-term effects.

This is supported by Barrett (1997) who reviewed various studies on separation and found that securely attached children sometimes cope reasonably well, whereas insecurely attached children become especially distressed.

Bowlby's research led to social change in the way that children were cared for in hospital.

▶ Lesson notes p. 43

Psychology storytime

'Happy birthday', said Katie's Mum as she handed over a box wrapped in bright pink paper with a matching bow secured to the top.

Katie had been waiting for the date – 1 May 2040 – for what felt like forever. Her tenth birthday had finally arrived and she was silently praying she already knew what lay beneath the pretty pink wrapping.

Tearing off the paper to reveal the familiar, friendly face of the bear staring back at her, Katie said: 'Wow, thanks Mum!'

Excitement bubbled up inside her as she read on the back of the box how she could make her very own, real-life, walking, talking, Edward bear. Katie had become quite attached to her friend Lucy's bear; he was much friendlier than her mother's surly home robot, Robert.

Katie could barely wait for her birthday celebrations to finish so she could focus on the important task ahead of her. With all the industry of a steam train Katie forged ahead with her mission: cutting material, stuffing and sewing, until her work was done.

Inserting Edward's computer chip was the finishing touch. After clicking the chip into place, Katie held the finished article aloft. She eyed her creation as it sprang to life, blinked, and cautiously took in its surroundings. Katie followed Edward's eyes as they scanned the room and came back to rest on her face.

Something about the way Katie had sewn Edward's eyes slightly too close together and the way the stuffing didn't quite reach the full length of his limbs, gave Edward a somewhat haunted, empty look. Edward didn't look like Lucy's bear. His eyes didn't twinkle with cheeky charm, they glinted with what Katie thought, but didn't like to admit, was slightly sinister intent. Disappointed with the fruit of her labour, Katie stuffed Edward into a dark cupboard, leaving him to contemplate his bleak future.

Edward soon began to wonder if dark loneliness was all life had to offer him. He decided to leave Katie's house in search of something more.

Finding himself amongst humans and other robotic creatures was difficult for Edward. If anyone approached him he would respond with anger, pushing any potential friends away until they no longer tried to get to know him. He had also found himself with an inexplicable desire to destroy anything he came into contact with.

Since leaving Katie's house, Edward had taken to watching her from across the road. Seeing Katie playing happily with her friend Lucy and Lucy's bear filled Edward with rage.

Following Lucy home, Edward plotted to put an end to their fun for good.

He was about to remove and destroy the computer chip in Lucy's bear, when the light snapped on, illuminating his dark deed.

Lucy shrieked in horror, immediately summoning Katie to confront Edward.

When Katie arrived she demanded: 'Why have you done this?'

'Because of you', Edward replied.

A shiver ran through Katie as she absorbed his words.

► Lesson notes p. 46

Love Quiz!

A short version of the love quiz
• • • • • • • • • •

Question 1:

Which of the following best describes your parents' relationship with each other?

(a) My parents have a caring relationship and are affectionate with each other.

(b) My parents appear to have a good enough relationship with each other but are not especially affectionate.

(c) My parents have a reasonable relationship and are sometimes affectionate towards each other.

Question 2:

Which of the following best describes your relationship with your mother?

(a) My mother treats me with respect and is accepting and not demanding. She is confident about herself.

(b) My mother is humourous, likable and respected by others. She treats me with respect.

(c) My mother treats me with respect but is sometimes cold and rejecting.

Question 3:

Which of the following best describes your relationship with your father?

(a) My father is sometimes affectionate but can be unfair.

(b) My father is caring, affectionate and humorous.

(c) My father is reasonably caring.

Question 4:

Select the statement that best describes your experiences of intimacy.

(a) I find that others are reluctant to get as close as I would like.

(b) I find it relatively easy to get close to others and am comfortable depending on them and having them depend on me.

(c) I am somewhat uncomfortable being close to others; I find it difficult to trust them completely, difficult to allow myself to depend on them.

Question 5:

Select the statement that best describes your experiences of intimacy.

(a) I don't often worry about being abandoned or about someone getting too close to me.

(b) I often worry that my partner doesn't really love me or won't want to stay with me.

(c) I am nervous when anyone gets too close, and often romantic partners want me to be more intimate than I feel comfortable being.

Question 6:

Select the statement that best describes your experiences of intimacy.

(a) I enjoy relationships but am generally quite self-sufficient.

(b) I have been lucky in love and most of my relationships are rewarding. I still like the people I was involved with.

(c) At times I wish I could just melt into someone so we could get beyond our separateness.

Question 7:

Select the statement that best describes your attitudes towards love.

(a) The kind of head-over-heels love that is depicted in novels and in the movies does not exist in real life.

(b) It is easy to fall in love and I frequently find myself beginning to fall in love, though I am not sure that it really is love.

(c) Love is a positive and real experience.

Question 8:

Select the statement that best describes your attitudes towards love.

(a) It is rare to find a person one can really fall in love with.

(b) In some relationships romantic love never fades.

(c) Most of us could love many people equally well, there is no 'one true love'.

Question 9:

Select the statement that best describes your attitudes towards love.

(a) I think that romantic feelings do wax and wane.

(b) Romantic feelings wax and wane but at times they reach the intensity experienced at the start of a relationship.

(c) Intense romantic love is common at the start of a relationship but rarely lasts.

▶ Lesson notes p. 47

What's going on?

Imagine that a researcher conducts a longitudinal attachment study on 30 infants starting at 12 months of age. Initially, they use the Strange Situation observation technique to classify whether those infants have secure or insecure attachments with their parents/guardians.

They then test the same individuals' romantic adult attachment at 20 years of age using structured interviews.

At both stages the researcher converted the attachment behaviours indicated into an attachment score, with a high score indicating more secure attachment behaviours shown.

The researcher correlated infant attachment scores with their adult attachment scores in order to discover whether there had been **attachment stability,** i.e. whether the attachment styles had remained the same over the course of their life.

R was calculated at +.52. The scattergram below shows the results.

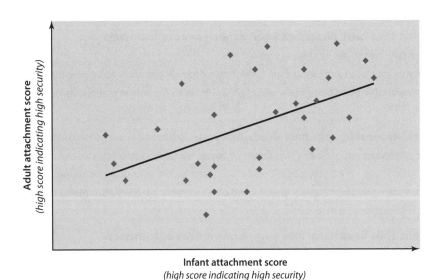

Infant attachment score
(high score indicating high security)

Tasks:

* What can you remember about the terms **secure attachment**, **insecure attachment**, and **internal working model** (Bowlby)?

* Describe the findings of the correlation study described and illustrated above.

* What would you conclude about the influence of childhood experiences on adult relationships from this study?

* What potential limitations are there to this study, for instance, in terms of the methodology used?

▶ Lesson notes p. 48

Confidence ratings

Attachment topic				
Caregiver interactions in humans: Reciprocity and interactional synchrony				
Stages of attachment identified by Schaffer				
Multiple attachments and the role of the father				
Animal studies of attachment: Lorenz and Harlow				
Explanations of attachment: Learning theory				
Explanations of attachment: Bowlby's monotropic theory. The concepts of a critical period and internal working model				
Ainsworth's 'Strange Situation': Types of attachment: Secure, insecure-avoidant and insecure-resistant				
Cultural variations in attachment, including van Ijzendoorn				

► Lesson notes p. 48

Confidence ratings

Bowlby's theory of maternal deprivation				

Romanian orphan studies: Effects of institutionalisation				

The influence of early attachment in childhood and adult relationships, including the role of the internal working model				

- **My strengths in relation to learning this topic were:**

- **Areas of my learning I need to develop during the next topic are:**

▶ Lesson notes p. 48

Statistical infrequency

Researchers placed questionnaires in a local vet's waiting room. Customers could choose to complete the questionnaire while waiting for their pets to be treated by the vet.

The questionnaire required participants to self-report the level of fear they would experience when asked to hold different animals. A rating of 1 indicated no fear at all, a rating of 10 indicated intense fear.

Data for fear of spiders was compiled in the graph shown opposite.

A graph to show self-reported fear of spiders.

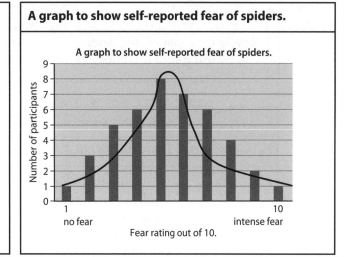

A graph to show self-reported fear of spiders.

What sampling technique was used by the researchers?
a) Random sampling
b) Volunteer sampling
c) Opportunity sampling

> Evaluate: What limitations might the researchers face using this sampling technique?

What question type was used to assess fear of spiders?
a) Closed question
b) Open question

> Identify: What type of data would this question type gather?

What distribution does the graph show?
a) Negatively skewed
b) Normal distribution
c) Positively skewed

> Analyse: What was the mode in this data set?

Frank was visiting the vet for his cat's annual check-up. He rated himself at level 9 for fear of spiders. Ralph, a tarantula owner, also completed the questionnaire and rated himself at level 1. Why might both participants be considered abnormal by the statistical infrequency definition of abnormality?

While visiting the vet surgery with her hamster, Molly completed the questionnaire and rated herself 7 out of 10 for fear of spiders. What challenges do researchers face in classifying her fear as normal or abnormal?

▶ Lesson notes p. 49

Deviation from Social Norms

Each task progresses in difficulty. Read all the tasks before choosing a task that you feel challenges your understanding, aim to complete this task and move at least one level higher by using your textbook, class notes, internet research or by collaborating with others.

Knowledge	Identify two social norms common to UK culture.
Comprehension	Explain the difference between social norms and statistical norms.
Application	Aisha has had a lucky teddy since primary school. She has always performed well in school assessments and formal examinations and attributes her academic success to having her lucky teddy in her bag at all times. Now she is off to university and is taking her teddy with her, to lectures, the library, he'll sit at her desk when completing essays and hide in her bag during formal exams. She feels she simply cannot pass assessments without teddy by her side. What aspects of Aisha's behaviour might be considered a deviation from social norms?
Analysing	In 1895 the playwright Oscar Wilde was jailed for two years for homosexuality, which was defined by law as illegal at the time. Homosexuality was classified as abnormal and regarded as a mental disorder. In 1967 The Sexual Offences Bill decriminalised homosexual acts between consenting adults (21 and over) in the privacy of their own home. Since 21 December 2005 homosexual couples have been able to have their relationship legally recognised as a civil partnership and the first same-sex marriages occurred in March 2014. What can you infer about social norms from this example?
Evaluating	**Point:** Thomas Szasz (1974) claimed that the concept of mental illness was simply a way to exclude non-conformists from society. **Point:** Making judgements on deviance is often related to the context in which the behaviour occurs. Use PEEL structure to create two effective evaluations of deviation from social norms as a definition of abnormality. P – state your evaluative point. Ev – give evidence to develop the limitation. Ex – explain how evidence comments on point made, give additional research. L – relate back to the usefulness of deviation from social norms as a definition.
Creating	Identify a number of public figures whose behaviour might be said to be unusual compared to the majority of society. Create a continuum to consider how far removed they are from social norms. Consider whether the deviation from social norms definition can be applied to their behaviour: what factors should you consider before reaching a conclusion?

▶ Lesson notes p. 50

Failure to function adequately

Your exam essays are marked out of 12 in the AS route and 16 in the A Level route. At AS, to access the top mark band (level 4), your AO3 discussion points need to be effective; the A Level route calls for thorough and effective evaluations. This means you need to make developed evaluations that are explicitly linked to the concept being discussed. This task requires you to match up the evaluation points from left to right in order to increase the effectiveness of your AO3 discussion points.

Weak → Basic → Reasonable → Effective

Weak	Basic	Reasonable	Effective
Who judges what functioning adequately is?	The DSM includes an assessment of ability to function called WHODAS (World Health Organisation Disability Assessment).	On the other hand, it may be that the individual is quite content with the situation and/or unaware that they are not coping. It is others that are uncomfortable with this behaviour and then judge it to be abnormal.	This may explain why lower-class and non-white patients are more often diagnosed with mental disorders; because their lifestyle is 'non-traditional' and may result in a judgement of failing to function adequately.
What may seem maladaptive to us may be adaptive to the individual.	If a patient is experiencing difficulties managing day-to-day life then he or she may themselves determine that this behaviour is undesirable.	This involves individuals rating each item on a scale of 1 to 5 and resulting in an overall score out of 180.	Some individuals who cross-dress make a living out of it, yet transvestism is in the list of mental disorders and is generally regarded as abnormal.
Can you really apply ideas of functioning in one culture to another culture?	This definition will likely result in different diagnoses when applied to people from different cultures.	For example, some mental disorders, (e.g. eating disorders) may lead to welcome extra attention for the individual.	For example, many schizophrenics do not feel they have a problem, but their behaviour can be distressing to others and may even be dangerous as in the case of the Yorkshire Ripper.
It should be noted that the definition is a useful means to judge abnormality.	Some dysfunctional behaviour can be functional for the individual.	This is because the standard of one culture is being used to measure another.	Listing behaviours and rating them provides a quantitative measure of functioning meaning an objective judgement can be made as to whether someone requires treatment.

▶ Lesson notes p. 51

Deviation from ideal mental health

Marie Jahoda (1958) suggested we could define mental health in the same way we define physical health: by looking for the positive aspects of functioning, by considering what a person can do rather than what they cannot do.

How is this definition different to Failure to function adequately as a definition or abnormality?

As a result of a review of mental health research, Jahoda identified six categories. These are characteristics that enable an individual to feel happy. The absence of these categories denotes mental ill health:

- Self-attitudes

- Personal growth

- Integration

- Autonomy

- Accurate perception of reality

- Mastery of the environment.

Match the category to its definition.

Being able to cope in the social world such as managing in stressful situations.

Being able to form a realistic judgement of themselves and the actions of others.

The ability to love, work, solve problems and adjust to new situations.

Self-actualisation: the extent to which a person develops to their full capacities.

Being an independent person who is of their own mind and able to make their own decisions.

Having high self-esteem and a strong sense of personal identity.

Chris visited his GP as he felt he was no longer able to cope with the demands of his current job. He mentioned that he had fallen out with a number of his friends in recent months and could not see a way to rectify the situation. A number of his comments indicated he had a poor opinion of himself claiming he was 'no good' and 'his friends were better off without him'.

What aspects of ideal mental health does Chris seem to be lacking?

Stretch: How can 'failure to function adequately' be applied to the case study shown above?

▶ Lesson notes p. 51

Act like an examiner

'Outline two limitations of the ideal mental health definition of abnormality.' (4 marks)

Candidate A The criteria Jahoda mentions are unrealistic. How can anyone live up to all these ideals? How many do we have to have missing for us to be classed as abnormal? How can we even measure each capacity? But, the definition is better than other attempts to define abnormality as it is a positive view rather than focusing on the negatives. This is reflected in the positive psychology movement.

Examiner response.

What did the candidate do well?

What does the candidate need to improve?

Mark awarded out of 4: _____

Candidate B

Many, if not all, of the criteria proposed by Jahoda are culture bound. If we apply these criteria from non-Western or non-middle-class social groups we find a higher incidence of abnormality. For example, the criterion for self-actualisation is relevant to individualistic cultures but not collectivist ones, where individuals strive for greater good of the community rather than for self-centred goals.

A second limitation is that these criteria could be considered to be unrealistic. Many of the criteria are difficult to reach and so many of us would be considered abnormal. Furthermore, the criteria are unrealistic in that they are hard to measure. For example, how can be objectively measure personal growth? This means Jahoda's criteria are interesting but not very useful when trying to identify abnormality.

Examiner response.

What did the candidate do well?

What does the candidate need to improve?

Mark awarded out of 4: _____

Level	Marks	Description
2	3–4 marks	Limitations are clear and coherent.
1	1–2 marks	Limitations are incomplete or partially accurate.
	0 marks	No relevant content/comments apply to another definition of abnormality.

▶ Lesson notes p. 52

Cultural relativism

Statistical infrequency

Behaviours that are _____ (statistically infrequent) in one culture may be more _____ (statistically more frequent) in another culture. For example, one symptom of schizophrenia is

_____ _____.

However, this is common in some cultures where religious leaders have claimed to have heard the voice of _____. This means that the statistical infrequency model is culturally relative.

Social norms

Social norms are bound by _____. Classification systems such as the DSM are almost entirely based on the social norms of the dominant culture in the West (_____ and _____ _____). However, the most recent revision to DSM acknowledges cultural differences. For example, _____ _____ make reference to uncontrollable crying in some cultures while difficulty breathing might be more common in other cultures.

Terms
adequate

common

diagnosis

God

hearing voices

lower-classes

non-white

rare

Cultural relativism

The view that behaviour cannot be judged properly unless it is viewed in the context of the culture in which it originates.

Terms
collectivist

culture

individualist

incidence

Jahoda's

middle class

panic attacks

white

Failure to function

_____ functioning is relative to cultural ideas of how one's life should be lived. Therefore this definition is likely to result in different _____ when applied to people from different cultures, because the standard of one culture is being used to measure another. This might explain why _____ _____ and _____-_____ patients are more often diagnosed with mental disorders.

Ideal mental health

Most, if not all of _____ criteria are culture bound. If we apply these criteria to people from non-Western or even non-middle class social groups we will most probably find a higher _____ of abnormality. For example, self-actualisation is relevant to members of _____ cultures but not _____ cultures where individuals strive for the greater good of their community rather than themselves

▶ Lesson notes p. 52

Characteristics of mental disorders

For each passage highlight the emotional, behavioural and cognitive characteristics mentioned in different colours.

Textbook extract

A phobia is most easily recognised by marked and persistent fear which, for the onlooker, is likely to seem excessive and unreasonable. For example, a wasp phobia may result in the sufferer refusing to eat outside during the summer months in an attempt to avoid the feared insect. If these actions are deemed to interfere significantly with day-to-day routines or social activities, and are accompanied with noticeable distress then a phobia would be diagnosed. While the phobic patient may acknowledge their fear is irrational, such as the fear of receiving an excruciating sting from a wasp, they cannot overcome their fear response in the presence of the phobic stimulus.

OCD patient

When you watch me, you see my compulsions which are rituals I carry out in an attempt to reduce the anxiety my obsessions create. My main obsession is that I have left electrical items plugged in and switched on when I am not in the house. I become very anxious about the idea this will lead to a fire. I have developed elaborate rituals involving tapping wall sockets and touching the pins in each plug to ensure electrical items are unplugged. If an obsession enters my head while I am away from home I find myself driving home to carry out my rituals. I cannot concentrate on anything else until my rituals are completed. This takes up a large part of my day and I spend a lot of time fighting rising feelings of anxiety as well as a sense of embarrassment should my friends and colleagues see my rituals.

Doctor's notes

Mr X appears to be suffering from depression. During our consultation he complained of a lack of energy, general sense of tiredness and feeling the need to sleep excessively. He mentioned this is a change from his usual level of activity and previously would have thought of himself as 'full of energy' and 'someone who likes to keep busy'. A number of comments Mr X made regarding his view of himself are concerning. Describing himself as 'a useless husband' suggests he has a negative self-concept and is struggling with feelings of worthlessness. He repeatedly stated he 'cannot see how things could get better' which implies he holds a negative view of the world, as if he expects his situation to remain in this negative state. On asking Mr X what activities he might engage in that might lift his mood, he explained that he used to enjoy cycling but has lost all enthusiasm for this hobby. He expanded upon this saying it simply felt too much of an effort to get into his cycling gear and feared he would feel overwhelmed trying to hide his true feelings to other members of the cycling club he used to attend on a weekly basis.

revision opportunity

Analyse each example using different definitions of abnormality.

- Statistical infrequency
- Deviation from social norms
- Failure to function adequately
- Deviation from ideal mental health

▶ Lesson notes p. 52

The behavioural approach:
The two-step model

As a child, Ali was bitten by a small dog when he was playing in the park. He had noticed the dog and reached out towards it. Unfortunately the dog attacked Ali's outstretched hand. Although the dog was quickly brought under control by its owner, the dog bite was considered serious and Ali needed a number of stitches on the palm of his hand. As a teenager Ali has a fear of all breeds of dog and becomes anxious when near dogs, especially if they are not on a lead. He never visits a friend's home if they own a dog and will leave the park if a dog is off their lead.

Step 1: Classical conditioning.

Watson and Rayner (1920) showed how a conditioned response could be created to a previously neutral stimulus. The original unconditioned stimulus was a loud noise (UCS) and the original unconditioned response was fear (UCR). By pairing the loud noise with a fluffy object, the fluffy object acquired the same properties as the UCS and produced the response of fear. The fear this fluffy object produced was called the conditioned response (CS). The fluffy object had become the conditioned stimulus (CS).

Apply this concept of classical conditioning to Ali's fear of all breeds of dog.

Step 2: Operant conditioning.

Classical conditioning explains how the phobia is acquired but not why individuals continue to feel fear and are driven to avoid the feared object. Operant conditioning is the second step in Mowrer's (1947) model.

Using the concepts of negative and positive reinforcement, explain Ali's continued fear and subsequent avoidance of dogs.

Social learning theory.

Social learning theory is not part of Mowrer's (1947) two-step model but is a more recent development of behaviourism which includes the role of indirect reinforcement and the involvement of cognitive factors.

If Ali's phobia continued into adulthood why might any children he has also show a fear of dogs?

▶ Lesson notes p. 53

Extended answer analysis

Discuss the behavioural approach to explaining phobias.
Refer to the experience of Ali as part of your answer.

How might **Ali's phobia of dogs** be **explained** by this approach?

Evaluate how useful this approach is in explaining **Ali's phobia.**

One limitation of the two-step model is that not every phobic person can recall a specific incident like Ali's childhood experience with the dog. Öst (1987) suggested that such traumatic events did happen, but have since been forgotten. Sue et al. (1994) provided an alternative explanation, stating different phobias might result from different processes. For example, agoraphobics (fear of open spaces) were most likely to explain their disorder in terms of a specific incident, whereas arachnophobia (fear of spiders) was most likely to cite modelling. While Ali's phobia might derive from the dog attack, other people might develop their fear through imitating others. Therefore, the two-step model in itself cannot be seen as an explanation for all phobias.

Focusing on phobias as being solely the result of learning might be misguided. DiNardo et al. (1988) found not everyone who is bitten by a dog develops a phobia of dogs. This could be explained by the diathesis-stress model. Ali might have inherited a genetic vulnerability for developing mental disorders. This disorder manifested itself after being triggered by being bitten as a child. Therefore, if the dog had bitten another child, who does not have this genetic vulnerability, a phobia would not develop.

The behavioural approach ignores adaptive pressures that may influence phobia development. Martin Seligman (1970) argued that animals, including humans, are genetically programmed to rapidly learn an association between potentially life-threatening stimuli and fear. Ali might be biologically prepared to learn a phobia for dogs as their sharp teeth, strong jaws and claws relate to ancient fears; things that would have been dangerous in our evolutionary past. Therefore, the phobic response is useful as it encourages us to actively avoid potentially harmful objects. This suggests that behavioural approach alone cannot explain Ali's phobia of dogs.

1. Complete the first section of the answer.
2. In your answer circle all key terms relating specifically to the behavioural approach to explaining phobias.
3. In the evaluation section circle all key terms relating to alternative explanations for phobias.
4. In both sections underline any comments that relate to Ali's phobia of dogs.
5. In the evaluation section highlight research evidence.
6. Annotate the evaluation section to identify P (point), Ev (evidence), Ex (expansion) and L (Link) in each paragraph.

▶ Lesson notes p. 53

Cut it down and build it up

Effective outline

Flooding involves one long session where the patient experiences their phobia at its worst, while at the same time practising relaxation. The session continues until the patient is fully relaxed in the presence of their phobia.

For example, a person who is scared of clowns is in a room full of them (*in vivo* – actual exposure). Alternatively, virtual reality can be used.

Patients first learn relaxation techniques before being exposed to the phobic item for two to three hours. A person's fear response (and the release of adrenaline underlying this) has a time limit. As this decreases, a new stimulus-response link can be learned between the feared stimulus and relaxation.

Systematic desensitisation

Basic summary

Flooding

Systematic desensitisation

Single sentence

Flooding

Systematic desensitisation

Key terms

Flooding

Systematic desensitisation

progressive muscle relaxation, classical conditioning, reciprocal inhibition, relaxation techniques, visualising a peaceful scene, counterconditioning.

▶ Lesson notes p. 54

Behavioural treatments: Evaluation graph

SD: One strength of SD is that it can be self-administered, a method that has proved successful with social phobia (Humphrey 1973). This makes self-administered SD a cheaper alternative to treatments such as cognitive behavioural therapy (CBT) which requires a trained therapist.

SD: Research has found that SD is successful for a range of phobic disorders. McGrath et al. (1990) reported that about 75% of patients with phobias responded to this treatment.

Flooding: Flooding is a highly traumatic procedure and so might not be for every patient (or for every therapist). Although patients are made aware of this before they begin, they may quit during the treatment as they find it overwhelming. This reduces the ultimate effectiveness of the therapy.

SD: Choy et al (2007) found *in vivo* techniques, where the patient comes into contact with the actual feared stimulus, seem to be more effective than just using pictures or imagination. Often a number of different exposure techniques are involved including modelling where the patient watches someone else coping well in the presence of the feared stimulus (Comer 2002).

SD: Őhman et al. (1975) suggested that SD may not be as effective in treating phobias that have an underlying evolutionary survival component (e.g. fear of the dark), than in treating phobias that have been acquired as a result of personal experience (e.g. fear of clowns).

Flooding: Choy et al. (2007) found flooding was more effective than SD.

Flooding: Craske et al. (2008) conducted a review of research and concluded that SD and flooding were equally effective.

SD and Flooding: Exposure might be a more important element of the treatments than relaxation. Klein et al. (1983) compared SD with supportive psychotherapy for sufferers of social phobias and specific phobias. They found no difference in effectiveness, suggesting that the success of the treatments (whether that be SD, flooding or psychotherapy) was the generation of hope that the phobia could be overcome.

SD and Flooding: Behavioural therapies might not work with certain phobias because the symptoms are the result of a deeper, underlying issue. If you remove the symptoms, the cause remains and symptoms will simply resurface later. Freud (1909) reported the case of Little Hans who suffered from a phobia of horses. Freud concluded the boy's actual problem was intense envy of his father which he could not express and so the anxiety was projected onto the horse. The phobia was cured when the boy accepted his feelings towards his father.

▶ Lesson notes p. 55

The cognitive approach: Beck's negative triad

Identify whether each statement is true or false. Be sure to develop the statements and make any corrections.

Statement	True	False
1. Aaron Beck developed a cognitive explanation for all mental disorders.		
Expansion OR correction.		
2. Beck believed that if our thinking is biased towards negative interpretations of the world, we are likely to suffer from depression.		
Expansion OR correction.		
3. A schema is a cognitive framework that helps organise and interpret information. Schemas help us make sense of new information.		
Expansion OR correction.		
4. Depressed people have developed a negative schema during adulthood.		
Expansion OR correction.		
5. Negative schemas are activated whenever a person encounters a new situation that resembles the original conditions in which the schemas were learned.		
Expansion OR correction.		
6. Negative schemas lead to systematic behavioural biases.		
Expansion OR correction.		
7. Negative schemas and cognitive biases maintain what Beck calls the negative triad: a pessimistic and irrational view of four key elements in a person's belief system.		
Expansion OR correction.		

▶ Lesson notes p. 56

Evaluating the cognitive approach

Evidence exists to support the role of irrational thinking in the development of depression. For example...

Yes, but the fact that there is a link between negative thoughts and depression does not mean that negative thoughts cause depression...

Are thoughts always irrational? Alloy & Abrahmson (1979)

The cognitive approach blames the patient rather than situational factors for their disorder. This can be helpful because...

However, there are disadvantages to this stance...

How might biological factors be involved in the development of depression?

▶ Lesson notes p. 56

Treating depression with CBT

Greta suffers from depression. She often experiences feelings of hopelessness and worries constantly that she is a burden to others; she feels guilty for having depression. This has affected her work, as she believes she cannot cope; some days she finds it difficult to even get up let alone travel to work. She reports losing interest in food and finds sleeping difficult. Previously Greta was in a relationship which she describes as very controlling. Following the breakdown of this relationship, Greta found herself staying at home more, avoiding friends and losing enthusiasm for life in general. Although she now realises her partner was very manipulative, she blames herself for how she was treated. Following a discussion with her GP, Greta has been referred to a psychologist for cognitive behavioural therapy.

Ellis' Rational Emotive Behavioural Therapy (REBT) is a form of CBT as it aims to resolve emotional and behavioural problems. Explain how the psychologist would use REBT to treat Greta.

Greta's psychologist has asked her to complete homework assignments between each session. What homework could her psychologist set to encourage her to test her irrational beliefs against reality?

During the CBT sessions, Greta and her therapist identify potentially pleasurable activities she could become involved in. Why is this an important component of her treatment?

Why should Greta's therapist use unconditional positive regard as part of the treatment process?

▶ Lesson notes p. 57

Peer assessment

Answer the following question on a separate piece of paper:

Evaluate, using PEEL paragraphs, cognitive behavioural therapy as a treatment for depression.

Now swap your work with another student and complete the assessment form below of any two paragraphs.

Evaluation point identified: _____ **Paragraph 1.**

Brief summary of evidence: _____

_____

_____

_____

_____

Further support/counterarguments: _____

_____

_____

_____

_____

Rate the evaluation paragraph:

Limited. Poorly focused or absent.	Limited effectiveness. Lacks clarity and accuracy.	Mostly effective. Clear and organised.	Effective. Detailed and coherent.

Evaluation point identified: _____ **Paragraph 2.**

Brief summary of evidence: _____

_____

_____

_____

_____

Further support/counterarguments: _____

_____

_____

_____

_____

Rate the evaluation paragraph:

Limited. Poorly focused or absent.	Limited effectiveness. Lacks clarity and accuracy.		

What advice would you offer the author to improve other paragraphs based on the two you assessed?

▶ Lesson notes p. 57

Triplets

All the words below relate to genetic explanations of OCD.
For each set, select three words and explain how they are linked.

COMT gene	Serotonin	Vulnerability
Decreased neurotransmitter levels	Dopamine	SERT gene
Diathesis-stress	Stressors	Increased neurotransmitter levels

Set A:

_____

_____

_____

Link:

_____

_____

_____

_____

_____

_____

Set B:

_____

_____

_____

Link:

_____

_____

_____

_____

_____

Set C:

_____

_____

_____

Link:

_____

_____

_____

_____

_____

_____

Team teaching

Your group is focused on one of the following areas of abnormality: neurotransmitters OR brain circuits.

Topic:

50 word summary:

Related research:

Key terms:

Interesting points:

Links to other areas:

Be sure to record details in your own words and work with your group to ensure you really understand this explanation. You will shortly be using this information sheet to teach someone else in the class.

▶ Lesson notes p. 58

Construct a commentary

In support of a genetic basis for OCD, Nestadt et al. (2000) compared 80 patients with OCD and 343 of their first-degree relatives to 73 control patients without mental illness and 300 of their relatives. They found that people with a first-degree relative with OCD had a five-times greater risk of having the illness themselves at some time in their life, compared to the general population.

→

What is meant by the term 'first-degree' relative? What % of DNA do they share?

→

Why can't this data be seen as conclusive evidence of a genetic basis for OCD?

Billett et al. (1998) conducted a meta-analysis of 14 twin studies of OCD. Concordance rates for monozygotic and dizygotic twins were calculated.

It was found that on average, monozygotic twins were more than twice as likely to develop OCD if their co-twin had the disorder than was the case for dizygotic twins.

→

What is meant by the terms monozygotic and dizygotic? What % of DNA does each twin type share?

→

Concordance rates are never 100%. What does this suggest about the genetic basis of OCD?

Many studies have demonstrated the genetic link to abnormal levels of neurotransmitters. Menzies et al. (2007) used MRI to produce images of brain activity in OCD patients and their first-degree relatives without OCD, as well as a group of healthy unrelated people. OCD patients and their close relatives had reduced grey matter in key regions of the brain including the OFC.

→

What is meant by the terms OFC? What functions of the OFC implicate this region in the development of OCD?

→

How have technological advances developed our diagnosis and understanding of OCD?

▶ Lesson notes p. 58

Six hats analysis

Edward de Bono's six hats is a way of looking at an issue from a number of different perspectives. Use this technique to consider drug therapy as a treatment for OCD.

White hat: Data	What data is available regarding the use of this therapy with sufferers?
Red hat: Feelings	What do you feel about the use of this therapy with sufferers of OCD? Does it seem like a useful form of treatment?
Black hat: Limitations	What problems does the therapy face? Who disagrees with the use of this therapy with OCD sufferers? Are there any limitations with the therapy?
Yellow hat: Strengths	What are the strengths of this therapy? Who supports the use of this therapy with OCD sufferers?
Green hat: Creativity	How can this therapy be used in the real world to improve people's psychological well-being?
Blue hat: Overview	Can we accept the data presented to us as giving an accurate overview of research into drug therapy as an effective treatment for OCD?

► Lesson notes p. 59

Confidence ratings

Psychopathology topic	I can identify key terminology in this topic.	I can give a detailed outline of research.	I can create effective evaluations of research.	I can apply my knowledge of this topic to novel scenarios.
Definitions of abnormality: Statistical infrequency and Deviation from Social Norms				
Definitions of abnormality: Failure to Function adequately and Deviation from ideal mental health				
Behavioural, emotional & cognitive characteristics for phobias, depression and OCD				
The behavioural approach to explaining phobias: Two-step model (classical & operant conditioning)				
The behavioural approach to treating phobias: Systematic desensitisation (relaxation, hierarchy) Flooding				
The cognitive approach to explaining depression: Ellis' ABC model Beck's negative triad				
The cognitive approach to treating depression: CBT (Challenging irrational thoughts)				

▶ Lesson notes p. 59

Confidence ratings

The biological approach to explaining OCD: Genetic explanations Neural explanations				
The biological approach to treating OCD: Drug therapy (SSRIs, Tricyclics, BZs)				

- **My strengths in relation to learning this topic were:**

- **Areas of my learning I need to develop during the next topic are:**

▶ Lesson notes p. 59

Key words are good for you!

The passage below could be simplified by the addition of key words. Use the key words and phrases beneath the passage to replace the phrases and explanations in bold:

The scientific methods used by natural scientists (such as biology and chemistry) were regarded as the only reliable methods for discovering reliable **[facts, information, gained through experience or education]** about the world. Therefore, in order to be accepted and to flourish as a subject in its own right, psychology had to adopt the methods of the natural sciences.

Wundt was the first person to call himself a psychologist, believing that all aspects of nature, including the human mind, could be studied scientifically. His aim was to study the structure of the human mind, and he believed that the best way to do this was to break down behaviours such as sensation and **[the process of extracting meaning from what we see, hear, touch etc]** into their basic elements. The technique he used was **[a person gaining knowledge about their mental states by examining their conscious thoughts and feelings]**; just as our perceptual ability enables us to observe and make sense of the outer world, this enables us to observe our inner world.

With training, Wundt argued that **[things people can do/experience with their minds]** such as memory and emotion could be observed **[with a clear system and ordered method]** as they occurred. For example, in Wundt's studies of perception, participants would be presented with carefully controlled stimuli (e.g. visual images) and asked to describe the inner processes they were experiencing as they looked at it. This made it possible to compare different participants' reports in response to the same stimuli, so as to establish general **[proposed and testable explanations]** about perception and other mental processes.

Wundt's approach to the study of human beings was based on the philosophical view of **[the belief that all knowledge should be gained via sensory experience]**. This new scientific approach was based on two assumptions. First the assumption of **[the idea that all events and behaviours have causes]**. Secondly, the idea that it is possible to predict how humans will behave in certain conditions.

The scientific method refers to the use of methods that are **[without bias or preconceived ideas]**, systematic and **[are able to repeated exactly by other researchers to determine whether the same results can be obtained]**.

Wilhelm Wundt.

Introspection
Knowledge
Determinism
Mental Processes
Replicable

Theories
Empiricism
Objective
Systematically
Perception

▶ Lesson notes p. 61

Connect 5

Empiricism…

↕ Link… ↕

Introspection…

↕ Link… ↕

Scientific Methods…

↕ Link… ↕

Hypotheses…

↕ Link… ↕

Determinism…

▶ Lesson notes p. 61

Explaining with classical conditioning

Key concepts:

Unconditioned stimulus (UCS): Something which naturally/automatically causes a response.

Unconditioned response (UCR): A natural reaction to a stimulus.

Neutral stimulus (NS): A stimulus that *initially* does not cause the target reaction or response.

Conditioned stimulus (CS): When the neutral stimulus causes the same response as the UCS on its own because they have become 'paired'.

The classical conditioning equation:

Before conditioning: UCS $\longrightarrow$ UCR

During conditioning: UCS + NS $\longrightarrow$ UCR

After conditioning: CS $\longrightarrow$ CR

Identify the UCS, UCR, NS, CS and CR in each of the examples below, then complete a classical conditioning equation for each example.

1. Saisha's grandfather, to whom she was very close, recently died. When travelling home from the funeral there was one song on repeat on her radio. Now, whenever that song is played, Saisha is upset and often cries.

2. Soldiers returning from a warzone have often become used to explosions and gun fire. One psychological issue they can have when they return to their normal lives is that they have a very anxious reaction to any loud bangs.

3. Grace used to love eating spaghetti bolognaise. Unfortunately, on one occasion, she made her favourite meal with mince that was out of date. As a result of food poisoning, Grace was very sick for the next 24 hours. Now, when Grace catches a glimpse of any spaghetti meal, it makes her feel sick.

4. Tia's dog, Fido, is a very laid-back and non-aggressive pet. However, one day, as a result of illness, Fido was irritated and barking; when Tia tried to comfort Fido he bit her on the leg. Now, whenever Fido barks, Tia flinches.

5. Harriet and Jamie's relationship is going through a difficult time. Harriet feels that all Jamie does is shout and yell at her when he thinks she has done something wrong. She explains to Jamie that she has started to feel tense whenever Jamie is around.

6. Steven is trying really hard to stop smoking. Most of the time he is able to resist the temptation. However, he finds it very hard to resist smoking when he is with his friends at the pub having a drink.

▶ Lesson notes p. 62

Operant conditioning: Reinforcements and punishments

Key concepts:

Positive reinforcement: When a behaviour produces a consequence which is satisfying and/or pleasant. Therefore, the behaviour is reinforced and therefore the behaviour is more likely to be repeated.

Negative reinforcement: When a behaviour removes something aversive (unpleasant). Therefore, the behaviour is reinforced and therefore the behaviour is more likely to be repeated.

Positive punishment: When a behaviour is followed by an unpleasant consequence. This punishment is 'added' to the situation, i.e. it would not have occurred without the behaviour. Therefore, the behaviour is less likely to be repeated.

Negative punishment: When a behaviour is followed by an unpleasant consequence. This punishment is caused by taking away something pleasant. Therefore, the behaviour is less likely to be repeated.

Identify which type of reinforcement or punishment is illustrated by the examples below:

1. Aaron's mother makes him a 'hot lemon' to help him with his flu symptoms.

2. Beth likes to tell jokes because her friends usually laugh.

3. When Charlie rides his bike too fast he usually falls off and scrapes his knees.

4. Whenever Debra is naughty her mother grounds her; she is not allowed to see her friends.

5. Emma's home is repossessed because she has not been keeping up with her mortgage payments.

6. Frank wears sunscreen to avoid getting sunburn.

7. Georgie ate so much food last Christmas that it made her feel sick. She has vowed never to do that again.

8. Harriet was promoted at work and given a wage increase as a result of her hard work.

9. Ian always does his homework so that he doesn't get any detentions.

10. James likes to volunteer at the charity shop because it is rewarding and makes him feel good about himself.

11. Katy's phone is taken away by her mother because she was rude to her.

12. Lewis tells his friends an inappropriate joke, his friends frown at him and suggest to him that the joke wasn't funny.

13. Michael regularly takes his pet to the vet to vaccinate her against fleas.

▶ Lesson notes p. 62

Social Learning Theory: Applying key concepts

Identification:

Mental representation:

Model:

Vicarious reinforcement:

Lucy loves celebrity websites and reading all the gossip about her favourite female idols. In particular, she likes to see what the celebrity females are wearing and whether their outfits are judged as 'HOT!' or 'NOT!' by the editors. On the websites, there are often articles about 'amazing' celebrity diets accompanied by photos of the celebrities' 'fabulous' body shapes. Lucy often likes to imagine her own photo on the websites and the editors praising her appearance.

Lucy's mother discourages her from visiting these websites, she is worried that they are causing her change in eating habits and recent weight loss. Her friends, however, have commented recently that she 'looks good' with her more slimline figure.

Reproduction/Imitation:

Task Instructions

- Write very brief definitions in each of the concept boxes. (If you are not confident, you could perhaps attempt the dominoes on **Handouts 107** and **108** *first.*)

- Read the scenario carefully.

- Underline parts of the scenario that you think demonstrate one of the concepts. Draw a line from the quote to the concept box.

- Using all six concepts in your writing… *'Explain how Lucy's recent weight loss can be explained by Social Learning Theory.' (4 marks)*

Direct reinforcement:

▶ Lesson notes p. 63

Bandura et al.'s (1961) research: Study deconstruction

Research method:		**Potential problem in this study:**	
Independent Variable (include all levels):			
Dependent Variable (operationalised):			
Experimental design:		**Potential problem in this study:**	
Directional hypothesis:			
Findings (by condition):			
Potential ethical issues in this study:		**How they might have been dealt with in this study:**	

▶ Lesson notes p. 63

Cognitive approach:
Evaluation & elaboration

Whether you are preparing for the AS or A Level exam, you should be aware that you could be expected to 'discuss' or 'outline and evaluate' the cognitive approach in psychology. This means you must prepare and revise evaluation points of the approach.

Your exam essays are marked out of 12 (AS Level) or 16 (A Level) and evaluation will be judged as part of the marking process. Many students miss out on evaluation marks because they do not *elaborate* their comments and evaluations in sufficient detail to get the full marks. Here are the general marking descriptors for evaluation: *(Level 1 = Evaluation/Discussion is limited), (Level 2 = Evaluation/Discussion is partly effective), (Level 3 = Evaluation/Discussion is mostly effective), (Level 4 = Evaluation is thorough/effective).* Obviously, the higher the level of evaluation, the more marks you are likely to be awarded.

Your task here is to match up the evaluation points from the left, further and further to the right in order to increase your evaluation marks.

Level 1 ....

A strength of the cognitive approach is that it has many applications.

Another strength of the cognitive approach is that it can be considered a scientific approach.

One major limitation of this approach is the use of computer models.

A further problem is that the cognitive approach appears to ignore important factors.

Level 2 ....

Although cognitive psychologists create theories and models of behaviour, they do this as a result of experimentation with human participants.

Although the cognitive approach tells us *how* cognitive processes take place, it doesn't tell us *why* they take place. The role of emotion and motivation are largely ignored.

For example, the cognitive approach to psychopathology has been able to explain dysfunctional behaviour in terms of faulty thinking processes.

For example, the approach uses terms such as 'encoding' and 'storage' for the mind which are borrowed from this field.

Level 3 ....

This has led to the development of treatments for illnesses such as depression with cognitive-based therapies.

This means that their conclusions are based on far more than common sense and introspection, which can give a misleading picture.

However, there are important differences between the human mind and computer programmes.

This may be a result of the computer analogy and the over-dependence of this approach on information-processing analogies.

Level 4!

For example, human minds make mistakes, can forget, and are able to ignore available information when necessary. These are all fundamental differences.

These treatments, which aim to change dysfunctional ways of thinking, have been shown to be successful in some mental disorders which suggests that the emphasis on mental processes for explaining mental disorders is valid.

Humans possess motivation and emotion, whereas information-processing machines do not.

As such, the approach can be seen as a systematic, objective and rigorous way for reaching accurate conclusions about how the mind works.

▶ Lesson notes p. 64

Biological approach: True/False

	T	F
1. This approach views human beings as biological organisms.	T	F

Extension / correction (circle)

	T	F
2. Heredity is the passing of characteristics from one generation to the next via culture.	T	F

Extension / correction (circle)

	T	F
3. The extent to which a psychological characteristic is determined by genes or environment is called the nature–nurture debate.	T	F

Extension / correction (circle)

	T	F
4. Phenotype is the genetic code that is 'written' in the DNA and genotype is the physical appearance that results from this information.	T	F

Extension / correction (circle)

	T	F
5. Each individual possesses a unique combination of genetic instructions.	T	F

Extension / correction (circle)

▶ Lesson notes p. 64

Biological approach: True/False continued...

6. The term heritability refers to the amount of variability in a trait within the population that can be attributed to environmental differences.	T	F

Extension / correction (circle)

7. The central nervous system (CNS) comprises the brain and spinal cord. The peripheral nervous system (PNS) comprises the somatic and autonomic nervous systems.	T	F

Extension / correction (circle)

8. The nervous system carries messages from one part of the body to another using muscles.	T	F

Extension / correction (circle)

9. The largest part of the brain is the cerebrum which makes up about 85% of the total mass of the brain.	T	F

Extension / correction (circle)

10. The outer surface of the cerebrum, the cerebral cortex, is responsible for 'lower-order' functions such as breathing.	T	F

Extension / correction (circle)

▶ Lesson notes p. 64

Biological approach:True/False continued...

11. When a nerve impulse reaches the end of one neuron, a chemical called a neurotransmitter is released.		T	F
Extension / correction (circle)			
12. Some neurotransmitters are 'excitatory', such as dopamine, which trigger nerve impulses in the next neuron.		T	F
Extension / correction (circle)			
13. Other neurons are 'inhibitory', which calm the brain and balance mood.		T	F
Extension / correction (circle)			
14. Hormones are chemicals produced by endocrine glands.		T	F
Extension / correction (circle)			
15. Hormones are secreted directly into their 'target cells.'		T	F
Extension / correction (circle)			
16. Organism behaviour is also influenced by evolution and natural selection.		T	F
Extension / correction (circle)			

▶ Lesson notes p. 64

Psychodynamic approach: Seeing the bigger picture

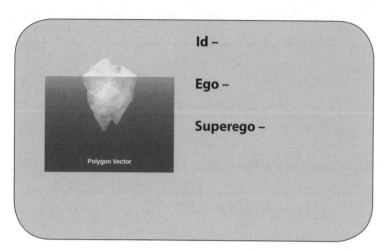

Id –

Ego –

Superego –

Polygon Vector

Defence mechanisms

Displacement

Repression

Denial

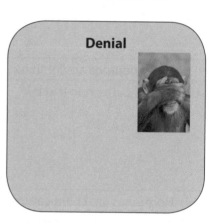

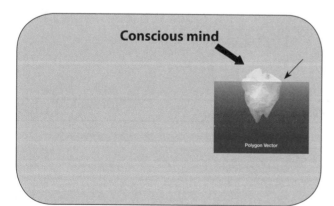

Conscious mind

Polygon Vector

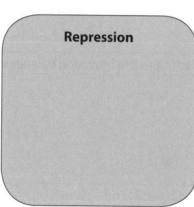

Unconscious mind

Polygon Vector

Conflict

▶ Lesson notes p. 65

Psychodynamic approach: Dominoes

Energy is expressed in different ways and through different parts of the body. Freud believed personality developed through the sequence of these stages where sexual energy is focused on different parts of the body.	**Unconscious mind**
The part that is inaccessible to conscious thought. Most of our everyday behaviours are controlled by this.	**Conscious mind**
The thoughts, feelings and perceptions that we are aware of.	**Freudian slips**
A verbal or memory mistake which is linked/influenced by the unconscious mind. They may reveal what is going on in the unconscious.	**Dreams**
The 'window' into the unconscious according to Freud.	**Defence mechanisms**
Used by the ego to prevent a person experiencing anxiety. These tend to operate unconsciously and work by distorting reality.	**Id**

▶ Lesson notes p. 66

Psychodynamic approach: Dominoes continued...

Operates in the unconscious. Operates according to the pleasure principle, it demands immediate gratification.	**Ego**
Mediates between the impulsive demands of the id, the reality of the external world and the moralistic demands of the superego.	**Superego**
The conscience (internalisation of the societal rules). It determines which behaviours are right/ wrong and causes feelings of guilt when rules are broken.	**Repression**
A type of defence mechanism. The unconscious blocking of thoughts and impulses.	**Denial**
A type of defence mechanism. Refusing to accept reality so as to avoid having to deal with any painful feelings that might be associated with an event.	**Displacement**
A type of defence mechanism. Involves the redirecting of thoughts or feelings in situations where the person feels unable to express them in the presence of the person they should be directed towards. Instead they 'take it out' on others.	**Psychosexual stages**

▶ Lesson notes p. 66

Goals and motivation: Hierarchy of needs

Task 1: Match the statements with the correct level of need.

1. I have developed into the person I always wanted to be. _____

2. I hope that they thought my presentation was interesting. _____

3. I hope that my roof will survive this storm. _____

4. I really hope that I get invited to the party my classmates are having. _____

5. I am extremely hungry. _____

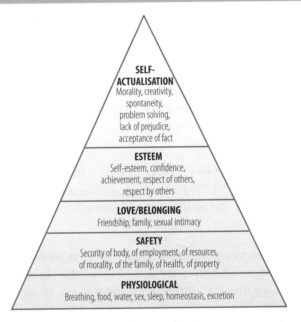

Task 2: Match the statements with the correct level of need. Think about a goal you would like to achieve and where the motivation to achieve this goal might come from.

1. Identify a goal you would like to achieve this year, or within the next few years.

_____

2. Write five reasons why you are motivated to achieve this goal and link the reasons to the level of need.

A. _____ Level of need: _____

B. _____ Level of need: _____

C. _____ Level of need: _____

D. _____ Level of need: _____

E. _____ Level of need: _____

▶ Lesson notes p. 66

Spot the deliberate mistakes

Free will: Unlike most other approaches, humanistic theories emphasise that people have full unconscious control over their own destiny, i.e. they have free will. However, we are also subject to many other forces, including biological and societal influences.

Maslow's theory: Maslow's hierarchy of needs emphasised the importance of personal growth and fulfilment. The most basic, physiological needs are represented at the bottom of the hierarchy and the most-advanced needs at the top. Each level must be fulfilled before a person can move up to a higher need.

1. *Love and belonging* needs are essential for survival and include basic necessities such as air, food, and water.
2. *Safety* needs include feeling physiologically safe and economically secure.
3. *Physiological* needs include emotional needs such as the need for love, friendship and intimacy.
4. *Self-actualisation* needs represent the need for social recognition and respect.
5. *Esteem* needs represent the highest level of human achievement and include personal growth, highly developed morality, and creativity.

Focus on the self: The self (or self-concept) refers to how we perceive ourselves as a person. Feelings of self-worth develop in adulthood and through further interactions with significant others (friends, spouse etc.). The closer our self-concept and our ideal-self are to each other, the lesser our feelings of self-worth and the greater our psychological health.

Congruence: When there is similarity between a person's ideal self and how they perceive themselves to be in real-life, a state of incongruence exists. The closer our self-image and ideal-self are to each other, the greater the congruence and the higher our feelings of self-worth.

Conditions of worth: The love and acceptance given by others may be conditional (conditional positive regard), when a person is accepted for who they are or what they do. Or, acceptance may be unconditional, when they are accepted only if they do what others want them to do. When people experience conditional positive regard they develop conditions of worth. These are the conditions that they perceive others (e.g. parents or a spouse) put upon them, and which they believe have to be in place if they are to be accepted by others. For example, a person may apply to study at university to please their parents, not because he or she wants to. Failure to meet these conditions of worth, claimed Rogers, results in incongruence and distress.

The influence on counselling psychology: Rogers (1959) claimed that an individual's psychological problems were a direct result of their conditions of worth and the conditional positive regard they receive from themselves. He believed that, with counselling, people would be able to solve their own problems in constructive ways, and move toward becoming a more fully functioning person.

Therapists provide empathy and conditional positive regard, expressing their acceptance and understanding, regardless of the feelings and attitudes the client expresses. This results in the client moving toward being more authentic and more true to self, rather than the person others want them to be.

▶ Lesson notes p. 67

Do you know your approaches?

Match the correct approach to the correct explanation!

APPROACH	Behaviour is determined by…
Behaviourist	…our own thought processes, which determine our behaviour. Therefore the individual has some degree of control over his or her behaviour.
Social learning	… observations of others (vicarious learning) and so behaviour is largely a product of our experience (i.e. it is *determined*). However, although the learning process provides the 'tools' to conduct a particular behaviour, it is up to the individual how and when to apply these tools (i.e. *free will*).
Cognitive	…our own free will. Psychologists such as Abraham Maslow and Carl Rogers believed that people exercise choice in their behaviour, rather than being at the mercy of outside forces such as biological predispositions or reinforcement history.
Biological	…unconscious factors, which are largely unknown to us and therefore beyond our conscious control.
Psycho-dynamic	…physiological (e.g. neurochemical and hormonal) factors and/or inherited (genetic) factors, both of which are outside of our control.
Humanistic	…the consequences of our behaviour (i.e. our reinforcement history), which determines the likelihood of a behaviour reoccurring. Skinner emphasised the importance of external forces in the environment (e.g. rewards and punishments) in shaping our behaviour (environmental determinism).

APPROACH	The origin of behaviour is…
Behaviourist	…*nurture*, as it is a consequence of our interactions with the environment and the consequences of our behaviour within that environment.
Social learning	…primarily *nurture* in that people learn as a result of observing others. However, it is generally assumed that the capacity to learn from an observation of others has some adaptive value, therefore is likely to be innate (i.e. *nature*).
Cognitive	…both *nature* and *nurture*, as thought processes may be a product of innate factors or our experiences. We all share the same means of information processing (*nature*), but problems may arise when people develop irrational thoughts and beliefs as a result of their experiences (*nurture*).
Biological	…primarily *nature*. Biological systems such as the CNS and the endocrine system are the product of innate factors (*nature*). However, experience may modify these systems, e.g. Maguire et al.'s study (2000) of London taxi drivers, which found structural changes in the brain as a result of having to learn to navigate London's complex road layout (see p000).
Psychodynamic	…both *nature* and *nurture*. The psychodynamic approach focuses on the *nature* side of human behaviour in the unconscious forces (e.g. the demands of the id) and conflicts that we must all deal with. However, how we cope with these is in a large way a product of our upbringing (i.e. *nurture*).
Humanistic	…both *nature* and *nurture*. The humanistic approach makes various assumptions about human nature, e.g. our drive to self-actualise (*nature*). However, it also acknowledges the problems in achieving self-actualisation that arise from our experiences and upbringing, e.g. our experience of conditional positive regard and conditions of worth (*nurture*).

▶ Lesson notes p. 68

Comparing the approaches

At A Level, you could be asked to compare the approaches. This means being able to explain the similarities and differences between the approaches.

This handout is designed to show you a clear and simple way of structuring these explanations.

Example:

Approach 1: *Behaviourist*

Approach 2: *Biological*

Similarity/difference: *Nature/Nurture emphasis*

Point	One difference between the behaviourist approach and biological approach is in their emphasis on nature and nurture.
Evidence from approach 1	The behaviourist approach suggests that all behaviour is the result of interactions in our environment and the consequences our behaviour has within that environment.
Evidence from approach 2	Whereas, the biological approach suggests that behaviour is primarily caused by innate factors such as genes, neurotransmitters and hormones.
Brief conclusion/link	As such, the behaviourist approach emphasises the environment and nurture, whereas the biological approach emphasises physical structures and nature.

Task: Use this box, and possibly handout 00, to plan your own approaches comparison paragraph. Then, use the reverse side of this handout to copy and complete the box above to help with the structure of your answer.:

Approach 1:

Approach 2:

Similarity/difference:

▶ Lesson notes p. 68

Confidence ratings

Approaches topic	I can identify key terminology in this topic.	I can give a detailed outline of research.	I can create effective evaluations of research.	I can apply my knowledge of this topic to novel scenarios.
Origins of Psychology: Wundt, introspection and the emergence of Psychology as a science				
Learning approach: the behaviourist approach, including classical conditioning and Pavlov's research, operant conditioning, types of reinforcement and Skinner's research				
Learning approach: Social learning theory including imitation, identification, modelling, vicarious reinforcement, the role of mediational processes and Bandura's research				
Cognitive approach: study of internal mental processes, the role of schema, the use of theoretical and computer models to explain and make inferences about mental processes. The emergence of cognitive neuroscience				
Biological approach: the influence of genes, biological structures and neurochemistry on behaviour. Genotype of phenotype, genetic basis of behaviour and evolution				
The psychodynamic approach (A Level): the unconscious, structure of personality (id, ego, superego), defence mechanisms including repression, denial and displacement, the psychosexual stages				
The humanistic approach (A Level): free-will, self-actualisation and Maslow's hierarchy of needs, focus on the self, congruence, conditions of worth. Counselling Psychology				
Comparison of approaches				

▶ Lesson notes p. 68

Confidence ratings

- My strengths in relation to learning this topic were:

- Areas of my learning I need to develop during the next topic are:

▶ Lesson notes p. 68

Hierarchies:
The nervous system

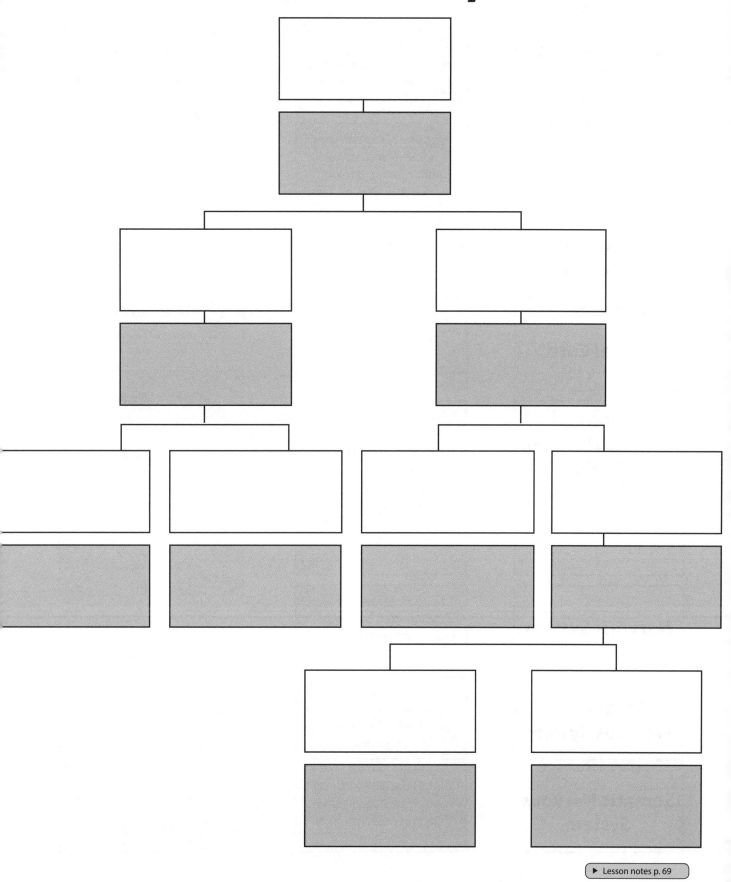

▶ Lesson notes p. 69

Hierarchies:
The nervous system

Parasympathetic Nervous System	*Governs the brain's involuntary activities (e.g. heartbeat, stress) and is self-regulating.*	*Sensory receptors, e.g. eyes, ears, skin etc.*
Central Nervous System (CNS)	*Responsible for carrying sensory and motor information to and from the CNS.*	*Spinal column*
Sympathetic Nervous System	*The part of the CNS responsible for coordinating sensation, intellectual and nervous activity.*	*Cerebrum, cerebellum, diencephalon, brain stem*
Spinal Cord	*Receives information from the senses and controls the body's responses.*	*2% of the body's weight*
Peripheral Nervous System (PNS)	*A bundle of enclosed nerve fibres which connects nearly all parts of the body with the brain.*	*Involved in reflex actions*
Brain	*Involved in responses that help us deal with emergencies (fight or flight).*	*Noradrenaline*
Nervous System	*The part of the nervous system that is outside of the brain and spinal cord.*	*Acetylcholine*
Autonomic Nervous System	*Network of nerve cells and fibres. Helps all parts of the body communicate with each other.*	*Heartbeat, digestion*
Somatic Nervous System	*Calms the body after an emergency state. Involved in energy conservation and digestion.*	*Increases blood pressure*
		Decreases blood pressure

▶ Lesson notes p. 69

Knowing the synapse

Add the following labels to this diagram of the synapse:

- Axon
- Receptor
- Neurotransmitter
- Synaptic vesicles
- Dendrites
- Synaptic cleft

Then use the grey 'function' box to explain the role each part plays in synaptic transmission.

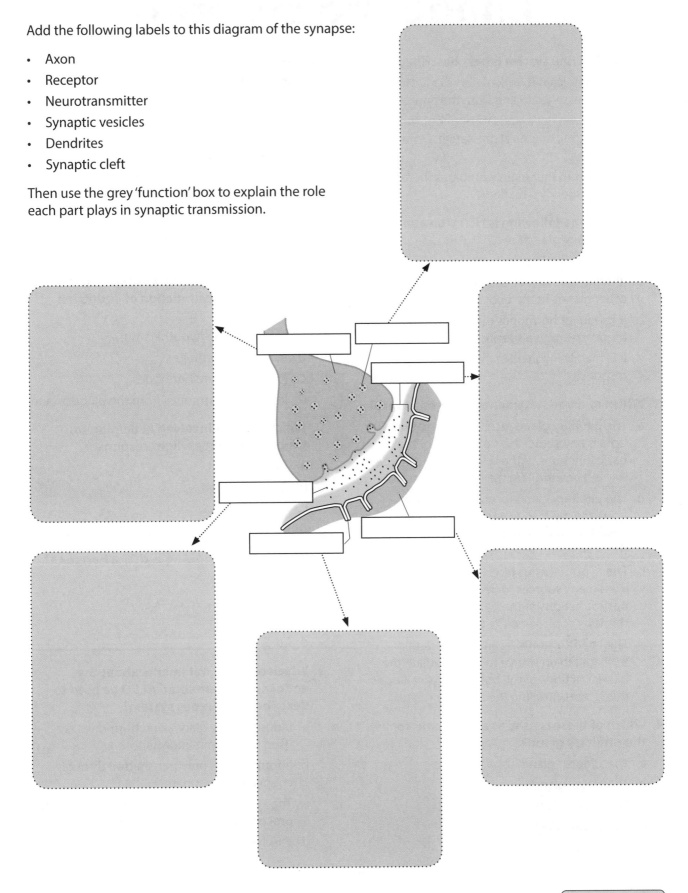

▶ Lesson notes p. 69

Multiple choice:
Endocrine system

1. **The endocrine system is best described as:**

   a. The complex network of nerve cells that carry messages to and from the brain.

   b. The network of glands throughout the body that secrete chemical messengers known as hormones.

   c. The system that mainly prepares the body for emergency situations.

2. **Which of the following is NOT true about the pituitary gland?**

   a. It is controlled by the hypothalamus.

   b. It influences the release of hormones from other glands in the body.

   c. It produces hormones that travel in the bloodstream to a specific target.

   d. It is mainly involved in the fight or flight response.

3. **Which of these statements is most accurate?**

   a. The pituitary gland receives information from many sources to help regulate the basic functions of the body. One way it does this is by controlling the hypothalamus.

   b. The pituitary gland receives information from one main source to help regulate the basic functions of the body. One way it does this is by controlling the hypothalamus.

   c. The hypothalamus receives information from many sources to help regulate the basic functions of the body. One way it does this is by controlling the pituitary gland.

   d. The hypothalamus receives information from one main source to help regulate the basic functions of the body. One way it does this is by controlling the pituitary gland.

4. **Which of these is used as a 'nickname' for the pituitary gland?**

   a. The 'biggest gland'.

   b. The 'clever gland'.

   c. The 'minor gland'.

   d. The 'master gland'.

5. **Which of the following is NOT true about hormones?**

   a. Hormones affect most of the cells in the body with which they come into contact.

   b. Hormones are chemicals that circulate in the blood stream and are carried to target sites throughout the body.

   c. Hormones affect 'target cells' which have receptors for that hormone.

   d. Hormones cause physiological reactions in target cells.

6. **Which TWO of the following statements best describe the function of endocrine glands?**

   a. To control the hypothalamus.

   b. To secrete hormones.

   c. To manufacture hormones.

   d. To remove hormones from the bloodstream.

7. **Which gland is involved in helping to trigger the fight or flight response?**

   a. Thyroid gland.

   b. Adrenal glands.

   c. Pituitary gland.

   d. Pancreas.

8. **Which of the following is NOT a hormone?**

   a. Adrenaline.

   b. Oestrogen.

   c. Serotonin.

   d. Cortisol.

9. **Which of these statements about the endocrine system could ALSO be used to describe the nervous system?**

   a. Blood vessels, glands and hormones are used to transmit information.

   b. Information is only transmitted through chemical messengers.

   c. The system is used to regulate physiological processes in the body.

   d. The system takes seconds to act.

▶ Lesson notes p. 69

Key concepts:
Fight or flight response

Adrenaline	Acute stressors	Adrenal cortex	Sympathetic nervous system
Parasympathetic nervous system	Hypothalamus	Energy	Adrenal glands
Amygdala	Glucose	Pituitary gland	Fight or flight
Adrenal medulla	Increased heartbeat, blood pressure	Chronic stressors	Adrenocorticotrophic Hormone (ATCH)
Cortisol	Decreased heartbeat, blood pressure	Digestion	HPA axis
Corticotrophin-releasing hormones (CRH)	Feedback		

Activities:

1. Use the 'traffic light' system to self-assess your understanding of each of these key concepts. Highlight in green the concepts you understand and can explain, highlight in orange the concepts you are unsure of, highlight in red the concepts you do not recognise.

2. Use your textbook to write brief definitions of your 'red' concepts.

3. Use your textbook to write brief definitions of your 'orange' concepts.

4. Cut out the 'acute stressors' box and place on the left-hand side of an A3 sheet. Cut out the 'chronic stressors' box and stick on the right-hand side of the A3 paper.

5. Cut out all of the other boxes and arrange them into a flow chart on the A3 paper. Do this by reading about how the body responds to acute and chronic stressors.

6. Stick down the boxes you have arranged into a flow chart. Draw arrows to connect concepts and explain on the arrows why you have connected them.

Extension:

7. *Read about the evaluations and further research on the fight or flight response (e.g. page 154 of the Complete Companion). Add relevant analysis to your diagram and choose appropriate locations to write that analysis, i.e. think about that evaluation/research and the specific element of the fight or flight response it is relevant to.*

▶ Lesson notes p. 70

Brain function
revision cards

Motor Cortex

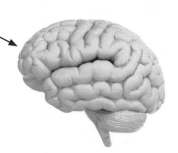

Primary function:

Description of location:

Shade the correct area

PTO for extra detail…

Somatosensory Cortex

Primary function:

Description of location:

Shade the correct area

PTO for extra detail…

Visual Cortex

Primary function:

Description of location:

Shade the correct area

PTO for extra detail…

▶ Lesson notes p. 72

Brain function revision cards

Auditory Cortex

Primary function:

Description of location:

PTO for extra detail…

Shade the correct area

Broca's area

Primary function:

Description of location:

PTO for extra detail…

Shade the correct area

Wernicke's area

Primary function:

Description of location:

PTO for extra detail…

Shade the correct area

▶ Lesson notes p. 72

Choose the right word!

Hemispheric lateralisation

The term brain lateralisation refers to the fact that the two halves of the human brain are [**completely dissimilar / not exactly alike / exactly alike**]. Each hemisphere has functional specialisations, i.e. neural mechanisms for some functions (such as language) are localised primarily in one half of the brain. For example, research has found that the [**left / right**] hemisphere is dominant for language and speech, whereas the [**left / right**] excels at visual-motor tasks. In 1861, Paul Broca established that damage in a particular area of the left brain hemisphere led to language deficits, yet damage to the same area of the right hemisphere did not have the same consequence.

However, this raises an important question. If language is located in the left hemisphere, how can we talk about things that are experienced in the right hemisphere? The answer is that the two hemispheres are [**connected / disconnected**]. This allows information received by one hemisphere to be sent to the other hemisphere through connecting bundles of nerve fibres such as the [**corpus callosum / cerebellum / Broca's area**].

The chance to investigate the different abilities of the two hemispheres came about when, in a treatment for severe epilepsy, surgeons [**connected / cut**] the bundle of nerve fibres that formed the corpus callosum. The aim of this procedure was to prevent the violent electrical activity that accompanies epileptic seizures crossing from one hemisphere to the other. Patients who underwent this form of surgery are often referred to as 'split-brain' patients.

Sperry and Gazzaniga's split-brain research

Roger Sperry and Michael Gazzaniga were the first to study the capabilities of split-brain patients. To test the capabilities of the separated hemispheres, they were able to send [**auditory / visual / olfactory**] information to just one hemisphere at a time in order to study what is known as hemispheric lateralisation.

Sperry and Gazzaniga took advantage of the fact that information from the left visual field goes to the [**left / right**] hemisphere and information from the right visual field goes to the [**left / right**] hemisphere. Because the corpus callosum is [**connected / cut**] in split-brain patients, the information presented to one hemisphere has no way of travelling to the other hemisphere and can be processed only in the hemisphere that received it. In a typical study, the split-brain patient would fixate on a dot in the centre of a screen while information was presented to either the left or right visual field. They would then be asked to make responses with either their left hand (controlled by the [**left / right**] hemisphere) or their right hand (controlled by the [**left / right**] hemisphere), or verbally (which is controlled by the [**left / right**] hemisphere).

For example, if the patient was flashed a picture of a cat to the right visual field and asked what they had seen, they would answer [**'cat' / 'nothing'**]. However, if a picture of a dog was flashed to the left visual field the patient would say that he or she sees [**'cat' / 'nothing'**]. Why is this the case? The information from the left visual field is processed by the right hemisphere, which [**can / cannot**] see the picture, but as it has no language centre, cannot respond verbally. The left hemisphere, which does have a language centre, does not receive information about seeing the picture, therefore cannot say that it has seen it.

▶ Lesson notes p. 73

Experiment:
Left brain right brain

Complete the following experiment with at least ten different participants:

- Using PowerPoint, or similar, present two words on a computer screen. One of these words should be on the left-hand side of the screen and the other should be on the right.

- Display the words for less than 100 milliseconds. The easiest way to do this is to add animations to a PowerPoint slide; set up the slide so that the words 'appear' on mouse click but 'disappear' after 00.10 seconds after they have appeared. (You could also copy and paste this slide and use different word pairs with the same participants if you have time.)

- Ask your participants to recall one of the words they saw on the screen and record whether they choose the word on the left or the right.

- Repeat this procedure with all of your participants, but this time, display two pictures instead of two words.

Independent Variable	
Dependent Variable	
Research design	
Possible extraneous variables and how they will be controlled	
Results *(draw a table of results)*	
Stats test required and three reasons	
Conclusions *(ensure that you explain the results in terms of left-brain and right-brain preferences)*	

▶ Lesson notes p. 73

Stepping stones

7a. Why? Refer to the hemisphere involved and the specialism of that hemisphere in your answer.

7b. Why? Refer to the hemisphere involved and the specialism of that hemisphere in your answer.

6a. A picture of a dog is presented in the RVF to a split-brain patient. They are then asked what they can see. What do you think they would say?

6b. A picture of a cat is presented in the LVF to a split-brain patient. They are then asked what they can see. What do you think they would say?

6. What cannot happen to information presented to one hemisphere in a split-brain patient?

5. What is meant by a *split-brain* patient?

4a. What functions does the brain's **LEFT** hemisphere specialise in?

4b. What functions does the brain's **RIGHT** hemisphere specialise in?

3. What is meant by the phrase *hemispheric lateralisation*?

2a. Which hemisphere (left or right) receives information from the RVF?

2b. Which hemisphere (left or right) receives information from the RVF?

1a. Look at the diagram on the right. What image is visible in the **RIGHT** visual field (RVF)?

1b. Look at the diagram on the right. What image is visible in the **LEFT** visual field (LVF)?

▶ Lesson notes p. 74

Finish these sentences...

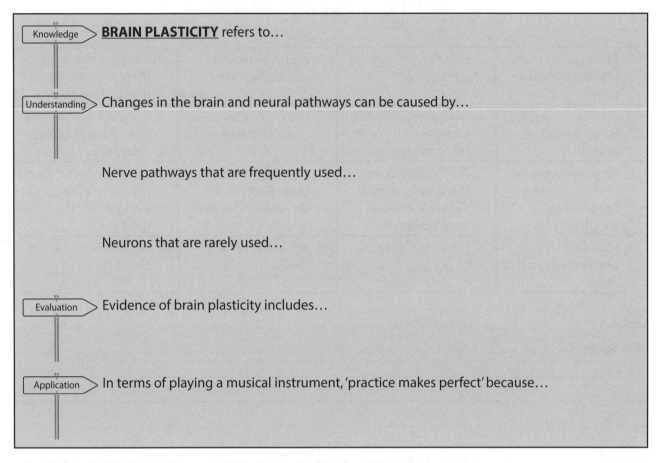

Knowledge	**BRAIN PLASTICITY** refers to...

Understanding Changes in the brain and neural pathways can be caused by...

Nerve pathways that are frequently used...

Neurons that are rarely used...

Evaluation Evidence of brain plasticity includes...

Application In terms of playing a musical instrument, 'practice makes perfect' because...

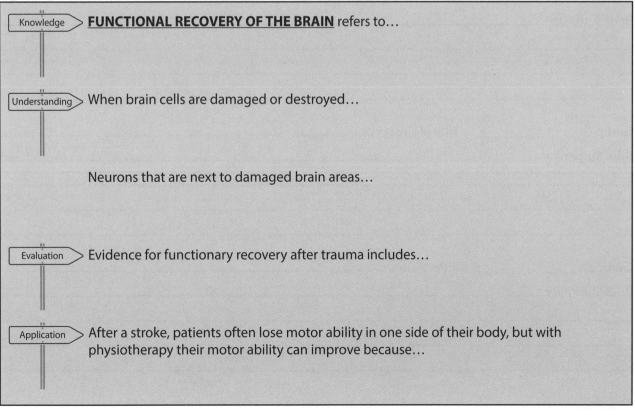

Knowledge **FUNCTIONAL RECOVERY OF THE BRAIN** refers to...

Understanding When brain cells are damaged or destroyed...

Neurons that are next to damaged brain areas...

Evaluation Evidence for functionary recovery after trauma includes...

Application After a stroke, patients often lose motor ability in one side of their body, but with physiotherapy their motor ability can improve because...

► Lesson notes p. 75

Studying the brain: Summaries

1. Examination of the actual, physical brain	2. Broca's work with his patient 'Tan'	3. Alpha, beta, delta and theta waves	4. If brain is more active, there is an increased demand for oxygen
5. Signals are graphed over a period of time	6. Measuring change in brain's activity while performing a task	7. Looking for lesions in abnormal cases	8. Generated before the first 100 milliseconds = sensory
9. Very small voltage changes in brain triggered by specific events	10. Electrodes placed on the scalp to detect electrical charges from brain cells	11. Data used to detect brain disorder, e.g. slow/spiking activity	12. Generated after the first 100 milliseconds = cognitive
13. High flow = high brain activity in that area	14. Difficult to detect	15. When the person dies	16. Measures changes in blood flow

Group A: _____ Title of Group: ....

Brief Summary: ....

....

....

....

Group B: _____ Title of Group: ....

Brief Summary: ....

....

....

....

Group C: _____ Title of Group: ....

Brief Summary: ....

....

....

....

Group D: _____ Title of Group: ....

Brief Summary: ....

....

....

....

▶ Lesson notes p. 75

Ultradian rhythm homework:
Sleep stages

In the boxes below you will find lots of information relevant to the sleep cycle – an ultradian rhythm.

Your task is to cut out these boxes and arrange them onto paper in a way that is structured, accurate and easy to understand.

You might like to think about which of the concepts below could be used as headings to structure this concept organiser. Some of the concepts might fit neatly into these categories, you may need to add annotations and write explanations for some of the others.

Stage four	4–5% of sleep	Very deep sleep	20–25% of sleep
Occasional muscle twitching	Rapid eye movement (REM)	Brainwaves speed up	Muscle activity slows down
		Rhythmic breathing	Muscles relax
EEG resembles that of an awake person	12–15% of sleep	Dreaming occurs	NREM
4–6% of sleep	Awake		Limited muscle activity
Stage three	Light sleep	Stage two	Breathing pattern and heart rate slows
Slow wave sleep	Slight decrease in body temperature	45–55% of sleep	Heart rate increases
	90–100 minutes		Breathing is rapid and shallow
Stage five	Stage one	Easily woken	Growth hormones produced
Alpha waves	Beta waves	Theta waves	Delta waves
Paradoxical sleep	K complexes	Sleep spindles	Body repair

▶ Lesson notes p. 76

Knowing your biological rhythms!

Key words

Ultradian	Circadian	Infradian

Definitions

A pattern of behaviour that occurs or recurs approximately every 24 hours.

Rhythms that have a duration of over 24 hours, and may be weekly, monthly or event annually.

Cycles that last less than 24 hours.

Examples

Hormone production	Core body temperature	Mood (e.g. seasonal affective disorder)

BRAC (alertness)	Sleep stages	Sleep–wake cycle	Menstrual cycle	Migration

Details

Light	Brainwaves	SCN	Progesterone	Free-running	Winter months

Pineal gland	EEG	Entrainment	Depression	36–38ºC	28 days

90–100 minutes	Melatonin	Ovulation	Early afternoon	Coffee breaks

Oestrogen	REM / NREM	Concentration

▶ Lesson notes p. 76

Cut and paste – Pacemakers and Zeitgebers

What do I need to know?

The role of endogenous pacemakers and exogenous zeitgebers

Endo = inside Occurring within the body	Keeps a rhythm	Exo = external Occurring outside the body	German word for time giver

- Using the challenge card provided (**Handout 130**) and the images shown below, create a visual representation of the role of the endogenous pacemaker (SCN) and exogenous zeitgebers (light) for the circadian sleep-wake cycle.
- If you need a little extra help, or think you have finished, ask your teacher for the check card.

- -

Pineal gland

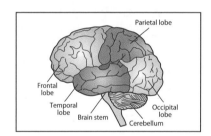

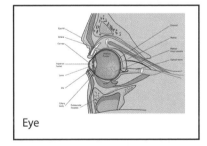

Eye

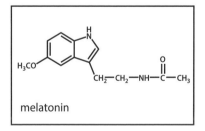

melatonin

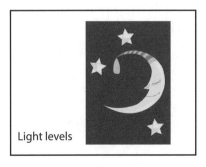

Light levels

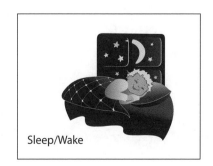

Sleep/Wake

▶ Lesson notes p. 76

Challenge and check cards

Challenge card

In mammals, the main endogenous pacemaker can be found deep in the brain, within the hypothalamus. It is a tiny cluster of nerve cells called the suprachaismatic nucleus (SCN). One SCN sits in the left hemisphere of the brain, the other in the right hemisphere. Both are located just above where the optic nerves from each eye cross over (the optic chiasm). Even with our eyes closed the SCN is able to receive information on light levels from the optic nerve. Special photoreceptors in the eyelids detect light signals and carry them to the SCN. In mammals another pacemaker known as the pineal gland can be found deep in the middle of the brain. This gland is able to receive information about light levels from the SCN as it contains light-sensitive cells. When light is sensed, the production of melatonin in the pineal gland is inhibited. When the level of light falls, the pineal gland is stimulated to produce melatonin. Melatonin is a hormone that induces sleep by inhibiting the brain mechanisms that promote wakefulness.

Check card

When night falls, light lessens. Tiny photoreceptors in the eyes pick up lessening light signals and carry them to the SCN, which lies in the hypothalamus. The main pacemaker in mammals is the SCN, it obtains information on light from the optic nerve. The SCN informs the pineal gland, which produces melatonin (the sleepy hormone). When light is detected, the pineal gland stops melatonin production. Melatonin causes us to become sleepy by inhibiting the brain mechanisms that make us feel awake.

▶ Lesson notes p. 76

Stepping stones 2

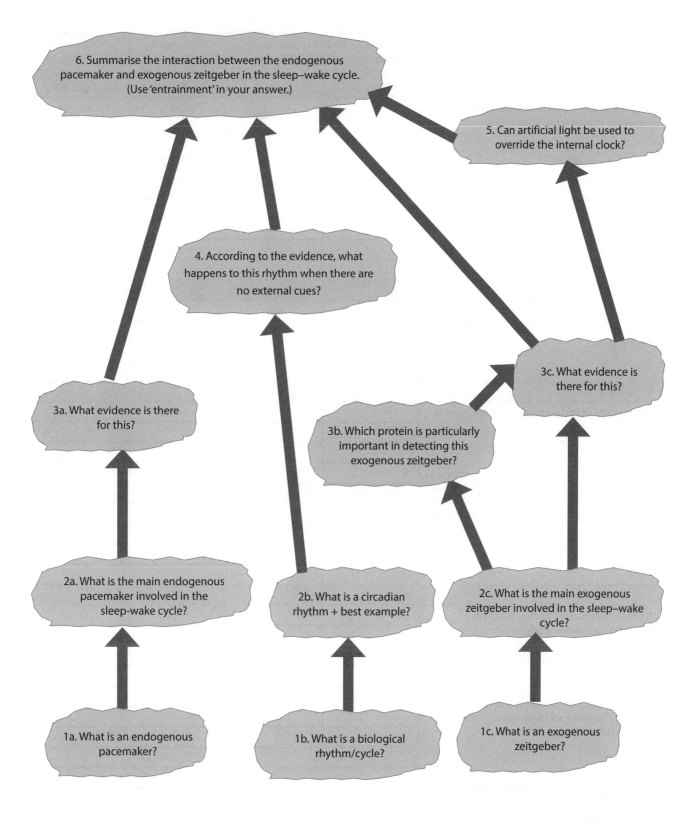

6. Summarise the interaction between the endogenous pacemaker and exogenous zeitgeber in the sleep–wake cycle. (Use 'entrainment' in your answer.)

5. Can artificial light be used to override the internal clock?

4. According to the evidence, what happens to this rhythm when there are no external cues?

3c. What evidence is there for this?

3a. What evidence is there for this?

3b. Which protein is particularly important in detecting this exogenous zeitgeber?

2a. What is the main endogenous pacemaker involved in the sleep-wake cycle?

2b. What is a circadian rhythm + best example?

2c. What is the main exogenous zeitgeber involved in the sleep–wake cycle?

1a. What is an endogenous pacemaker?

1b. What is a biological rhythm/cycle?

1c. What is an exogenous zeitgeber?

▶ Lesson notes p. 77

Confidence ratings

Biopsychology topic	I can identify key terminology in this topic.	I can give a detailed outline of research.	I can create effective evaluations of research.	I can apply my knowledge of this topic to novel scenarios.
Divisions of the nervous system: Central and peripheral (somatic and autonomic)				
The structure and function of sensory, relay and motor neurons				
The process of synaptic transmission, including reference to neurotransmitters, excitation and inhibition				
The function of the endocrine system: glands and hormones				
The fight or flight response including the role of adrenaline				
(A Level) Localisation of function in the brain and hemispheric lateralisation: motor, somatosensory, visual, auditory and language centres; Broca's and Wernicke's areas, split brain research				
(A Level) Plasticity and functional recovery of the brain after trauma				
(A Level) Ways of studying the brain: Including functional magnetic resonance imaging (fMRI), electroencephalogram (EEGs), event-related potentials (ERPs) and post-mortem examinations				

▶ Lesson notes p. 77

Confidence ratings

Biopsychology topic	I can identify key terminology in this topic.	I can give a detailed outline of research.	I can create effective evaluations of research.	I can apply my knowledge of this topic to novel scenarios.
(A Level) Biological rhythms: Circadian, infradian and ultradian and the difference between these rhythms				
(A Level) The effects of endogenous pacemakers and exogenous zeitgebers on the sleep–wake cycle				

- **My strengths in relation to learning this topic were:**

- **Areas of my learning I need to develop during the next topic are:**

▶ Lesson notes p. 77

The experimental method

Aim: statement of intent

How does the aim differ from the hypothesis?

Hypothesis: *predicted outcome.*

Extraneous variables: variables extra to the IV that should be controlled to avoid their impact on the DV.

A group of psychology students wanted to investigate recall for different types of information. It was hypothesised there would be a difference in recall between participants who learnt 20 words and those who learnt 20 images. An advert was placed in the school's termly newsletter informing parents of a memory test to be held at the Year 12 parents' evening. On the night it was decided that the first 20 people to volunteer would be given two minutes to learn 20 words, while the following 20 people who volunteered would have two minutes to learn 20 images (mirroring the words in the other condition). After the learning period volunteers were asked to recall as many items as possible in any order (free recall). No time limit was set for recall. Once participants had finished the aim was explained and they were thanked for their time.

When would you use a directional hypothesis?

Independent variable: variable the researcher manipulates.

Dependent variable: variable the researcher measures.

Why is it important that the IV and DV are operationalised?

Ethical considerations: issues that might impact on participants' well-being and how to deal with them.

Standardised procedure: elements of the experiment that were the same for each participant.

Why is it important that the procedure is the same for each participant?

▶ Lesson notes p. 78

Operationalisation

When conducting research it is important researchers state their variables in a form that can be easily tested. This ensures readers understand what was done and enables the research to be replicated to test for reliability and/or validity, both of which are important features of scientific research.

Research summary	IV/DV spotted	IV?DV operationalised
Researchers were interested in gender differences in procedural memory. Men and women were taught a simple origami technique to make a paper crane (a bird). Two weeks later they were asked to make the paper crane without the aid of instructions. Each correct paper fold made was awarded one mark (25 folds in total were needed to make the crane).	IV: Gender.	IV: Gender (male or female)
	DV: Memory of how to make a paper crane.	DV: number of correct paper folds made in creating a paper crane.

EXAM TIP
If asked to identify the IV or DV only operationalised variables score full marks.

Research summary	IV/DV spotted	IV?DV operationalised
Adults identified as having secure or insecure attachments as children (based on their responses in a questionnaire), were asked to score their satisfaction in their current relationship with their partner on a scale of 1 (very unhappy) to 10 (very happy).	IV: Childhood attachment type.	IV:
	DV: Satisfaction with adult relationship.	DV:

Research summary	IV/DV spotted	IV?DV operationalised
Participants were shown a film clip of a conversation between two actors where one actor hugs the other. They were later asked to identify this actor from 50 headshots. A week later the same participants were shown a film clip of two actors arguing where one actor pushes the other. They were later asked to identify this actor from 50 headshots.	IV:	IV:
	DV:	DV:

▶ Lesson notes p. 78

Speak like a psychologist

Psychology can be difficult because not only are you learning about new research and theories, you are learning a new language at the same time. Keeping a log of key terms will help you understand text and answer exam questions.

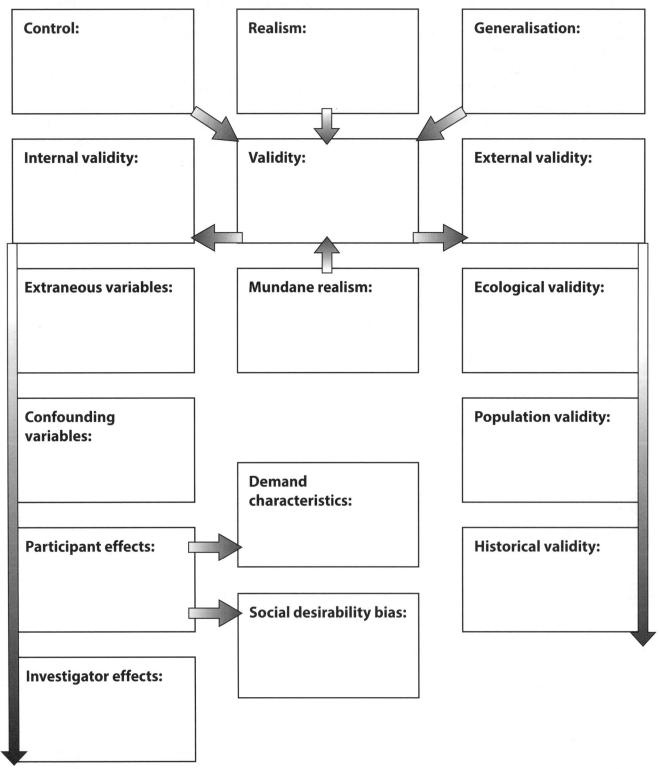

Control:

Realism:

Generalisation:

Internal validity:

Validity:

External validity:

Extraneous variables:

Mundane realism:

Ecological validity:

Confounding variables:

Population validity:

Demand characteristics:

Participant effects:

Historical validity:

Social desirability bias:

Investigator effects:

▶ Lesson notes p. 79

Class research project 1

What was the aim of the investigation? *(2 marks)*

State the operationalised independent variable (IV). *(2 marks)*

State the operationalised dependent variable (DV). *(2 marks)*

Write a directional hypothesis for this investigation. *(2 marks)*

What research design was used? *(1 mark)*

Why might the researchers have carried out a pilot study prior to this investigation? *(3 marks)*

Why did the researchers include the name matching task? *(2 marks)*

What conclusions can you draw from the data gathered? *(2 marks)*

▶ Lesson notes p. 79

Project 1 materials

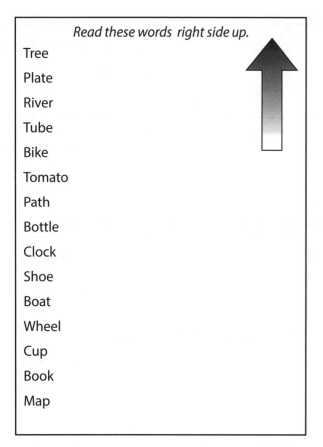

Read these words right side up.

Tree
Plate
River
Tube
Bike
Tomato
Path
Bottle
Clock
Shoe
Boat
Wheel
Cup
Book
Map

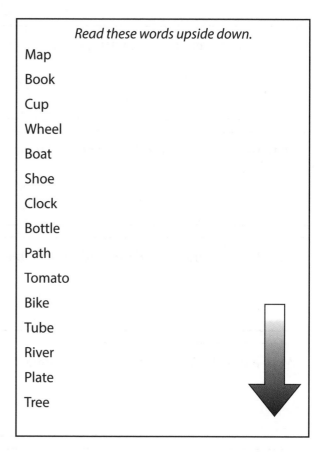

Read these words upside down.

Map
Book
Cup
Wheel
Boat
Shoe
Clock
Bottle
Path
Tomato
Bike
Tube
River
Plate
Tree

Match the first name to the surname.

Mickey	Thumb
Winnie	Flintstone
Donald	Pan
Peter	Mouse
Tom	Bob
Fred	Godmother
Sponge	Simpson
Bart	Pooh
Fairy	Duck

Match the first name to the surname.

Mickey	Thumb
Winnie	Flintstone
Donald	Pan
Peter	Mouse
Tom	Bob
Fred	Godmother
Sponge	Simpson
Bart	Pooh
Fairy	Duck

▶ Lesson notes p. 79

Experimental design

Gavin wants to investigate coding in STM. He intends to compare recall of visual items (pictures of everyday objects) with recall of acoustic items (common nouns, e.g. table, letter).

Two separate groups may be better for Gavin's memory study as the participant may have become muddled in the second condition as they have already been exposed to one list (pictures). This could interfere with learning of the second list (nouns). Therefore, **any risk of this is** eliminated by having the participants only take part in one level of the independent variable.

What experimental design is referred to?

Why might Gavin choose to randomly allocate participants to each condition?

Hugo is interested in memory performance at different times of the day. He wants to compare participants' results on a test they have taken in the morning with another test they have taken in the afternoon.

One weakness of using **this research design** is that if participants have already sat a test in the morning they may be bored sitting another test in the afternoon and so do not try as hard as they might on the second test. Therefore, their second score would suggest they found the afternoon test harder when really they had a lower score because they did not try as hard (this is an example of an order effect).

What experimental design is referred to?

Why does Hugo want to use this design for his memory experiment?

Possible ways of dealing with this weakness could be to vary the order in which participants sit each test.

Half the participants sit TEST A in the morning then TEST B in the afternoon.

The other participants sit TEST B in the morning and TEST A in the afternoon.

Possible ways of dealing with this weakness could be to change the experimental design to matched pairs.

Hugo could match participants by age and academic ability. For example, a 16 year old GCSE student sitting TEST A has an equivalent participant (another 16 year old GCSE student) sitting TEST B.

What is meant by the term counterbalancing?

What are the limitations of matched pairs for this study?

▶ Lesson notes p. 80

Types of experiments

Peterson and Peterson (1959) showed participants consonant syllables (e.g. TWY). Participants were then given an interval task involving counting backwards. Finally participants tried to recall the consonants they had seen. The interval task varied in length: 3, 6, 9, 12, 15 or 18 seconds.

Aspects of a laboratory experiment seen here are…

Johnson and Scott (1976) participants sat in a laboratory waiting to take part in an investigation. A staged conversation took place in the room which participants overheard. Then a confederate left the room holding a greasy pen. In the second condition the conversation was hostile and the confederate left the room holding a bloodied letter opener. In both conditions the confederate was seen for four seconds. Participants were asked to identify the person they had seen from a choice of 50 images.

Aspects of a field experiment seen here are...

How do field experiments differ from natural experiments?

Sheridan and King (1972) investigated gender differences in obedience by asking participants to administer actual electric shocks of increasing strength to a puppy. They compared the percentage of participants who would administer the maximum shock level.

Aspects of a quasi-experiment seen here are…

▶ Lesson notes p. 80

Evaluating natural and quasi-experiments

For each evaluative paragraph highlight the (P)point, (Ev)evidence, (Ex)pansion and (L)ink.
The first one has been done for you.

In both natural and quasi-experiments the researcher has no control over the independent variable. In a natural experiment the psychologist studies an IV that could not have been manipulated due to practical or ethical reasons, so it occurs naturally. In a quasi-experiment the IV occurs due to the natural differences between people such as gender or age. This lack of control can be a problem as we cannot say for certain that any change in the DV was caused by the IV. If there were also uncontrolled confounding variables then observed changes in the DV might not be due to the IV. For example, if studying the effect of early experiences in an institute in orphans adopted before or after six months of age a confounding variable might be whether the child had been born with any developmental disabilities that had not been previously diagnosed. This would mean researchers could not make a causal conclusion about the effects of privation on development.

P

Ev

Ex

L

In an experiment with an independent groups design, participants are randomly allocated to conditions. This is not possible in natural or quasi-experiments. This means that there may be biases in the different groups of participants. In the case of institutionalisation studies into attachment, there may be other variables that varied systematically with the IV that were not controlled such as the friendliness of the baby. It might be that the infants adopted before six months of age were seen as more friendly than the infants adopted after six months of age. Friendly infants might reach out to adults more, smile more and cry less than those infants seen as less friendly. This confounding variable might explain why that group of children were emotionally better adjusted than the late adopted group. So, the lack of random allocation means there were uncontrolled confounding variables.

Stretch task → **A study investigates the anti-social effects of computer games by monitoring whether people who are excessive game players (more than 3 hours a day) are more aggressive than those who do not play computer games.**

What is the IV in this experiment? How would you measure the DV?

What uncontrolled confounding variables may be present in this investigation?

▶ Lesson notes p. 81

Sampling methods

ACROSS

4 Type of sampling where people who are easily available are approached to take part in the study.

6 A sample consisting of people who have put themselves forward to take part in the study.

8 Type of sampling which uses a predetermined system to select participants such as every 5th person on a class register.

9 Applying the findings of a particular study to the population.

10 Type of sampling where every person in the population has an equal chance of being selected.

11 Type of sampling where participants are drawn at random from each subgroup in proportion to their occurrence in the population.

DOWN

1 Group of people drawn from the population to take part in a study.

2 Pulling names out of a hat to select participants for a study.

3 The group of people that the researcher is interested in. From this group participants are selected.

5 Type of sampling where the researcher places an advert in a newspaper or noticeboard asking people to take part.

6 Subgroups within the population for example, children, adolescents, adults, older adults.

7 Distortion affecting the sample as a result of the method used to gather participants.

Ethical issues bingo

Confidentiality	Code of ethics	Anonymity
Deception	Informed consent	Respect
Right to withdraw	Privacy	Protection from harm

Epstein & Lasagna (1969)	Confidentiality	Code of ethics
Deception	Anonymity	Respect
Protection from harm	Integrity	Informed consent

Zimbardo (1973)	Privacy	Respect
Competence	Anonymity	Epstein & Lasagna (1969)
Confidentiality	Integrity	Deception

▶ Lesson notes p. 82

Ethical issues bingo

Zimbardo (1973)	Informed consent	Respect
Competence	Code of ethics	Responsibility
Integrity	Baumrind (1985)	Privacy

Baumrind (1985)	Privacy	Responsibility
Protection from harm	Competence	Epstein & Lasagna (1969)
Confidentiality	Integrity	Deception

Baumrind (1985)	Respect	Responsibility
Deception	Competence	Epstein & Lasagna (1969)
Zimbardo (1973)	Integrity	Informed consent

▶ Lesson notes p. 82

Improve the answers

Use your knowledge of observations to improve the candidates' answers.
Think about the extra little details needed to help develop the ideas they express.

Explain what is meant by participant observation. (2 marks)	Improvements
An observation where the researcher is also a participant.	

Explain the difference between a naturalistic observation and a controlled observation. (4 marks)	Improvements
In a naturalistic observation the participants are in their own environment. Events occur as they normally would in everyday life. In a controlled assessment the researcher will control some variables in the environment, and may even be carried out in a laboratory.	

Identify and explain one ethical issue related to cover observations. (2 marks)	Improvements
One ethical issue would be lack of informed consent and invasion of privacy.	

Over to you: apply your understanding of exam technique to answer the question.

Give **one** limitation and **one** strength of using non-participant observation as a method of collecting data. (2 marks + 2 marks)

▶ Lesson notes p. 83

Select a method

Suggest a suitable self-report technique for the following research scenarios. Be sure to justify your decisions and how any potential problems may be overcome. The first one has been done for you.

> A psychologist wishes to discuss the effects of OCD on patients' daily lives. Using volunteer sampling he identified five participants to take part in the research.

I would recommend the psychologist use an unstructured interview to gather this information. They may begin the interview with certain questions such as, 'How easy is it for you to get ready in the morning?' but as the interview progresses, comments from the patient may lead to issues the psychologist has not thought of and would now like to explore. However, this technique can take longer than a structured interview with pre-set questions which may limit the number of participants that can be interviewed. As the psychologist has only five patients this may be a suitable number for this self-report method.

> A team of researchers is interested in finding out about attitudes to drug taking in first year university students. They want their sample to include students from a wide range of degree courses at two local universities.

> A researcher wants to study participants' recall of film clips arousing various levels of anxiety from low level (two cars driving past each other) to medium level (two cars bump into each other) to high level (multi-car incident).

▶ Lesson notes p. 84

Similarities and differences

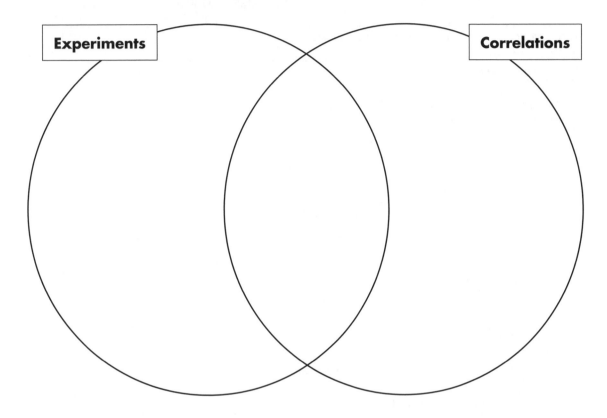

For each concept shown below decide whether it refers to experiments only, correlations only or can be applied to both research methods. Record the number in the appropriate segment of the Venn diagram.

1. Independent measures design	2. Matched pairs design	3. Repeated measures design	4. Hypothesis
5. Independent variable	6. Dependent variable	7. Co-variable 1 and co-variable 2	8. Continuous variables
9. Looking for a relationship	10. Looking for a difference	11. Quantitative data	12. Correlational coefficient
13. Bar charts	14. Scattergram	15. Testing data significance	16. Cause and effect

Stretch question: Why might a researcher choose to use a correlation rather than an experiment?

▶ Lesson notes p. 85

Mathematical skills audit

Topic	Skill	I cannot perform this skill.	I can perform this skill with guidance.	I can perform this skill alone.	I can confidently teach other this skill.
Arithmetic and numerical	Recognize and use expressions in decimal and standard form.				
	Use fractions, percentages and ratios.				
	Estimate results. For example, the fraction 19/36 is close to 18/36 which is the same as half (50%) so I can estimate my answer should be slightly more than half.				
Handling data	Use an appropriate number of significant figures. For example, 8,000,000,000 = 1 significant figure.				
	Make order of magnitude calculations				
	Understand simple probability.				
	Understand the principles of sampling as applied to scientific data.				
	Understand measures of central tendency: mean, median and mode.				
	Be able to calculate arithmetic means.				
	Understand measures of dispersion: range and standard deviation.				
	Use a scattergram to identify a correlation between two variables.				
	Construct and interpret frequency tables and diagrams, bar charts and histograms.				
	Know the characteristics of normal and skewed distributions.				
	Understand the differences between qualitative and quantitative data.				
	Understand the difference between primary and secondary data.				
	Understand when and how to use the sign test to reach a conclusion about significance of data collected.				
	Be aware of a range of statistical tests and know when to apply them.				
	Use statistical tables to determine significance.				
	Distinguish between levels of measurement: nominal, ordinal, interval and ratio.				
Algebra	Understand and use the symbols: =, <, <<, >>, >, α, ~				
	Substitute numerical values into algebraic equations using appropriate units for physical quantities.				
	Solve simple algebraic equations.				
Graphs	Translate information between graphical, numerical and algebraic forms.				
	Plot two variables from experiments and other data.				

"Grey cells refer to A Level route, not required for AS route."

▶ Lesson notes p. 86

Back to basics

You have probably met these concepts at GCSE but that may seem like a long time ago now, especially if you are no longer using maths in your other subject choices. Complete the table below to give your skills an update.

Concept	Explanation	Over to you
Calculating fractions.	A fraction is part of a whole number such as ½ or ¾. You may want to present results from a study as a fraction. For example, if there were 120 participants and 40 of them took part in condition A then what fraction is this? 1. Divide 40 by 120 = 40/120. 2. Reduce the fraction by dividing the numerator (40) and the denominator (120) by the lowest number that divides them both equally (the lowest common denominator). In this case it is 40/40 = 1 and 120/40 = 3 so the fraction would be 1/3.	During a debriefing of 80 people who had been deceived as part of a conformity study, 32 of these participants stated they felt upset by the deception. Express this as a fraction.

Concept	Explanation	Over to you
Calculating percentages: changing a fraction to a percentage.	The word 'percent' means 'out of 100'. Therefore 5% means 5 out of 100. For example, a participant recalled 12 words out of 30 on a memory test (12/30). To work out the percentage of correct answers on a test, use a calculator to divide the participant's score by the maximum score possible and multiply by 100. 1. 12 divided by 30 = 0.4. 2. 0.4 multiplied by 100 = 40%	Using the Strange Situation a researcher found 45 out of 75 infants (45/75) were classified as securely attached. Express this as a percentage.

Concept	Explanation	Over to you
Ratios.	A ratio says how much there is of one thing compared to another thing. There are two ways to express a ratio: 1. Part-to-part ratio. Used in betting, e.g. odds of 4 to 1 (4:1) meaning that out of a total of five events you would be expected to lose four times and win once. 2. Part-to-whole ratio. In this case 4:5 would refer to four losses out of five occurrences. Part-to-whole ratios can be easily changed into a fraction, 4:5 is 4/5. Ratios can be reduced to a lowest form in the same way fractions are, so 10:15 would more simply be 2:3 (both parts of the fraction have been divided by 5).	A psychologist placed a questionnaire in a newspaper. 27 men and 63 women returned completed questionnaire. Express this as a ratio in its lowest form.

▶ Lesson notes p. 87

Data analysis

Aim: To investigate age differences and conformity.

Sample: Placing an advert in a local school newspaper led to a volunteer sample of 10 Year 7 students and 10 teachers (aged over 25).

Procedure: During a specified break time students and teachers met in a quiet classroom to complete the questionnaire. Participants sat on separate desks so as not to see responses from other participants and were given the whole break time (20 minutes) to complete the questionnaire. The questionnaire asked participants to identify how they would act in a range of hypothetical situations with choices ranging from non-conformist to high level of conformity. A high score indicated a high level of conformity (max. score 50).

Findings:

Participant	Year 7 pupils	Teachers
1	34	40
2	19	27
3	40	39
4	21	22
5	34	37
6	6	46
7	35	31
8	20	28
9	31	42
10	38	23
Mode		
Median		
Mean		
Standard deviation	10.80	8.39

Identify the operationalised independent variable.

Identify the operationalised dependent variable.

Write a non-directional hypothesis for this study.

Calculate the measures of central tendency. What problems can you identify with these calculations?

What do the standard deviations tell us about the data in the two conditions?

What conclusions would you draw from the data you have calculated?.

▶ Lesson notes p. 87

Graphical match up

Use your understanding of different ways to display quantitative data to match up key terms, with graphical images and explanations.

Bar chart	Line graph	Histogram	Scattergram

Negative skew	Normal distribution	Positive skew

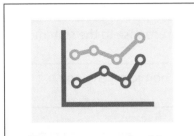

Mean memory score (y axis) and Year group (x axis)

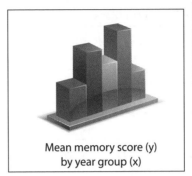

Mean memory score (y) by year group (x)

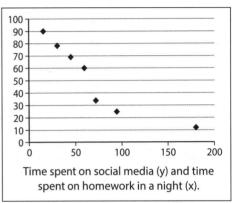

Time spent on social media (y) and time spent on homework in a night (x).

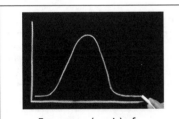

Frequency (y axis) of scores on IQ test (x axis)

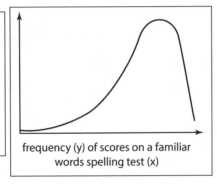

frequency (y) of scores on a familiar words spelling test (x)

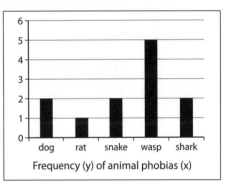

Frequency (y) of animal phobias (x)

This graph represents continuous data on the x-axis and there is a dot to mark the top of each bar and each dot is connected by a line.

This graph represents continuous data on the x-axis so you cannot draw this type of graph if data is in categories. The vertical axis (frequency) must start at zero and there should be no gaps between bars.

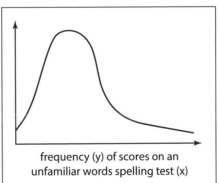

frequency (y) of scores on an unfamiliar words spelling test (x)

This distribution may occur when there are a few extreme high scores which has a strong effect on the mean, pulling it higher than the median and mode.

The height of each bar represents the frequency of each item. This graph is suitable for non-continuous data with a space between each bar representing this lack of continuity.

This distribution has a classic bell-shaped curve. Many human characteristics are normally distributed such as height and intelligence. The mean, median and mode are all in the exact mid-point with data distributed symmetrically around this mid-point.

This distribution may occur when scores were plotted for a test that was too easy. Many people would have scored highly as it was not difficult to perform well.

This graph is used to represent data gathered from correlations. Each dot represents a single participant in relation to the two variables that are measured.

▶ Lesson notes p. 87

Research project –
Aim and procedure materials

Aim:	How do non-psychology students view the usefulness of psychology?
Independent variable:	Knowledge of psychology. Condition 1: no understanding of how psychology can contribute to the public good. Condition 2: some understanding of how psychology can contribute to the public good (knowledge gained from reading of a passage).
Dependent variable:	Rating given on a scale of 1–10 (1 = no role, 10 = vital role) in response to the statement, 'Psychology plays a role in improving the lives of people'.
Directional hypothesis:	Participants will give a higher role-rating after reading the economic psychology passage than they gave before reading the it.

Procedure	Each participant completes both conditions as a repeated measures design is being used. We are testing attitude change after exposure to information.
Condition 1	Please read the following statement and rate your opinion on the scale below. **'Psychology plays a role in improving our lives.'**

No role									Vital role
1	2	3	4	5	6	7	8	9	10

Condition 2 Passage	Please read the following passage. The mission statement for the British Psychological Society is to be 'responsible for the development, promotion and application of psychology for the public good'. For example, through psychological research, a technique called the cognitive interview has been developed to improve the amount of accurate information collected from eyewitnesses. This reduces the amount of wrongful arrests and ensures that criminals are caught. Research into attachment (the bond between a child and their care-giver) and the importance of emotional care has influenced childcare polices. Before this research many people believed that physical care was all that was necessary. Furthermore, research into social influence has been used to inform health campaigns such as reducing drink driving and smoking behaviour by considering the psychology behind attitude and behavioural changes.
	Now, please read the following statement and rate your opinion on the scale below. **'Psychology plays a role in improving our lives.'**

No role									Vital role
1	2	3	4	5	6	7	8	9	10

▶ Lesson notes p. 88

Research project – Recording and analysing data

Participant	Rating before reading passage	Rating after reading passage	Difference (after – before)	Sign
example	5	7	2	+
example	6	3	3	-
example	8	8	0	n/a
1				
2				
3				
4				
5				
6				
7				
8				
9				
10				
11				
12				
13				
14				
15				

To analyse the data you will carry out a sign test because you have related data (repeated measures design). This is an inferential statistical test which allows you to work out the probability of whether the data collected was simply the result of chance.

Step 1	Remind yourself of the hypothesis, 'Participants give a higher role-rating after reading the economic psychology passage then they gave before reading the passage'. This is a directional hypothesis so a one-tailed test will be used.
Step 2	Record the rating scores (before and after reading the passage) in the table shown above. Remember you are comparing each participant on their response in the two conditions so make sure you enter the correct data for each participant on the two conditions.
Step 3	For each participant subtract the 'after rating' from the 'before rating' and record the sign, whether the answer was negative or positive. See the *example cells* for guidance.
Step 4	Count up the number of positive signs and the number of negative signs recorded in the end column. The calculated S value will be the lower of these two numbers.
Step 5	Find the critical value needed to compare your calculated value to N = number of participants in the study 0.05 = this is the usual level of probability chosen (1 in 20 likelihood results are due to chance also stated as 5% chance) One-tailed = select this when a directional hypothesis has been chosen Two-tailed= select this when a non-directional hypothesis has been chosen.
Step 6	For data to be significant (and the hypothesis to be accepted) the calculated value of S must be EQUAL to or LESS THAN the critical value identified.

▶ Lesson notes p. 88

Research project – Reaching a conclusion

The S value calculated was =

The critical value identified was =

Therefore data is significant / insignificant (circle)

'Are the signs in the expected direction? Yes / no (circle answer)

The directional hypothesis is accepted / rejected (circle)

Strengths of this research study were…

Limitations of this research study were…

These limitations could be overcome by…

Table of critical values of S		
One-tailed	0.05	0.01
Two-tailed	0.10	0.02
N		
5	0	
6	0	0
7	0	0
8	1	0
9	1	1
10	1	1
11	2	1
12	2	2
13	3	2
14	3	2
15	3	3
16	4	3
17	4	4
18	5	4
19	5	4
20	5	5
25	7	7
30	10	9
35	12	11

Calculated value of S must be EQUAL to or LESS THAN the critical value in this table for significance to be shown.

Stretch question.

The level of probability for this study was set at 0.05 meaning a 5% probability that the results would have occurred by chance. This level states there is a 5% chance that ratings would have changed even without reading the passage.

Explain the probability level 0.01.

▶ Lesson notes p. 88

Triplets

All the words below relate to the scientific process and the role of peer review. For each set select three words or phrases by writing their number on each line and explain how they are connected to each other.

1. refereeing	9. Research Excellence Framework	17. open reviewing
2. anonymity	10. burden of proof	18. experts
3. university research rating	11. positive results	19. revolution
4. status quo	12. assessment	20. Philica
5. research funding	13. existing theory	21. government bodies
6. wisdom of the crowds	14. social world	22. misperception of results
7. publication bias	15. charities	23. future funding
8. academic journals	16. post comments online	24. twentieth century

Set A ___ ___ ___	
Set B ___ ___ ___	
Set C ___ ___ ___	
Set D ___ ___ ___	
Set E ___ ___ ___	

▶ Lesson notes p. 89

Reading record

Five sentence summary of psychology's contribution to the economy.

1

2

3

4

5

Glossary of key terms

Specific examples of psychology's contribution to the economy taken from the text and /or class notes.

In 2008 Richard Thaler and Cass Sunstein published a book called *Nudge: Improving decisions about health, wealth and happiness.* They reasoned that a kind of 'soft paternalism' could be used to nudge people to make better decisions (better for themselves and society) without taking away freedom of choice. Following this, the UK government set up the Behavioural Insights Team, also called the 'Nudge Unit'. Their research has included a project on increasing payment of car tax through easy to understand, personalised letters to non-payers.

What is meant by the term 'soft paternalism'?

Why might placing junk food above eye level at supermarkets be seen as an example of nudging people into making better decisions?

If you worked for the Nudge Unit what might you like to research with the aim of encouraging people to make better decisions?

▶ Lesson notes p. 89

Confidence ratings

Research methods	I have a basic awareness of the concept/ method.	I have a secure understanding of the concept/ method.	I can apply this concept/ method to novel scenarios.
Methods			
Experimental method. Types of experiment: laboratory and field experiments, natural and quasi-experiments.			
Observational techniques. Types of observation: naturalistic and controlled observation, covert and overt observation; participant and non-participant observation.			
Self-report techniques. Questionnaires; interviews, structures and unstructured.			
Correlations. Analysis of the relationship between co-variables. The difference between correlations and experiments.			
Scientific processes			
Aims: stating aims, understand the difference between aims and hypotheses.			
Hypotheses: directional and non-directional.			
Sampling: the difference between population and sample; sampling techniques including: random, systematic, stratified, opportunity and volunteer; implications of techniques, including bias and generalisation.			
Pilot studies and the aims of piloting.			
Experimental designs: repeated measures, independent groups, matched pairs.			

▶ Lesson notes p. 90

Confidence ratings *(Continued)*

Observational design: behavioural categories; event sampling; time sampling.			
Questionnaire construction, including use of open and closed questions; design of interviews.			
Variables: manipulation and control of variables, including independent, dependent, extraneous, confounding; operationalisation of variables,			
Control: random allocation and counterbalancing, randomisation and standardisation.			
Demand characteristics and investigator effects			
Ethics, including the role of the British Psychological Society's code of ethics; ethical issues in the design and conduct of psychological studies; Ethics, dealing with ethical issues in research.			
The role of peer review in the scientific process.			
The implications of psychological research for the economy.			
Data handing and analysis.			
Quantitative and qualitative data; the distinction between quantitative and qualitative data collection techniques.			
Primary and secondary data; including meta-analysis.			
Descriptive statistics: measures of central tendency – mean, median, mode; calculation of mean, median, mode; measures of dispersion; range and standard deviation; calculations of range;			

▶ Lesson notes p. 90

Confidence ratings *(Continued)*

▶ Lesson notes p. 90

Descriptive statistics: calculations of percentages; positive, negative and zero correlations.			
Presentation and display of quantitative data; graphs, tables, scattergrams, bar charts			
Distributions: normal and skewed distributions; characteristics of normal and skewed distributions.			
Introduction to statistical testing; the sign test.			

- **My strengths in relation to learning this topic were:**

- **Areas of my learning I need to develop during the next topic are:**